Population in Asia

WARREN C. SANDERSON
JEE-PENG TAN

Avebury

Aldershot · Brookfield USA · Hong Kong · Singapore · Sydney

Published in association with The World Bank by
Avebury
Ashgate Publishing Ltd
Gower House
Croft Road
Aldershot
Hants GU11 3HR
England

Ashgate Publishing Company
Old Post Road
Brookfield
Vermont 05036
USA

British Library Cataloguing in Publication Data

Sanderson, Warren C.
    Population in Asia
    1. Demography - Asia 2. Asia - Population
    I. Title II. Tan, Jee-Peng, 1954- III. World Bank
    304.6'095

      IODN 1 05972 309 0

Library of Congress Cataloging-in-Publication Data

Sanderson, Warren C.
  Population in Asia / by Warren C. Sanderson, Jee-Peng Tan.
    p. cm.
  Includes bibliographical references and index.
  1. Asia–population 2. Birth control–Asia. 3. Fertility,
Human–Asia. I. Tan, Jee-Peng, 1954– . II. Title.
HB3633.A3S26 1995
304.6095–dc20   94–41460
                                    CIP

Reprinted in hardback

Printed in Great Britain by Ipswich Book Co. Ltd., Ipswich, Suffolk.

Contents

Text Figures

Appendix Tables

Appendix Figures

Foreword

IN RECOGNITION OF THE SIGNIFICANT IMPACT that population has on economic and social development, the World Bank has played and continues to play an active role, through both lending operations and analytical work, in support of countries' efforts to address population issues. The present study adds to the Bank's growing stock of analytical work on population. It is a product of broader efforts in the World Bank's East Asia and South Asia Regions to deepen our understanding of social sector issues facing countries in the region.

The study capitalizes on the large amounts of data typically collected by World Bank staff in their work on particular projects in individual countries. In this study, such data have been consolidated in a common framework to facilitate comparative analyses. Although country-level data have obvious limitations, the authors have drawn on the diverse experiences among Asian countries to illustrate both the scope for policy action to influence fertility and population growth as well as the potential effectiveness of alternative policy options. The main results of the study—which the authors summarize in chapter 1 as three key messages—provide a useful starting point for consideration of population-related policy issues in Asia and elsewhere.

Given the potentially adverse effects of high fertility and population growth on economic and social welfare, an important objective of public policy in most countries consists not only of reaching but also sustaining low levels of fertility. How effective are countries' family planning programs in this regard? Are they designed for the challenges of the 1990s and beyond—in terms of cost-effectiveness, effective targeting of services to the neediest populations, and financial sustainability under fiscal austerity? What program features warrant emphasis at different stages of the demographic transition? What lessons can be drawn from the experiences of countries that have made (for example, Korea and Thailand) or are making (for example, Indonesia) successful transitions from high to low levels of fertility? In demographically more mature countries (such as China) what programmatic changes, if any, are needed to help maintain fertility at low levels? What institutional arrangements in the delivery of services are most likely to ensure sustained success? What role can donors play in ensuring long-term support for family planning programs?

Adequate answers to the foregoing questions will obviously require detailed, country-specific studies. Comparative data and analysis nonetheless offer a vantage point from which to embark on such studies. Based on the data for Asian countries, the authors conclude that the speed and sustainability of fertility decline depend significantly on countries' "social capacity"—that is, the capability of institutions, particularly the government, in its regulatory and provider roles, to deliver social services to the population, as well as the capability of individuals to use those services appropriately. Differences in countries' social capacity raise important questions about policies to promote fertility decline. If, for example, the costs of averting births through family planning services rise steeply in poorly educated populations, it may be appropriate for public policy in such settings to place relatively more emphasis on expanding social capacity (for example, by educating girls) than on simply delivering contraceptive services, at least in the initial stages of efforts to lower fertility.

The present study also draws attention to the long-term dynamics of demographic processes: simulations for Asian countries show that even in those that have already reached replacement fertility in recent years, their populations will continue to grow, often substantially, over the next forty years. The largely unavoidable changes in population size and structure are, of course, not an excuse for complacency with regard to family planning programs. They do mean, however, that the context of overall development policies is changing and thus needs explicit attention in policy design. For example, population trends in Asian countries (especially as reflected in such predictable variables as dependency ratios and age structures) imply substantial changes in the demand for social services, the supply of labor, and the delivery of such personnel-intensive services as schooling and health. They raise questions about the viability of current arrangements in social security, the sustainability of current land use patterns in urban and rural areas, and so on. The question is whether or not current policies are adequate to address future challenges in these diverse spheres.

The views and interpretations set forth in the study are, of course, the views of the authors alone. It is my hope that the dissemination of their views among Bank staff and others will stimulate debate, thinking, and additional work on population issues, and thereby contribute toward enhancing the effectiveness of development policy in Asia and elsewhere.

Daniel Ritchie
Former Director
Asia Technical Department

Acknowledgments

WE ARE HAPPY TO RECOGNIZE THE CONTRIBUTIONS of many people in the preparation of this study. Oktay Yenal first suggested the idea of a cross-country study on population in Asia addressed to general policymakers. His support and interest helped to shape and sustain the project, while his probing questions helped to sharpen the study's findings and conclusions. We have also benefited enormously from comments on the manuscript by Gobind Nankani, Vinod Thomas, Ram Argarwala, Estelle James, Nancy Birdsall, Mark Montgomery, Daniel Ritchie, Judith Banister, Paul Gertler, Jack Molyneaux, Antonio Estache, Sudershan Sudhakar, Maureen Lewis, Tom Merrick, Paul Isenman, James Socknat, Richard Skolnik, Susan Stout, Frances Plunkett, Maria MacDonald, Christopher Chamberlin, Badrud Duza, Samuel Lieberman, and Randy Bulatao. Participants at an East and South Asia Regions population seminar at the World Bank on July 10, 1992, also offered extremely helpful suggestions for improvement.

In a large study such as this, the data needs are highly demanding, and we have depended on many who went beyond the call of duty to provide us with the needed information. Among them, we would like especially to thank Fred Arnold, Christine Peterson, Ok Pannenborg, Bigyan Pradhan, Shaikh Hossain, Faruque Ahmed, Aminul Haque, S. Nizamuddin, B. S. Minhas, Minja Kim Choe, Nam-Hoon Cho, John Ross, Cheng Hong Fong, Nai Peng Tey, Jo Martins, Kedar Mathema, Carmen Garcia, Jovencia Quitong, A.T.P.L. Abeykoon, Tanaporn Poshyananda, Charuwan Jongvanich, Bates Buckner, Amy O. Tsui, Andrew Mason, Indra Pathmanathan, Eduard Bos and My T. Vu.

Abdo Yazbeck helped to produce many of the graphs, while Jae Shin Yang typed and retyped several versions of the manuscript with grace and skill. Nancy Levine, Jenepher Moseley, and Beverly Logan gave us expert editorial advice. We are also grateful for helpful comments from four anonymous referees. The World Bank's Research Committee granted partial funding which made it possible to complete the study. Finally, we would like to thank our respective spouses, Carol and Kok-Eam, for their constant support during the study's long gestation; to them we dedicate this book. All of the above persons helped us to improve our work; however, as authors, we alone are responsible for any remaining errors.

Warren C. Sanderson
Jee-Peng Tan

1

Introduction and Overview of Findings

POPULATION ISSUES ARE A VITAL COMPONENT of policy discussion on social and economic development. They encompass a broad set of concerns, ranging from questions about the rationale for and design of appropriate interventions to reduce fertility, improve the health of mothers and children, encourage better birth spacing, and reduce population growth, to concerns about coping with unavoidable short-run increases in population size, changes in the age composition associated with past and current fertility and mortality trends, as well as shifts in the urban-rural and other geographic distribution of the population.

These diverse issues have received ample attention in the literature, with perhaps more focus on fertility-related topics than on migration and mortality.[1] Building on the existing literature, this study attempts to draw together quantitative information on the countries of East and South Asia to inform policy dialogue on a broad range of issues relating to fertility and population growth. The countries included in this study are Bangladesh, Bhutan, Cambodia, China, India, Indonesia, the Republic of Korea, the People's Democratic Republic of Korea, Lao People's Democratic Republic, Malaysia, Myanmar, Nepal, Pakistan, Papua New Guinea, the Philippines, Sri Lanka, Thailand, and Viet Nam.[2] As available, we occasionally also include data on Mongolia. We use data for these countries to highlight the nature of the population issues in the region and the options potentially available to address them. The primary audience is policymakers with a general and broad interest in population matters.[3]

Literature Background

Leaving aside studies on migration and mortality, the literature[4] falls broadly into three categories, each serving different audiences: (a) the consequences of population growth on development; (b) the determinants of fertility; and (c) contraceptive practices and the operational design of family planning programs.

Studies in the first category generally rely on country data to assess the effects of population growth on development.[5] The findings are still very unsettled, however. The views of one group of scholars are coalescing around what Kelley (1988) calls the "revisionist" view—that the consequences of population growth on development are, on balance, probably negative, but that the net adverse effect is probably limited. Other scholars, led by Ehrlich and Ehrlich (1991),[6] maintain that population pressures could have catastrophic consequences for life on earth.

Simon (1981) and others, on the other hand, believe that in the very long run, population growth has a favorable effect on economic growth, even though its short-run effects may be negative.

On the determinants of fertility, the literature generally consists of statistical analyses involving individual, contextual, and policy variables.[7] The best of these studies offer insights into the responsiveness of fertility to specific interventions.[8] When combined with cost information, the results can guide the design of appropriate policies to influence fertility.

Studies in the third category—on family planning practices and programs—focus mainly on patterns of contraceptive use and the practical aspects of program implementation.[9] They deal, for example, with issues of contraceptive method mix, discrepancies between fertility intentions and contraceptive use, and differences among population groups in the practice of contraception. Also considered are the institutional structures and modes of delivering family planning services, the development of client-provider relationships, the training needs of the program, the work schedules of front-line family planning workers, the location of service outlets, the selection of services offered, and so on.

The literature thus spans a broad spectrum of topics, providing a useful starting point for considering population issues in Asia. Most of the studies are addressed, however, to specialized audiences, given their focus on specific aspects of the issues.[10] In some, the technical complexity of the methodology or uncertainty about how the results apply in particular situations, or both, also make them inaccessible to nonspecialists, increasing the difficulty of distilling lessons to inform overall policy formulation.

The present study takes a broader approach because its primary audience is policymakers with a general, rather than specific, interest in population issues. It attempts to give this audience a factual basis for considering overall directions and emphases in the formulation of population and related policies. Because population policy dialogue takes time to produce plans for specific projects, which themselves take time to materialize and yield results, the study takes a long-term perspective on policymaking. Although the findings are too abstract to be used to design country-specific policies and projects, it is hoped that they will be useful in conceptualizing such work.

Scope and Limitations of the Study

The study addresses three separate aspects of population issues, with countries as the units of observation: (a) the demography of Asian populations and the power of policies to affect fertility and future population size; (b) the design of current interventions to lower fertility through family planning programs; and (c) population prospects and their implications in selected sectors.

In a study on policies to influence fertility and population growth, a consideration of the rationale for government intervention might be a natural starting point. This topic is not treated in detail here, however. The main arguments are well known and reported elsewhere.[11] Moreover, since the 1960s and 1970s, almost all the countries in Asia have adopted policies directly aimed at lowering fertility and slowing population growth. A discussion of the rationale for such policies would be redundant, if not out of step with what governments are, at least in rhetoric, already committed to doing.

Suffice it to note that policies to lower fertility and slow population growth are motivated by a variety of reasons whose importance relative to one another may change as a country's socioeconomic conditions evolve. The possible adverse effects of more rapid population growth on economic development and environmental quality are frequently cited reasons. In the poorest countries, an additional consideration is that rapid population growth (a) exacerbates the tradeoffs between present consumption and the investments in human capital and infrastructure needed to bring higher consumption in the future; (b) constrains improvements in the health of mothers and children; and (c) dilutes the effect of efforts to reduce poverty. Further considerations for intervention include the need to counteract the bias in favor of large families caused by public subsidization of health and education services; the inability or unwillingness of private providers to enter the market for contraceptive information and services; and the existence of other market failures. The fact that public intervention to lower fertility is justified does not, of course, imply that all, or even most, family planning services should be provided by the government. One role for the government is to encourage the private provision of services, perhaps by lifting unnecessary restrictions on private sector activity, or perhaps by selective subsidization of private services. The arguments for direct public provision of services appear to be strongest where private services are not viable (for example, in rural areas and other localities with high concentrations of poor people).

Given the foregoing rationales, policies and programs can be evaluated according to such criteria as the power of policies to influence population growth, the conditions under which their effects are maximized, the extent to which they compensate for the effects of market failure in contraceptive information and commodities, and the extent to which they increase access of target populations to family planning services. To address some of these policy issues meaningfully, it is necessary to consider each country's particular situation. This report, therefore, provides extensive factual documentation about Asian countries' demographic circumstances and policy environments. The data allow comparative analysis, and the results enable policymakers to consider other countries' experiences and assess the situation in their own countries from a comparative perspective. The study is not a substitute for more detailed country-specific studies, and is intended only to help provide a framework for structuring such studies.

By its very nature, a cross-country study, such as the present report, has certain limitations. First, because of the large number of countries included, many details for individual countries could not be presented. For example, important regional differences within many Asian countries are ignored here. Second, in discussing the data and in the choice of case studies, we have paid particular attention to the larger countries for two reasons: (a) because of the greater size of these countries, policy choices affecting fertility trends influence the lives of more people; and (b) the data for some of the smaller countries are incomplete, and where they do exist, are of much lower quality. Third, to ensure comparability across countries, we have recompiled information in a similar format, but this task could not always be accomplished on all the indicators used, thus limiting the breadth of the cross-country comparisons. In addition, some of these recompilations are unique to this report and cannot readily be compared with other data.

A Guide to the Contents

The report contains eight chapters, divided into three parts. Part I, comprising three chapters, provides the demographic context for population policies. Chapter 2 documents population growth rates from 1950–54 through 1985–89. In chapter 3, the discussion considers the power of policies to alter fertility and population growth, focusing on the effects of such policy-dependent factors as contraceptive prevalence and method mix. The next part of the report—consisting of three chapters—focuses on current programmatic interventions to influence fertility and population growth. Chapter 4 documents the cost of these programs and how they are financed, emphasizing the division of responsibility between the public and private sectors. Because the government is the predominant actor in service delivery in most Asian countries, chapter 5 gives additional details on how those services are organized, whom they benefit, and how those services can be strengthened through partnership with nongovernmental organizations and other private providers. Chapter 6 examines the family planning programs in China, India, and Indonesia, countries whose large populations and diverse experiences attract particular interest. The third part of the report comprises two chapters which examine the population prospects of Asian countries. In chapter 7, we consider the future population sizes of Asian countries and the sensitivity of the projections to alternative assumptions about underlying demographic processes. Because all the developing countries of Asia will experience considerable population growth in the foreseeable future, even in the best of circumstances, chapter 8 focuses on the implications of future population growth for environmental management, the provision of social services, employment-related policies, and the development of urban infrastructure.

Overview of Findings

Between 1950 and 1990, population growth rates in Asian countries were among the highest in the world. The total number of people in the eighteen countries in this study rose from 1.2 billion to 2.7 billion—an increase of 125 percent in those forty years. During the same period, the world's total population increased by 112 percent, from 2.7 billion to 5.3 billion. The prospects are for continued population growth. Under standard World Bank assumptions, by 2030 the total population of the eighteen Asian countries is projected to reach 4.3 billion—about 60 percent larger than the total in 1990. Future population growth is thus expected to be slower than past increases. Projected population increases are nonetheless still large in absolute terms, and could be exceeded by actual increases if the underlying assumptions are not met. The prospect of population increase in Asia thus continues to attract considerable concern among policymakers and others, particularly about the design of appropriate population policies and activities.[12]

The policy context in the region today is vastly different from what it was a decade or more ago, when most countries were at early stages of considering and launching family planning programs to lower fertility and slow population growth. Countries then were generally characterized by slow and uncertain gains in contraceptive use and family planning programs with more promise than accomplishment. Today in most Asian countries, knowledge about contraception and its use are widespread, family planning services are often, though not always, reasonably accessible, and many of the easiest-to-reach clients are already being served. Although programs vary in strength and maturity across countries, their existence is now the rule in Asia, not the exception.

In part because of the success of these programs, the 1980s in particular has been a decade of impressive gains in the spread of contraceptive knowledge and use. In India, for example, the share of currently married women who had ever used contraception rose from 39 percent in 1980 to 50 percent in 1988–89; and in Bangladesh, the corresponding share increased from 22 percent in 1979 to 45 percent in 1988–89. In Pakistan, the proportion of ever users of contraception among currently married women is still modest, 21 percent in 1990–91, but knowledge of contraceptive methods is nonetheless widespread, with 78 percent of the women reporting knowledge of at least one (usually modern) method in that year compared with 62 percent in 1984–85.

Assuming continuation of the existing family planning programs in Asia, the study's concern is, for the most part, with policies and program design needed, in the 1990s and beyond, to make continued gains. The purpose is to inform discussions on these matters by highlighting, in a cross-country perspective, the nature of the issues involved and the options for addressing them.[13] The study's primary audience is policymakers with a broad rather than specialized interest in population problems.

Policies to lower fertility and slow population growth are motivated by a variety of considerations which may change in relative importance as countries' demographic and other conditions evolve. Broadly, these considerations include (a) the possible adverse effects of more rapid population growth on socioeconomic development, environmental quality, the health of mothers and children, and poverty; (b) the inability or unwillingness of private providers to enter the market for contraceptive information and services, or the existence of other market failures; and (c) the possible need to counteract biases in favor of large families caused by the public subsidization of health and education services. Given these rationales, policies and programs can be assessed on a set of criteria, including their potential effects on population growth, the conditions under which the effects are likely to be maximized, and the efficiency with which they bring family planning services to target populations.

Three Key Messages

The study's analysis of a broad set of population issues in Asia—the demographic context for population policies, the current design of family planning programs, and the prospects for future population growth—yields three broad conclusions:

- Family planning programs in Asia have helped to lower fertility and population growth by increasing the spread of contraceptive knowledge and contraceptive use. Their effectiveness in sustaining further fertility decline can be improved. Additional resources are warranted in countries at earlier stages of fertility decline, particularly where current spending levels are relatively modest. In many other countries, better allocations and targeting of available resources are needed.

- Investments in family planning services are essential, but not sufficient, to bring sustained fertility declines to replacement level. Needed as well are investments to improve social and economic conditions (leading, for example, to increased access for women to education and employment as well as higher family incomes) in order to encourage the demand for small families. At earlier stages of fertility decline, bottlenecks in the supply of family planning services often limit fertility decline, but as services become more widely available and accessible, progress toward lower fertility depends increasingly on strengthening the demand for small families.

- Substantial population increase in Asian countries in the short run—say, the next forty years—is unavoidable because of their relatively youthful populations.[14] Because the age structure effect is strong, policies that lower current fertility affect population size mainly in the long run[15] and are most effective in this regard when they support a sustained decline toward a low level of fertility that continues to be maintained. Even under such policies, coping with increased population, as well as the accompanying changes in age structure and rural-urban distribution of the population, will continue to present significant challenges for economic development policies.

The Demographic Context for Population Policies in Asia

This study considers, from a comparative perspective, patterns of past population growth, as well as the relationships between demographic variables—especially those sensitive to policy influence—and fertility and population growth.

Past Patterns of Population Growth

At the end of the 1980s, population growth rates of the developing countries of Asia were highly diverse. China, the two Koreas, Sri Lanka, and Thailand had relatively low rates of increase, whereas Bangladesh, Lao People's Democratic Republic, Cambodia, Nepal, Pakistan, and Papua New Guinea had relatively high rates of increase. It is not often recognized, however, that in the recent past the former group of countries, on average, experienced much faster population growth than the latter group. Indeed, at its peak, the average rate of population growth in today's slowest growing countries was much higher than ever attained by today's most rapidly growing countries. The time profiles of population growth in the two groups thus cross each other.

The crossover pattern was due to differences in the time paths of the underlying birth and death rates. In the 1950s, the average birth rates in the two groups of countries were comparable, but, in general, the death rates in today's lower-fertility countries were much lower and also falling much more rapidly. As a result, their populations grew faster and their rates of population growth accelerated. At the beginning of the 1970s, the birth rates in today's lower-fertility countries began falling rapidly, while the decreases in death rates began to decelerate, translating into substantial declines in population growth rates. On the other hand, in today's high-fertility countries, death rates tended to fall slowly, while their birth rates remained high longer, beginning to decrease only in the early 1980s. As a result, population growth in those countries has been climbing steadily since the 1950s.

One possible explanation of the observed crossover pattern is that those Asian countries that reduced their fertility first were not a random subset, but rather those with the most social capacity to effect changes in mortality and fertility. Social capacity encompasses those characteristics of the social, political, and economic organization of a country that enhance the capability of institutions, particularly the government, to provide social services to the population as well as enhance the capacity of individuals to use those services appropriately. To reduce mortality, governments or private institutions must provide medical facilities, trained staff, and medicine, among other things, and the populace must want to and be able to make use of that care. The sorts of institutional arrangements necessary to provide modern health care are similar to those needed to provide family planning services. Thus, given this interpretation, it should be no surprise that countries which, in the 1950s, showed themselves capable of organizing effective programs to reduce mortality, were also capable, in the 1970s and 1980s, of organizing effective family planning programs.

This interpretation suggests that public interventions to lower fertility would achieve different results depending on the level of social capacity. Today's higher-fertility countries in Asia may not necessarily follow the road taken by today's lower-fertility Asian countries. The difference between the two groups in terms of social capacities implies that what worked at the early stage of the fertility transition in the lower-fertility countries may not work as well in the countries with high fertility today. Where the fertility transition is still incomplete, two offsetting factors need consideration when assessing prospects for future population change: social capacity tends to increase over time as investments in institutional development and education bear fruit, but as some countries complete their fertility transitions, those left behind are, generally, countries with lower social capacity. Where social capacity remains poorly developed, family planning programs face a double burden because the delivery of services is weak, and social conditions discourage the demand for small families. In these circumstances, progress toward lower fertility would require a broad set of interventions beyond simply supplying contraceptive services, particularly investments in broad-based education.

Links between Demographic Variables and Population Growth

The rate of population growth depends on the age structure of the population, the average number of children women have over their reproductive lives (that is, the total fertility rate), and the average age at which women have children. The total fertility rate itself depends on a number of factors, including the contraceptive prevalence rate (the proportion of currently married women of reproductive age who are using contraception), the mix of contraceptive methods, marriage patterns, abortion rates, and other fertility-influencing variables, especially breastfeeding practices, which determine the length of postpartum nonsusceptibility (the period of noncontraceptive protection against pregnancy following a birth). Some variables, such as contraceptive use and the timing of births are sensitive to policy influence, whereas others, such as the population's age structure, are much less so.

To assess policy options, it is important to understand how these underlying determinants of fertility and population growth have changed over time and to compare countries' diverse experiences. The major reason for recent fertility declines in Asian countries has been the substantial increases in contraceptive use. For example, the contraceptive prevalence rate in Bangladesh rose from 7 percent in 1972–76 to 31 percent in 1989; and in Thailand it rose from 24 percent in 1972–76 to 68 percent in 1987.

In addition to changes in contraceptive prevalence, there had been important changes in other fertility determinants. In this regard, the demographic histories of such countries as Nepal and Sri Lanka are revealing. Between 1975 and 1982–86, Nepal's contraceptive prevalence rate rose from 2 percent to 11 percent, yet the total fertility rate remained relatively stable at about 6 births per woman during this period. In Sri Lanka, contraceptive prevalence rates rose, from 30 percent in 1971–75 to 48 percent in 1978–82. Again, the total fertility rate hardly budged during this period. Comparison across countries is also instructive. During 1984–88, the Philippines, for example, had a contraceptive prevalence rate of 44 percent and a total fertility rate of 4.3 births per woman. In Malaysia the contraceptive prevalence rate was comparable, at 42 percent in 1987, but the total fertility rate was only 3.5 births per women.

To understand the sources of these differences across countries and over time, we developed an analytical framework for cross-country analysis, based in part on a method associated with John Bongaarts. Analysis of the data for eleven Asian countries using this framework suggests that people influence their fertility in a large number of ways that can offset or complement the fertility-reducing effects of increases in contraceptive prevalence. Population policies can affect the outcome because they can, for example, affect the use-effectiveness of various contraceptive methods, influence the extent to which infant formula is substituted for breastfeeding, increase mothers' awareness of the health benefits of avoiding short birth intervals, and help couples maintain some traditional practices that are used to lengthen birth intervals.

Because of the aggregate nature of the data used, the results can only hint at these potential explanations of fertility differences across countries. They raise questions rather than answer them, highlighting the still inadequate state of our current knowledge of underlying fertility processes in Asian countries. Better understanding of these processes would help to enhance the effectiveness of family planning programs.

Other dimensions of fertility in addition to contraceptive prevalence may be relevant in some circumstances. Simulations using data for China provide an illustration. In 1988, the mean age at marriage was 22 years, and the mean age at childbearing was 26. The latter was the lowest among all Asian countries studied here. If China had instituted policies that caused the mean age at marriage to increase to 25 years and the mean age at childbearing to rise to 30 years, its population growth rate would have been reduced, from 1.5 percent a year to 0.9 percent a year—clearly a very substantial decrease. Policies that persuade women to delay childbearing can have a potent effect on China's population growth rate.

The Design of Family Planning Programs

To implement interventions to reduce fertility, almost all governments in Asia have organized and financed family planning programs. The study considered selected aspects of program designs with two objectives in mind, the first being to set individual country programs in comparative perspective, and the second, to document individual countries' initial conditions as a context for considering future policy options.

Aspects of Program Finance

In Asia, governments spent very different amounts on family planning programs in the late 1980s, ranging from a high of 0.37 percent of GNP in Bangladesh, to a low of 0.02 percent of GNP in the Republic of Korea and Malaysia (see chapter 4 for other indicators of expenditure levels). According to this measure, spending was relatively high in India and Nepal, and relatively modest in the Philippines,

Thailand, and Viet Nam. Foreign assistance varied in importance across countries, with four countries being supported relatively generously in 1989—60 percent of program expenditures in Bangladesh, 46 percent in Indonesia, 44 percent in the Philippines, and 35 percent in Nepal. The next tier of countries comprises Viet Nam (17 percent) and India (13 percent). Countries that depended least on foreign aid in the late 1980s include China (6 percent), Republic of Korea (4 percent), Malaysia (6 percent), and Thailand (2 percent). These patterns suggest that donor activity has concentrated mostly on the high-fertility countries, and the level of support tended to decline as countries approached replacement level fertility.

The level of spending in Bangladesh is noteworthy: it was more than twice the next highest level of spending in the sample and represented nearly 40 percent of the country's total public health expenditure in 1989. Fertility has fallen particularly rapidly in Bangladesh in the 1980s, a trend that may well be due, at least in part, to the strong financial support for the family planning program. Although the data are imperfect and cross-country comparisons of aggregate spending levels form an incomplete basis for judging efficiency, the very high level of spending in Bangladesh nonetheless signals that further investigation to determine the potential scope for improving program efficiency may be appropriate at this time.

In the Philippines, domestic spending—at 0.02 percent of GNP in 1988—is very low compared to other countries, and program activity has been supported to a large extent through foreign assistance. Domestic spending on family planning in India, in contrast, was 0.15 percent of GNP in 1989. On the basis of cross-country comparisons, a case can be made for increased public spending on family planning services in the Philippines, particularly in light of the still high level of fertility in this country. Domestic spending is also relatively low in Viet Nam, another high-fertility country, and a similar case can be made for increased public support for family planning services.

Patterns of Resource Allocation

Family planning programs in Asia are characterized by striking differences in resource allocation, revealing sharp variation in program design. The study examined allocation across four specific program components: (a) contraceptive supplies; (b) training of staff; (c) information, education, and communication (IEC); and (d) incentive payments to acceptors of family planning, particularly sterilization. These components were selected because, unlike staff remuneration, capital spending, and other input expenditures that are often shared with health services, they can be identified closely with family planning programs. These data thus offer a better basis for cross-country comparisons.

Comparisons between India and Indonesia are noteworthy. In the late 1980s, whereas India allocated 60 percent of its spending on these four components to incentive payments, Indonesia allocated nothing at all to this category. Indonesia allocated the bulk of its spending, 63 percent, on contraceptive supplies, whereas spending on this category reached only 28 percent in India. The two countries also show wide differences in their allocations for training and IEC activities: India spent 12 percent on these items, while Indonesia spent 38 percent. Evidence in the study suggests that India's concentration on sterilization and accompanying incentive payments may have reduced its de facto ability to accommodate the demand for temporary methods of contraception.

In the late 1980s, the family planning programs in Malaysia, Sri Lanka, and Thailand shared an almost exclusive emphasis on providing contraceptive supplies, with this item absorbing more than 80 percent of the total spending on the four components of expenditure. In these countries, such an allocation of spending may be appropriate because basic education was already very widespread by the 1970s, and there may have been little need to promote family planning through IEC and other interventions. Further research would be needed, however, to assess the appropriateness of this allocation of spending in other settings.

Public-Private Sector Roles

In all Asian countries in the sample, the public sector predominates as a provider of services. On average, 75 percent of contraceptive users currently rely on a public source of supply in Asia, compared to 44 percent in Latin America and 65 percent in Sub-Saharan Africa. In six Asian countries—China, India, Indonesia, Sri Lanka, Thailand, and Viet Nam—the public sector serves more than 80 percent of all users. In some of these countries, especially where the private sector is relatively well developed in the economy, the large role of public provision of services may have crowded out private providers. In such Asian countries especially, the study suggests there is scope for increased targeting of public services to segments of the population not readily reached by the private sector. This need appears to be recognized in Indonesia and Thailand, and steps are being taken there to redirect program resources accordingly.

Public family planning services are offered free of charge in most Asian countries. Although the provision of free services may be motivated by concerns that cost recovery would discourage users, the evidence—on the actual incidence of free services and the price elasticity of demand—is to the contrary, particularly among higher-income groups. As countries proceed with their demographic transitions, and as the population of users expands, it may not be fiscally sustainable, or even desirable, to offer free services to everyone, especially in view of the growing number of women of reproductive age. Empirical evidence in this study suggests that there is, indeed, scope for some cost recovery for public family planning services, and an expanded role for the private sector.

Aspects of Service Delivery

Public family planning programs in Asia are organized under different institutional arrangements, with varying degrees of integration with the provision of health services. Most programs began as vertical structures, but relatively few are still organized as autonomous entities today. Of those which continue to retain a strong element of autonomy, clinical family planning services are nonetheless provided through existing health facilities. The diversity of institutional structures suggests that no single setup is superior in all situations.

Service quality has recently attracted attention as a policy concern. Quality is difficult to quantify, but there is consensus that good-quality services should, at a minimum, be available and accessible, and should be provided by trained personnel with adequate supervision. Surveys reporting on these attributes of quality show improvements in virtually all the family planning programs in Asia during the 1980s. It is especially heartening to observe that quality improved in a period of rapid expansion in quantity of services delivered. Sustaining this performance will remain a challenge, however, because in most Asian countries, the number of women of childbearing age is expected to continue growing in the coming decades.

The delivery of family planning services requires investments in "hardware" and "software" components. The hardware includes, for example, buildings and equipment; the software includes, for example, contraceptive supplies and trained personnel. Budget constraints force obvious tradeoffs between these components of program design. This study made cross-country comparisons on the hardware component using data on the ratio of married women of reproductive age (MWRA) to the number of static (as opposed to mobile) public facilities providing family planning services.

Across countries in the sample, the ratio ranged from 990 MWRA per static facility in Thailand, to 5,182 in Bangladesh. It may come as a surprise that India's ratio—1,092 MWRA per static facility—is the second lowest in the sample. Although countries such as Malaysia and Indonesia have substantially higher ratios than India—2,409 and 1,504 respectively—they are not normally thought of as countries where women have difficulty finding accessible services. The density of static facilities is obviously only one dimension of service accessibility, because their effectiveness in providing accessible services can be seriously compromised if investments in the software components are inadequate. Ratios as low as those observed in India raise the question about whether the program should continue emphasizing investments in the hardware components. This question takes on particular relevance in light of results from the case study on Indonesia reported in this study, showing that incremental investments in family planning outlets seem to explain relatively little of the substantial fertility declines during the 1980s. Since Indonesia has fewer family planning outlets per married woman of reproductive age than India, these results reinforce the case for examining the effectiveness of further expansion of physical facilities in India's family planning program.[16]

One rationale for public intervention in family planning is that certain segments of the population may not otherwise be served. A way to address this concern is to target public services to rural areas. The available data suggest that Asian programs achieve this objective better than those in Latin America and Sub-Saharan Africa. Within Asia, public family planning services in Thailand and Malaysia are especially oriented to the rural areas. The programs of Indonesia, Nepal, and the

Philippines target the rural areas least well, and there is clearly scope for improvement in this dimension of their program design.

Lessons from Selected Case Studies

The study considered in greater detail the family planning programs of China, India, and Indonesia, both to learn more about their unique features and to distill potential lessons for policy design. To clarify the discussion, we distinguish between policies on the supply-side that affect fertility through the availability, quality, price, or ease of use of contraceptive services, and policies on the demand-side such as general education or advertising campaigns promoting small family norms.

CHINA. The government began implementing antinatal policies in earnest after 1970. With a campaign of "later, longer, fewer" in the early 1970s, the government encouraged couples to marry at older ages, wait longer between births, and stop at fewer births. Under that policy, the total fertility rate fell from 5.8 births per woman in 1970 to 2.8 in 1979. In 1979, the government adopted a "one-child policy" under which couples are required to adhere to strict births limits, usually one child per couple. Under this policy, China's total fertility rate fell to 2.0 births per woman in 1993. Data for 1987 show a fertility rate of 1.4 births per woman in urban areas, and 2.9 births per woman in rural areas.

The Chinese government is the only one in Asia that requires married women, by law, to practice contraception. The government sets strict family size limits and uses very strong measures, including substantial financial incentives and penalties, to ensure compliance. Total public spending to supply family planning commodities and services amounted to about 0.10 percent of the GNP in the late 1980s, and spending on financial incentives for single-child families amounted to over 0.20 percent of GNP, making the program the most costly in Asia after Bangladesh's. The overwhelming emphasis on incentives is unique, as is the use of negative incentives to deter pregnancies and births. What lessons, if any, does China's experience hold for countries with voluntary programs?

In the early phase of fertility decline, the provision of widely available services had been an important element. The very rapid transition between 1970 and 1979 suggests that Chinese couples did not resist the shift from bearing 6 children to only 3 per couple. As fertility reached relatively low levels, the government of China felt it necessary to supplement its strategy with further measures to influence the demand for children. If all the decline in total fertility between 1979 and 1993 were attributed to the influence of those additional demand-side factors, their effect would amount to a decline of 0.75 births per woman. The package of parity-related incentives and penalties, along with severe restrictions on the number of births, thus had a relatively limited effect on fertility. In the 1980s, economic conditions in China were not stagnant but improving rapidly. Even so, fertility declined only slowly in both rural and urban areas. One lesson is that even in the best of circumstances, the ability of demand-side interventions of the type used in China to reduce fertility further in a low-income context is limited.

Several aspects of China's family planning program are nonetheless noteworthy, suggesting possible application elsewhere. In particular, the Chinese program is a model of successful decentralization, involving all levels of government and local communities in program finance and execution. At many levels of government, decisionmakers in China are given the flexibility to use various combinations of inputs, depending on local circumstances, to achieve program goals. Defining results in terms of fertility rather than the contraceptive prevalence rate is also an important feature.

INDIA. Launched in 1951, the Indian family planning program is the oldest in the world. In the early years, the program mounted large-scale information-education-communication campaigns to spread contraceptive knowledge and promote small family norms. Over time, the principal channel for delivering family planning services—a network of health facilities with primary health centers and subcenters at the lowest levels in the system—has gradually expanded and today serves an impressively large part of the population. Other program interventions include intensive campaigns to recruit acceptors of sterilization as well as social marketing schemes to distribute pills and condoms. Private providers are active mainly in providing contraceptive supplies and services other than sterilization, serving 50 percent or more of the clients using IUDs, pills, condoms, and other resupply methods.

Most observers agree that continued fertility decline in India depends critically on changes in both demand- and supply-side factors. In the past, the family welfare program has focused on the supply of family planning services as the chief means to reduce population growth. This focus was arguably appropriate and effective in earlier years, when the supply of services was still too small relative to the existing latent demand for family planning. On the other hand, because socioeconomic and health conditions—particularly female education, employment opportunities for women, and children's health—have improved only slowly in India, the demand for children appears to have declined modestly (at a decrease of 0.05 children a year in desired family size between 1980 and 1988, compared with 0.09 children a year in Bangladesh between 1975 and 1989), and so the effectiveness of a supply-driven program inevitably levels off. Thus, without substantial changes in those conditions, continued expansion of the program may not reduce fertility to the same extent as it has in the past.

At the same time, the family welfare program itself suffers from serious inadequacies. Data from the National Sample Survey of 1986/7 show that as the family welfare program is currently organized, the stress on sterilization is indeed excessive, because it has severely compromised the system's capacity to supply temporary methods, particularly to lower-income populations. Because these methods appeal to younger women and are used to space births, their poor availability is a serious obstacle to slowing down population growth. The data show that compensation payments tied to sterilization accrued disproportionately to couples from lower-income groups, but that these groups also had less access to temporary methods of birth control. In India, changes in the way resources are allocated among program inputs and services delivered may be needed to enhance the program's effectiveness.

INDONESIA. The last few decades witnessed rapid demographic changes in Indonesia, with population growth rates slowing during the 1980s in contrast to an accelerating pattern during the previous three decades. These trends reflect an important transformation of fertility behavior. Whereas Indonesian women exceeded an average of 5 births each up until the mid-1970s, their fertility declined, on average, by about 2 children each by the late 1980s, with the decline being most rapid in Java-Bali.

Indonesia's fertility decline occurred in the context of a widespread public family planning program. Under the National Family Planning Coordinating Board (BKKBN), by the mid-1980s the program had developed a broad menu of widely available services. These included clinic-based services provided through the health ministry's maternal and child health program; house-to-house motivation by fieldworkers; and a network of Village Contraceptive Distribution Centers (VCDC), which supply oral pills, distribute condoms, and offer contraceptive and other information. To supplement clinic-based services, training programs were also mounted for mobile teams—consisting of para- and nonmedical personnel as well as medical staff—to bring family planning services, especially information-education-communication (IEC) activities, to villages without clinics. In addition, community meetings (*posyandus*) were organized by village heads, with volunteer help and technical support from health clinic staff, to offer integrated maternal and child health services. In general, the public sector was the dominant force in service delivery, with an 80 percent share of the country's contraceptive clientele in 1987. Beginning in 1986, however, the KB Mandari ("self-reliant") movement was launched to attract greater private involvement in service delivery and financing.

As part of this study, we commissioned a separate statistical analysis by Paul Gertler and John Molyneaux to assess the relative importance of demand- and supply-side factors in bringing about the rapid fertility decline in Indonesia during the 1982–86 period. Their analysis used data on individual women from the 1987 Indonesian Demographic and Health Survey, supplemented by data on community level variables. It focused on measuring the effect of changes in demand factors (proxied by education profiles and male and female wage rates) and family planning program inputs (proxied by monthly family planning team visits, VCDCs, health clinics, and number of family planning fieldworkers). The results (relating to women in Java-Bali) indicate that during the mid-1980s, changes in contraceptive use and fertility were influenced mainly by changes in the demand-side factors. Although better and more recent data are needed for a rigorous confirmation, the findings imply that incremental investments in the *specific family planning inputs considered in the analysis* contributed much less to fertility decline in Indonesia during the mid-1980s than did increases in education and wages.

What are the implications of these findings for policy analysis? In the mid-1980s, Indonesia had already developed a dense system of infrastructure (for example, clinics, health centers, and distribution outlets) and a ubiquitous cadre of workers supplying family planning services—investments that are generally considered crucial in the early phases of fertility decline. Additional investments in such inputs during the mid-1980s seem to have had less payoff, possibly because Indonesia had approached diminishing marginal returns to a policy that emphasized public supply interventions, particularly in the form of infrastructure investments. Indonesian authorities apparently recognized this and, in 1986, they initiated an aggressive program to increase the participation of the private sector in service delivery while concentrating public investments in lagging areas. The findings in this study provide strong support for this shift in policy strategy.

An Agenda for Future Work

The overview of cross-country experiences in this study suggests broad directions for future policies. The results are, however, inadequate for formulating country-specific strategies, particularly in large countries where substantial regional differences exist in current demographic conditions and government policies. For this purpose, additional data and analytical work are needed. Specifically, the agenda for future work could usefully focus on three broad topics. First, because sustainable policies are vital to reduce future population increases significantly, analyses focused on identifying the design of long-term strategies to help countries reach and stay at replacement level fertility would offer a particularly useful guide for policy discussions. Second, because contraceptive use and fertility behavior depends on the social and economic context, analyses about couples' choices under different conditions would help in the design of effective family planning policies. Third, because population momentum will lead to inevitable increases in population in all Asian countries in the next few decades, identifying the best way to cope with the increase will also be an important area for future work.

Supporting Sustainable Policies

Government interventions can slow population growth, and governments in Asian countries have indeed taken steps to do so, often with success. The effect of interventions materializes mainly in the long run, however, in large part because short-run increases in population size are heavily influenced by the relatively young age structures of Asia's populations—a demographic characteristic difficult to alter immediately via current policies. If reducing long-run population size is a goal, policies must aim to sustain declines in fertility *and* maintain fertility at low levels over relatively long periods of time.

Sustained policies are important for other reasons as well. In particular, they are more likely to bring about gradual rather than abrupt changes in the age structure of the population. Gradual changes in this population characteristic is preferred because the demand for many public services are age-sensitive, and because rapid expansion and contraction of their provision are difficult to manage.

What does long-term sustainability in population policies entail? At a minimum, it requires attention to the building of a durable institutional framework that ensures the availability of appropriate family planning services. The government has a decidedly important role as a direct supplier of services, particularly to lower-income and rural populations, as well as in the early phases of the demographic transition, when knowledge about contraception is poor, the physical infrastructure is sparse, and private providers are not willing to risk investments in areas where the demand is limited.

Three issues, however, could limit the sustainability of a purely public program over the long run: (a) the effects of political exigencies; (b) mismatch between available public services and the preferences of the target clientele; and (c) constraints on the financing of services for an ever-growing population of users. These concerns could be addressed by diversifying the sources of finance and provision for family planning services. In Asia, the private sector currently has a relatively small role in family planning—with commercial providers servicing, on average, 14 percent of all contraceptive users, compared with 40 percent in Latin American countries. Increased involvement of the private sector would contribute toward program sustainability, particularly in the more successful, lower-fertility countries.

Government policies can influence the viability of private providers, not only by regulating their operations, but also through the pricing of public sector services. Controls are needed to protect public safety, but overly stringent controls—for example, permitting only doctors to refill prescriptions for contraceptive pills—can stifle private business. With regard to financing policies, widespread and heavily subsidized contraceptive services could attract more users, but they could also hurt the financial survival of private providers. As a result, use could increase in the short run, but possibly not in a manner that is easily sustainable in the long run.

As contraceptive use spreads, it becomes important to identify population groups for whom heavily subsidized services are no longer essential to encourage use. Attention to this issue would allow sharper targeting of public family planning subsidies and services to the disadvantaged and other population groups for whom private services are either too costly or simply unavailable. Involvement of the private sector would in this way enhance the effectiveness of government intervention in family planning.

Improving Knowledge for Policy Formulation

In general, data availability, coverage, and quality have improved steadily over time in most Asian countries, making it easier to conduct the needed analyses. Whereas earlier surveys focused mostly on women's contraceptive and fertility histories, more recent surveys have been expanded to generate information on the use of public and private services and the personal costs of obtaining services. Survey questionnaire design has also improved, eliciting better responses from respondents. The expanded and improved data generally permit more detailed analyses of fertility behavior, contraceptive choice, and the incidence of public subsidies and services. In addition, the increased frequency of surveys, particularly in countries experiencing rapid fertility changes, also allows closer monitoring of demographic changes and their implications for planning the provision of such services as health and education.

There is, nonetheless, scope for improvement, especially to increase the availability of data on such policy-relevant variables as levels of public spending, types and density of services provided, skill mix of personnel providing the services, and other community-level data. Linking such data to information on individuals' contraceptive and fertility histories in a single data set opens up new possibilities for addressing questions about the effect of alternative policies on family planning outcomes across population groups in different socioeconomic settings. Tracking changes over time is especially desired to minimize technical problems associated with results based on single-period, cross-sectional data.

The case study on Indonesia reported in this study illustrates an analytical approach with possible application elsewhere. Asian countries face diverse population problems, so the precise specification of the models would need to differ. In some countries, for example, expenditure levels and allocations may warrant closer attention, whereas in others, better targeting of public subsidies may deserve more focus. Evaluating alternative options would be facilitated by analyses of contraceptive and fertility behavior under alternative supply interventions in different socioeconomic and population settings. Filling such knowledge gaps in policy analysis would contribute to improved policies to deepen and sustain Asian countries' hitherto impressive record of achievements in family planning.

Coping with Population Increase and Change

In part because of Asian governments' substantial efforts to promote family planning, fertility rates in the region can be expected to continue declining in the future. Under World Bank population projection assumptions (described in detail in chapter 7), by 2015 the majority of countries in the region will have reached replacement level fertility, a situation where the average adult woman produces roughly 2.1 births over her reproductive life span. Under these assumptions, Asian populations are projected to grow more slowly during 1990–2030 than they did during 1950–90. Over the next forty years, increases in absolute numbers will generally be smaller, or not much bigger, than the increases experienced in the past forty years. The increments nonetheless remain substantial: for example, between 1990 and 2030, the population of Bangladesh is projected to grow from 107 million to 184 million; China's population, from 1,134 million to 1,648 million; and India's population, is projected to grow from 850 million to 1,407 million.

An important reason for this growth has to do with the young age structures of the current populations of these countries. Because of this factor (called *population momentum*), population growth would remain substantial even if replacement fertility were reached immediately. Under the assumption that women average around 2.1 births over their reproductive life span from 1995 onward, Bangladesh's population, for example, would grow by 62 percent instead of the 74 percent under standard World Bank projections. In other words, over 80 percent of projected population growth in Bangladesh during 1990–2030 is virtually inevitable.

Different policies could lead countries to attain replacement level fertility at different dates and affect future population sizes. The total population of the eighteen Asian countries included in this study was 2.7 billion in 1990. Under standard World Bank assumptions, their aggregate population is projected to be 4.4 billion in 2030, 4.9 billion in 2050, and 5.2 billion in 2075. A delay in the onset of replacement level fertility by 20 years from the dates assumed in standard World Bank projections would result in aggregate (or average) increases that are 9 (or 12) percent larger than in the standard projections in 2030, 14 (or 18) percent larger in 2050, and 18 (or 24) percent larger in 2075, corresponding, respectively, to absolute differences of 410 million over 40 years, 660 million over 60 years, and 930 million over 85 years. The percentage differences are substantially larger in countries where the demographic transition is still at an early stage, such as Cambodia, Lao People's Democratic Republic, Nepal, Pakistan, and Papua New Guinea. Initiating and sustaining fertility declines in these countries would have relatively large effects on their long-run population sizes.

The unavoidable increase in the size of most Asian populations over the next forty years, as well as the attendant changes in the age composition and geographic distribution of the population, will present significant policy challenges in such areas as environmental management, education and health service delivery, employment creation, and urban development. The study does not address these issues in detail, but documents the demographic dimensions of the problems involved as a point of departure for discussing policies to address them.

ENVIRONMENT. Asia has significant environmental problems, some caused, in part, by rapid population growth. Some of these problems would be relieved if population density were reduced, but because the effect of population policies are slow to materialize, such policies do not, in themselves, provide the total, nor indeed the primary answer to environmental problems. For example, in the Philippines, if per capita income grew at 5 percent a year, population grew according to standard World Bank assumptions, and the level of pollution (or any other form of environmental degradation) per unit of income remained constant, pollution in 2030 would be 12 times the level in 1990. If fertility were reduced immediately to replacement level from 1990 onward, pollution in 2030 would be 10 times the 1990 level. The reduction in fertility clearly relieves environmental stress, but pollution levels would still be 10 times worse in 2030 than in 1990. This simulation, and those for other Asian countries in the study—while based on simple assumptions—suggests that the lion's share of the burden of solving environmental problems, at least over the next forty years, clearly rests with policies directed at reducing pollution per unit of income.

EDUCATION. According to World Bank projections, increases in Asia's school-age population between 1990 and 2000 will range from -12 percent (Republic of Korea) to 136 percent (Cambodia). The demographic trends are especially relevant for education planning in primary education because most governments consider universal enrollment at this level a basic policy objective. In some Asian countries—including Bhutan, Lao People's Democratic Republic, Nepal, Pakistan, and Papua New Guinea—grade-one entry is still incomplete, and substantial increases in the primary school-age population are projected. More investments in physical facilities and teacher training are needed to expand coverage, but increases in such investments would leave fewer resources to improve schooling conditions unless overall funding for primary education increased. Mobilizing the needed resources and making the right tradeoffs in resource allocation are central issues in these countries.

In countries such as India and Indonesia, first-grade entry is widespread and the primary school age population is not expected to grow significantly. Continuation rates in primary education nonetheless remain poor, particularly in India, where currently less than 40 percent of the 83 percent of the population who enter grade one eventually reach grade five. As the demographic pressures ease, improving education quality becomes increasingly feasible. An important policy challenge is to identify cost-effective school input mixes to enhance continuation rates and student learning.

The policy issues are markedly different in such countries as the Republic of Korea, Sir Lanka, and Thailand, which share the prospect of a shrinking school-age population. This development implies potential savings which could be used to upgrade education quality, but rigidities in the education system could prevent such savings from materializing. In these countries, policymakers may need to consider substantial restructuring of the system in light of the emerging demographic realities.

The implications of population prospects in China and Cambodia are also noteworthy. Because of their disrupted demographic histories, these countries expect large shifts in the size of school-age cohorts over relatively short periods—changes giving rise to unique problems in education planning. For example, because it takes time to train teachers and because teachers are not easily transferred or discharged, pupil-teacher ratios are likely to swing widely from one period to the next, causing significant changes in schooling conditions. In these circumstances, appropriate policies regarding teacher training and employment are critical to minimize the adverse effects of these swings on learning outcomes. Similarly, policies regarding investments in and use of physical facilities are needed to avoid excessive crowding or underutilization.

HEALTH. Overall demographic trends in Asia over the next two decades point to lower crude death rates, as cohort sizes expand more rapidly in the low-mortality age groups than at other ages. Except in China and the Republic of Korea, countries which are furthest along in the demographic transition, well over 75 percent of the population in 2010 would still be under 45 years of age.

This salutary prospect implies changing, rather than lessened, demands on health services. The elderly population is increasing from a tiny base, and would, for at least the next two decades, still constitute a small share of the total population. Over the longer term, however, institutions must be developed—for example, health insurance systems—to ensure that the chronic health needs of the aged are addressed in a cost-effective manner without imposing heavy tradeoffs in public budgets against other basic health services.

The more immediate challenges concern health services for children and women. In the 1980s, the population of children below age 5 in Asia increased, on average, by over 30 percent, but in the 1990s, the increase is projected at only 5 percent, and in the 2000s, a modest decline is actually anticipated. In purely quantitative terms, growth in the demand for basic health services for young children, particularly immunizations, can be expected to slow in the next two decades relative to the 1980s, making further gains in coverage easier to attain. Declining fertility in Asia is, however, likely to increase the demand for better-quality child health services. At the same time, contraceptive use can be expected to increase. In the mid- to late-1980s, contraceptive prevalence averaged 43 percent across Asian countries for which data are available. If prevalence rises toward the levels characterizing fully contracepting populations (around 70 to 75 percent), substantial increases in the demand for contraceptive services can be expected, raising issues about burden-sharing in the financing of those services.

EMPLOYMENT. In most countries in Asia, a slowdown in the growth of the working-age population is expected. Whereas this population increased, on average, by 30 percent between 1970 and 1980, the increase was 27 percent between 1980 and 1990, and is projected at 25 percent between 1990 and 2000, and 24 percent between 2000 and 2010. In purely quantitative terms, these trends suggest a possible modest easing of pressures on employment creation in Asian countries in the coming decades compared to the past. Landlessness, however, may rise in rural areas and significantly increase pressures on urban labor markets as people move there in search of employment.

Most Asian countries will experience large cohorts of young people entering the labor force for the first time, on a scale similar to that in the 1980s, but much smaller than in the 1970s. Job readiness training and the school-to-work transition among youth are therefore likely to remain important challenges in the 1990s. In a few countries, including China, Cambodia, Sri Lanka, and Myanmar, past fertility and mortality trends have created large swings in the cohort size of the youthful population, relaxing the demand for job creation in one decade but exacerbating it in the next. In all these countries, the swings in labor supply conditions will test the responsiveness of existing labor market institutions and add to the political stress of addressing unemployment and related problems among youths, particularly during supply upswings.

URBANIZATION. Asian countries are typically less urbanized than Latin American or African countries. In 1990, 30 percent of Asia's populations lived in urban areas, compared with over 70 percent in Latin America and nearly 35 percent in Africa.

The potential for increased urbanization in Asia is thus substantial. According to projections by the United Nations, Asia's main urban centers are projected to expand, on average, by 50 percent in the decade between 1990 and 2000 alone. In absolute terms, the scale of projected increase in population in some cities is truly gigantic: from 6.4 million to 11.3 million in Dhaka; 11.1 million to 15.4 million in Bombay; 9.4 million to 13.2 million in Jakarta; 7.7 million to 11.7 million in Karachi; and 8.4 million to 11.5 million in Manila.

The scale and speed of urbanization will add enormous pressure on what are still inadequate and unreliable basic physical infrastructure and services, presenting demanding challenges for urban management and development. Past models of urban development reserved a leading role for central governments in the financing and provision of services, but experience with such models has been less than satisfactory. Notably, policy has tended to focus on public investment, failing to recognize the critical role of local institutions in the operation and maintenance of infrastructure as well as the importance of establishing incentives to maximize the contribution of private sector activity. The public sector's dominance has also constrained and skewed responses to the burgeoning demand for shelter, infrastructure, and services in urban areas. Given these experiences, the prospects for population growth in urban areas only strengthen the case for substantial restructuring of the government's role to support sustainable urban development in the coming decades.

Notes

1. This emphasis may, in part, reflect the greater scope for influencing population growth through policies to alter fertility rather than migration or mortality.

2. On some topics, the full sample could not be analyzed because data were lacking. Pakistan was originally excluded from the study because, prior to December 1991, it was administratively classified in a different geographic region by the World Bank. As the study proceeded, data for Pakistan were added to the extent possible within the time constraints on the study.

3. This audience might include, for example, macroeconomists and non-population-sector specialists. While not having a direct role in implementing population policies and programs, these people have more than a passing interest in population problems because countries' demographic makeup and prospects provide the overall context for social and economic development. Population specialists will be familiar with much of the material covered here but may nonetheless find interest in the study's comparative perspective on population issues, as well as the factual information presented on program characteristics.

4. This discussion is not intended as a review of the literature on population and development. It is meant simply to alert readers to the place of this study in the general literature. For a useful discussion on population and development, see Birdsall (1988) and the citations therein.

5. See, for example, Johnson and Lee (1987). A small number of studies also rely on individual data to assess the effect of high fertility on household and individual welfare (see, for example, Knodel and Wongsith 1991 and Havanon, Knodel, and Sittitrai 1989).

6. See also Ehrlich (1968), which had earlier excited much interest in the adverse effects of population growth.

7. There are numerous citations to this literature, many of which appear in, for example, Bulatao and Lee (1983); Easterlin and Crimmins (1985); Schultz (1986); and Montgomery (1988).

8. Cochrane and Guilkey (1991, 1992), and Guilkey and Cochrane (1992) are recent examples.

9. See, for example, Lapham and Simmons (1987), and World Bank 1992.

10. An exception is the World Bank's *World Development Report 1984*.

11. See, for example, World Bank 1984.

12. Although population policies can address issues of migration and mortality, this study focuses on those related to fertility.

13. Although differences in demographic conditions within countries are obviously important to consider in formulating country-specific policies, the large number of countries surveyed here makes it difficult to analyze these differences in adequate detail. These analyses must await further work.

14. Between 1990 and 2030, the populations of the eighteen Asian countries in this study are projected by the World Bank to increase by an average of 82 percent (unweighted by population size). On average, nearly 70 percent of this increase

would occur even if fertility fell immediately to replacement levels of around 2.1 births per woman.

15. For example, the populations of Asian countries in 2075 would, on average, be 25 percent larger than in World Bank projections if replacement level fertility began twenty years later than assumed in those projections.

16. It bears reiterating that the simple cross-country comparisons made here are merely suggestive. Because of cultural and other differences in social conditions between India and Indonesia, it may well be that a higher density of outlets is needed in India to compensate for the disadvantages of poor institutions, weak infrastructure (such as roads), or inadequate social development. Whether or not investment in the hardware components of the family planning program has run into diminishing returns in India cannot be determined on the basis of simple cross-country comparisons. This would require the kind of analysis performed with Indonesian data in chapter 6 of this study.

2

Population Size and Growth in Asian Countries

POPULATION GREW UNUSUALLY RAPIDLY in Asia between 1950 and 1990. The populations of most Asian countries more than doubled over that period, and the populations of some of these countries increased nearly three-fold. What fueled this extraordinary increase in population? What similarities and differences characterized Asian countries in their patterns of population growth? This chapter addresses these questions by documenting the main determinants of population growth in Asia's recent past. It considers trends in birth and death rates as well as examines the effect of changes in such factors as mortality, fertility, and the age structure on these components of population growth.[1] Beyond demographic accounting, the chapter also distills a lesson from Asia's demographic past.

Population Sizes in 1950 and 1990

Table 2.1 presents the population sizes for a sample of eighteen selected developing Asian countries plus Japan, which is included for comparison. All the countries, except Japan, are now considered either low- or middle-income countries by the World Bank. In 1950, all of them, again except Japan, would have been considered low-income countries. The total population of these eighteen Asian countries was 1.2 billion people in 1950, compared with 2.7 billion people in 1990—more than a doubling, at an average growth rate of 2.0 percent a year during this period. For every person alive in 1950 there were 2.25 alive in 1990.

Differences across countries are striking. Relatively small increases were registered in Japan, where 1.48 persons were alive in 1990 for each person alive in 1950; in Bhutan, where 1.95 persons were alive in 1990 for each person alive in 1950 (because of extremely high mortality throughout the period); and in Cambodia, where the corresponding figure is only 1.98 persons alive in 1990 for each person alive in 1950 (because of the massive casualties inflicted by the Pol Pot government). In the rest of the sample, no country's population in 1990 was less than double what it was in 1950. China is the most populous country in the group; its 1950 population of 555 million had, by 1990, more than doubled to 1,134 million. India, with a population of 358 million in 1950, had grown to 850 million in 1990. In 1950, Indonesia had slightly fewer people than Japan, 80 million compared with 84 million respectively. By 1990, Indonesia had a population almost 50 percent larger than that of Japan (178 million relative to 124 million).

Table 2.1: Population Sizes of Selected Asian Countries in 1950 and 1990

Country	1950	1990	Ratio of 1990 population to 1950 population
Bangladesh	41,783	109,820	2.63
Bhutan	734	1,433	1.95
Cambodia	4,346	8,610	1.98
China	554,760	1,133,683	2.04
India	357,561	849,514	2.38
Indonesia	79,538	178,232	2.24
Japan	83,625	123,537	1.48
Korea, DPR	9,726	21,771	2.24
Korea, Republic of	20,357	42,869	2.11
Lao PDR	1,755	4,140	2.36
Malaysia	6,110	17,763	2.91
Myanmar	17,832	41,825	2.35
Nepal	8,182	18,916	2.31
Pakistan	39,513	112,351	2.84
Papua New Guinea	1,613	3,875	2.40
Philippines	20,988	61,480	2.93
Sri Lanka	7,678	16,993	2.21
Thailand	20,010	56,303	2.81
Viet Nam	29,954	66,233	2.21
Asia[a]	1,222,440	2,745,811	2.25 (2.38)

a. Excludes data for Japan; figure in parenthesis refers to the unweighted average of the country data.

Source: United Nations 1991d for 1950 data; Bos and others 1994 for 1990 data.

The two most rapidly growing countries were the Philippines and Malaysia. Both countries had 2.9 persons in 1990 for each person in 1950. Two countries—Pakistan and Thailand—had populations which had around 2.8 residents in 1990 for each resident in 1950. On the other hand, two countries—China and the Republic of Korea—had populations which only slightly more than doubled.

Every country in the sample thus has had to accommodate a substantial increase in its population. China had one of the slowest-growing populations in the sample, but because of its high initial size, over a half billion people were added to its population in the forty-year period, more than twice as many as currently live in the United States. India's initial population was smaller than China's, but a relatively fast pace of population growth resulted in an increase of about 492 million people between 1950 and 1990. This *increase* was greater than *ten times* the population of Bangladesh in 1950. The population of the Philippines was 21 million in 1950 and 61 million in 1990. The *increase* to the Philippine population in that period was around *twice* the population of the Republic of Korea in 1950. This period of population growth was probably the fastest that these countries had experienced in centuries.

Trends in Population Growth Rates

Between the early 1950s and late 1980s, governments and donors alike invested resources and effort to slow population growth. Yet the rates of population increase during 1950–54 and 1985–89 were virtually identical (figure 2.1)![2]

Closer examination of the data reveals that the rate of population growth did not, in fact, remain constant between 1950 and 1989 (figure 2.2). It rose from around 2 percent a year during 1950–54, to 2.5 percent a year during 1965–69, falling back to about 2 percent a year by 1985–89.

In light of these trends, it is not surprising that interest in reducing population growth rose in the late 1960s and early 1970s. Population growth rates were not only high, but at that point, they had been increasing substantially for over a decade. In a sense, there is good news and bad news in the observation that population growth rates were the same in 1950–54 as in 1985–89. The good news is that population growth rates have been falling for over twenty years now. The bad news is that it took the entire twenty years of falling rates, from 1965–69 to 1985–89, to undo the rise in population growth rates which occurred in the 1950s and 1960s. Perhaps the best news, though, is that as population growth rates continue to fall in the 1990s, they will finally fall below the early 1950s level of 2 percent per year.

Crossover Pattern among Currently Low-, Medium-, and High-Fertility Countries

The average time profile of population growth masks differences across countries. To further investigate the pattern of rising and then falling average population

Figure 2.1: Population Growth Rate in Asia, 1950–54 and 1985–89

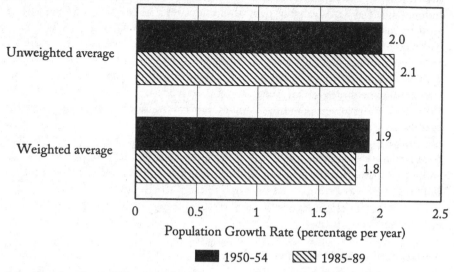

Population Growth Rate (percentage per year)

■ 1950-54   ▨ 1985-89

Source: Based on data in UN 1990; data for 1950-54 omit the Koreas which were at war.
Note: Figure excludes data for Bhutan and Pakistan.

Figure 2.2: Population Growth Rates in Asia, 1950–89

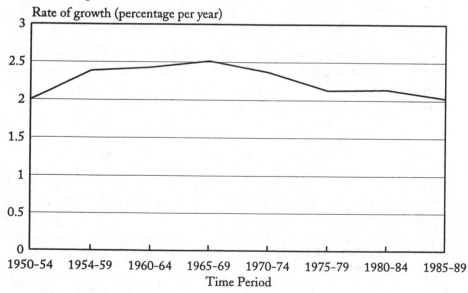

Source: Unweighted data from UN 1990.
Note: Figure excludes data for Bhutan and Pakistan.

growth rates, the sample of countries was divided into three groups based on their level of fertility in the 1985–89 period.[3] The low-fertility group includes China, the two Koreas, Sri Lanka, and Thailand. The medium-fertility group consists of India, Indonesia, Malaysia, Myanmar, the Philippines, and Viet Nam. The high-fertility group is composed of Bangladesh, Cambodia, Lao People's Democratic Republic, Nepal, and Papua New Guinea. Do these groups of countries exhibit differences in their time profiles of population growth rates?[4]

There are, indeed, marked differences in the time profiles of population growth rates among the three groups (figure 2.3). As expected, the low-fertility countries in 1985–89 had the lowest population growth rates in the 1985–89 period; the high-fertility countries had the highest population growth rates, and the medium-fertility countries had intermediate population growth rates. What is unexpected is that the *low* population growth rate group in 1985–89 was the *high* population growth group in the 1950s, and that the countries with the *highest* population growth in the 1980s had the *lowest* population growth in the 1950s.

This crossover pattern is very striking. Only the group with intermediate fertility in 1985–89 shows a time profile of population growth rates which looks like the average pattern in figure 2.2. The other two groups have almost opposite behavior. Among the high-fertility countries in 1985–89, population growth rates have been climbing almost continuously, from 1.73 percent a year in 1950–54 to 2.51 percent per year in 1985–89. The low-fertility countries, on the other hand, reached their

Figure 2.3: Population Growth Rates in Three Groups of Asian Countries, 1950–89

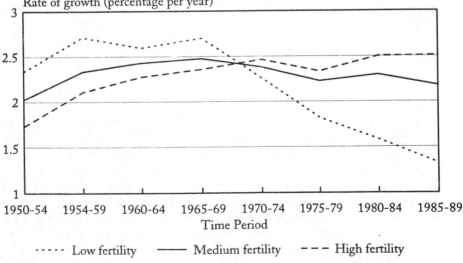

Low fertility ····· Medium fertility ───── High fertility ─ ─ ─

Source: Unweighted data from UN 1990 for countries grouped according to fertility in 1985-89.

highest population growth rate, 2.71 percent a year, in 1955–59, and beginning in the early 1970s, their population growth rates began to fall rapidly, reaching an average of 1.33 percent a year in 1985–89. Neither the high- nor the medium-fertility group of countries even approached the peak population growth rate of the low-fertility group of countries at any time during the 1950–90 period.

What factors produced the crossover phenomenon? Why was the earlier population growth rate of those countries, which are now so successful in reducing their population growth, so high? Was the phenomenon of high prior rates of population growth associated, in any way, with their currently low rates of population growth? What about the reverse? In the currently high-fertility countries, were the earlier low rates of population growth connected, in any way, with the higher subsequent population growth rates? Finally, did population policies have any influence on the crossover pattern? These are important and relevant questions for understanding the past as a context for future population policies. Answering them requires, as a first step, a consideration of the determinants of population growth rates.

The Determinants of Population Growth: Crude Birth and Death Rates

The populations of countries grow mainly because of the excess of births over deaths.[5] Other things being equal, larger populations generate both more births and more deaths. To account for differences in population size, demographers often use the concepts of *crude birth rate* and *crude death rate*. The crude birth (death) rate is the number of births (deaths) divided by the size of the population and multiplied by 1,000. In other words, the crude birth (death) rate is 10 times the percentage of births (deaths), where the base of the percentage is size of the population. Ignoring international migration, the rate of population growth in percent is just the difference between the crude birth rate and the crude death rate, divided by 10.

General Trends

To see how changes in crude birth and death rates produced the patterns of population growth rates observed above, consider figure 2.4, which shows the unweighted average of the crude birth rates and the crude death rates for 16 of the 18 sample countries (that is, excluding Bhutan and Pakistan). In 1950–54, the average crude birth rate was 44.45 and the average crude death rate was 23.39. Therefore, the rate of population growth, ignoring international migration, was 2.1 percent a year [(44.45 - 23.39)/10 = 2.1]. Between 1950–54 and 1965–69, the crude birth rate fell very little, by only 3.76 points, to a value of 40.69. In contrast, the crude death rate fell quite quickly in that period, by 7.90 points. Because the death rate fell by more than the birth rate, the rate of population growth increased. Between 1965–69 and 1985–89, the reverse occurred. The crude birth rate fell by 10.22 points, while the crude death rate fell by only 5.54 points. The more rapid fall in birth rate was the

Figure 2.4: Trends in Crude Birth and Death Rates in Asia, 1950–89

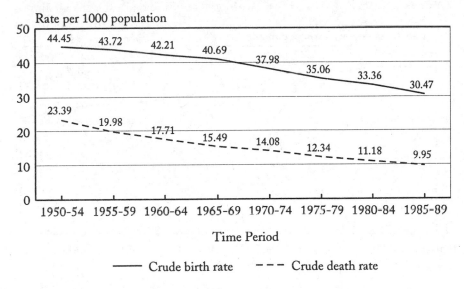

Source: Unweighted data from UN 1990.
Note: Figure excludes data for Bhutan and Pakistan.

cause of the observed decline in the rate of population growth after 1965–69. The rate of population growth was roughly the same in 1985–89 as it was in 1950–54 because decreases in the crude birth rate and crude death rate over that span were almost identical. The pattern of increasing and then decreasing population growth rates occurred because the more rapid portion of the mortality decline preceded the more rapid portion of the fertility decline.

Decomposition of the Crossover Phenomenon

Differences in the time profile of crude birth and death rates among countries in the three fertility groupings help to explain the crossover phenomenon identified above. Figure 2.5 shows the crude birth rates of the countries in each group. Notice that the crude birth rate graphs never cross. The low-fertility countries always have the lowest crude birth rates, the medium-fertility countries always have intermediate levels of the crude birth rate, and the high-fertility countries always have high crude birth rates. A second interesting feature is the closeness of the crude birth rates of all three groups of countries in the 1950s and 1960s. It was only in the 1970s that the crude birth rates of the low-fertility countries began to drop rapidly. The medium-fertility group had a fairly uniform and slower decline in their average crude birth rate

Figure 2.5: Trends in Crude Birth Rates in Three Groups of Asian Countries,
1950–89

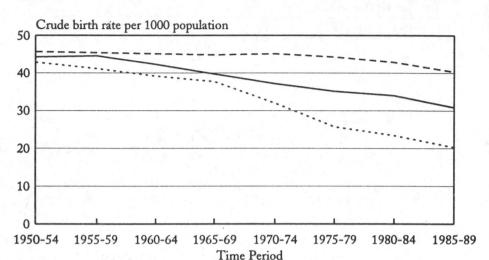

Source: Unweighted data from UN 1990 for countries grouped according to fertility level in 1985-89.

from the late 1950s onward. The high-fertility group did not show any appreciable change in its crude birth rate until the 1980s. Thus, two decades of rather similar crude birth rates were followed by another two decades in which the gap between the crude birth rates of the low and high groups continuously widened.

The crude death rates among the three country groups also show no crossover pattern, but their time profile differs from that of the crude birth rates (figure 2.6). In 1950–54, the crude death rate in the low-fertility group was 18.57, while in the high-fertility group it was 25.82. The crude death rate of the low-fertility countries fell fairly rapidly at first, but then flattened out. Between 1970–74 and 1985–89 there has been little decline in the crude death rate. The medium-fertility countries experienced the most rapid declines in their crude death rate, and by 1985–89, the difference between the crude death rates of the low- and medium-fertility groups was smaller than it had ever been since 1950. Nevertheless, the crude death rates of medium-fertility countries also appear to exhibit a tendency to stop falling so rapidly. The high-fertility countries, on the other hand, had crude death rates which were still falling rather rapidly in the 1980s.[6]

The foregoing patterns in crude birth and death rates help to explain the crossover phenomenon noted earlier. Crude birth rates were similar among the three groups

Figure 2.6: Trends in Crude Death Rates in Three Groups of Asian Countries, 1950–89

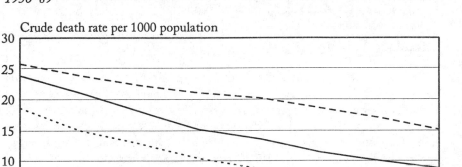

Crude death rate per 1000 population

Source: Unweighted data from UN 1990 for countries grouped according to fertility in 1985-89.

of countries in the 1950s and 1960s, but their crude death rates were very different. The lower-fertility countries had lower and rapidly falling crude death rates in the 1950s and 1960s, and so experienced more rapid population growth in this period. The high fertility countries had higher crude death rates and comparable crude birth rates, so that their population growth was lower. The medium-fertility countries had intermediate levels of crude death rates and so had intermediate levels of population growth.

After 1970, the low-fertility countries experienced rapidly falling crude birth rates and more slowly falling crude death rates. The result was a rapid fall in their population growth rates. The high-fertility countries experienced higher initial, but steadily falling, crude death rates. When this was combined with high and fairly constant crude birth rates, it caused an increase in the population growth rates. In the 1980s, crude birth rates in the high-fertility countries began to fall, but crude death rates were falling more rapidly so that the population growth rate continued to increase.

The changes in crude birth and death rates reflect the effects of underlying trends in fertility and mortality interacting with shifts in population age structures. In particular, the crude birth rate depends on the rate at which women of reproductive age bear children and the number of women in the reproductive ages. The crude death rate depends on the rates at which people die at each age and the number of males and females at each age. Below we examine how each of these factors have evolved over time in Asian countries.

Trends in Fertility

The rate at which women of reproductive age bear children is conveniently summarized by the *total fertility rate*, defined as the number of children a woman would bear over an entire reproductive span if she experienced the fertility rates observed in a particular period. Replacement fertility is a particularly important level of the total fertility rate. In an environment with no mortality before the mean age at childbearing and in which 50 percent of all births are girls, women of childbearing age would need to produce an average of 2 children each just to replace themselves. Where mortality is not negligible, the total fertility rate would need to be higher. In countries with low rates of mortality, the 1990 replacement level fertility would be around 2.1 births per woman. In countries like Bangladesh where mortality is still high, replacement level fertility could be as high as 2.5 births per woman or even higher. One advantage of the total fertility rate is that, unlike the crude birth rate, it is independent of the age structure of the population and, therefore, reflects underlying fertility behavior more accurately than does the crude birth rate.

All the countries in the low-fertility sample started with total fertility rates exceeding 5 births per woman in 1950–54 (figure 2.7). A few country highlights in this group are noteworthy. China's total fertility rate fell from 6.24 births per woman in 1950–54 to 5.40 in 1955–59. The decline was due to a severe famine induced by the policies of the Great Leap Forward. As the famine eased in the early 1960s, fertility rose, almost fully regaining its previous level by 1965–69, when the total fertility rate reached 5.99 births per woman. The spectacular falls—from 5.99 births per woman in 1965–69 to 4.76 in 1970–74 and then to 2.90 in 1975–79— coincided with the earlier phase of China's family limitation program, the campaign of "later, longer, fewer." The one-child family policy was introduced in 1979 and brought the total fertility rate down from 2.90 births per woman in 1975– 79 to 2.41 in 1985–89.

The total fertility rate in the Republic of Korea fell substantially in each five-year period from 1955–59. In 1985–89 it reached 1.60 births per woman, well below replacement level. At that rate, the average woman in the reproductive span would produce only around three-quarters of a daughter to replace herself. If this level of fertility persisted long enough for the age structure to adjust, the population would fall by one-quarter in every generation.[7]

In 1985–89, Thailand, with a total fertility rate of 2.20 births per woman, was on the verge of below-replacement fertility and is quite likely to have below-replacement fertility at this writing (1994). If so, Thailand would be the world's poorest country to experience below-replacement fertility under a voluntary policy

Figure 2.7: Trends in Total Fertility Rates in Currently Low Fertility Asian Countries, 1950–89

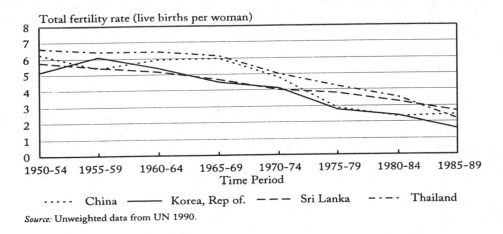

Source: Unweighted data from UN 1990.

regime, although with a GNP per capita of US$1,200 in 1989, it is the third richest of the eighteen developing Asian countries in the sample. The richest, the Republic of Korea, with a per capita income of US$4,400 in 1989, also had below-replacement fertility. The second richest, Malaysia, with a per capita GNP of US$2,160 in 1989, had a total fertility rate of 3.70 births per woman during 1985–89, much above replacement, but its government had adopted a pronatalist stance in the 1980s. Is the minimum income level at which below-replacement fertility is achieved likely to fall even further? If fertility in Sri Lanka descends below replacement in this decade, as is assumed under current World Bank projections, that income threshold would fall to around US$500 (in 1989 prices). Certainly it is possible that, given time, other low-income countries could achieve below-replacement fertility as well.

In the medium-fertility group, four of the six countries experienced comparable declines in their total fertility rates between 1980–84 and 1985–89 (figure 2.8). Those decreases were 0.55 births per woman in India, 0.57 in Indonesia, 0.54 in Malaysia, and 0.59 in Myanmar. The Philippines had the smallest change in fertility over the course of the 1980s, a decline of 0.38 births per woman. Viet Nam, on the other hand, had the most rapid change, a decrease of 0.72 births per woman. In all these countries, fertility is on a clear downward course.

The time paths of the total fertility rates in the high-fertility countries appear in figure 2.9. The most remarkable feature of this graph is the extraordinary decline in the total fertility rate of Bangladesh from 1970–74.[8] The country has sustained fertility decreases for around two decades now. It has the fastest falling fertility among the high-fertility countries, but most of the others are experiencing some

Figure 2.8: Trends in Total Fertility Rates in Currently Medium Fertility Asian Countries, 1950–89

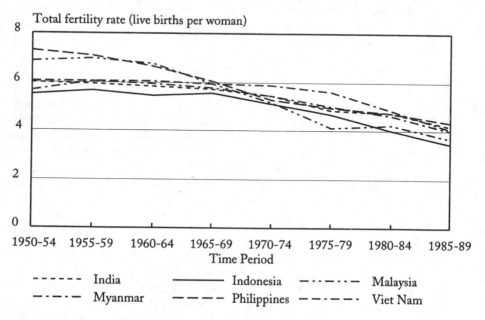

Source: Unweighted data from UN 1990.

decline as well. From 1980–84 to 1985–89, the total fertility rate fell in Cambodia by 0.31 births per woman, in Nepal by 0.31, and in Papua New Guinea by 0.33. These are not large changes, but they indicate significant downward movement in countries where fertility had been slow to fall. Only in Lao People's Democratic Republic, where the fertility data are not reliable, is there no sign of a fertility decrease.

Changes in Mortality

Mortality rates can be reflected succinctly in two measures: life expectancy at birth and the infant mortality rate. Throughout Asia, changes in these measures have contributed to declines in crude death rates. In all countries in the region, people have been living longer (table 2.2). Still, substantial disparities remain. A number of countries—China, the two Koreas, Malaysia, Sri Lanka, and Thailand—have made such substantial progress in lowering mortality rates that their aggregate life expectancy at birth was over 65 years in 1985–89. Malaysia aside,

*Figure 2.9: Trends in Total Fertility Rates in Currently High Fertility Asian
Countries, 1950–89*

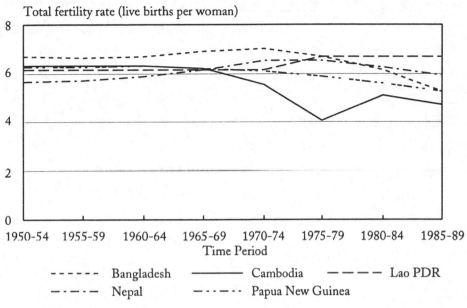

Total fertility rate (live births per woman)

1950-54	1955-59	1960-64	1965-69	1970-74	1975-79	1980-84	1985-89

Time Period

- - - - - - Bangladesh   ———— Cambodia   — — — — Lao PDR

— · — · — Nepal   — · · — · · Papua New Guinea

Source: Unweighted data from UN 1990.

these are all countries in the low-fertility group. On the other hand, there are
countries where life expectancy at birth was still below 55 years in 1985–89,
sometimes significantly below, including Bangladesh, Cambodia, Lao People's
Democratic Republic, Nepal, and Papua New Guinea. These countries are in the
high-fertility group. Countries where the life expectancy at birth was between 55
and 65 years in 1985–89 include India, Indonesia, Myanmar, the Philippines, and
Viet Nam. Generally, countries in the middle group of life expectancy also fall in
the middle of the distribution of total fertility rates. Life expectancy and fertility
thus appear to be closely related.

Biologically, females are more robust than males, and one would expect them
to have higher life expectancies. The sex differential in life expectancy is,
however, not simply biological. It also reflects the care and nutrition given to
girls relative to boys, the probability of dying in childbirth, and a host of other
factors. In two countries in the sample—Bangladesh and Nepal—the life
expectancies are greater for males than for females. In India, male life expectancy
was historically higher than female life expectancy, but they have recently

*Table 2.2: Life Expectancy at Birth in Selected Asian Countries, 1950–54
and 1985–89 (Years)*

| Country | Both sexes | | 1985–1989 | | |
	1950–54	1985–89	Male	Female	Male–Female
Bangladesh	36.6	50.7	51.1	50.4	−0.7
Bhutan	36.3	47.9	48.6	47.1	−1.5
Cambodia	39.4	48.5	47.0	49.9	2.9
China	40.8	69.4	68.0	70.9	2.9
India	38.7	57.9	57.8	57.9	0.1
Indonesia	37.5	60.2	58.5	62.0	3.5
Japan	63.9	78.3	75.4	81.1	5.7
Korea, DPR	47.5	69.8	66.2	72.7	6.5
Korea, Rep. of	47.5	69.4	66.2	72.5	6.3
Lao, PDR	37.8	48.5	47.0	50.0	3.0
Malaysia	48.5	69.5	67.5	71.6	4.1
Mongolia	42.3	61.3	60.0	62.5	2.5
Myanmar	40.0	60.0	58.3	61.8	3.5
Nepal	36.6	50.9	51.5	50.3	−1.2
Papua New Guinea	35.1	53.9	53.2	54.7	1.5
Philippines	47.5	63.5	61.6	65.4	3.8
Sri Lanka	56.6	70.3	68.3	72.5	4.2
Thailand	47.0	65.0	63.0	67.1	4.1
Viet Nam	40.4	61.5	59.2	63.6	4.4
Country average[a]	42.0	59.9	58.5	61.3	2.8

a. Excludes data for Japan.
Source: United Nations 1990.

converged and are now practically identical. In these three countries in particular, women's health care, including reducing mortality from maternal mortality, needs serious attention.

Countries in the sample where the differential in life expectancies in favor of women is three years or less include Bangladesh, China, India, Cambodia, Lao PDR, Nepal, and Papua New Guinea. In other words, the unusually small differential in life expectancies occurs in all five of our high-fertility countries, plus China and India. In the high-fertility countries, some portion of the low differential is attributable to high rates of maternal mortality. In China, where fertility is quite low and life expectancy, in general, quite high, maternal mortality probably is not an important reason for the small differential. Although India has higher fertility than China and lower life expectancy, it does not seem likely that maternal mortality is the dominant factor explaining the small differential there either. After all, India is alone among the six intermediate-fertility countries in having such a low differential. The more likely reason is that parents in both China and India have a strong preference for sons, which is manifested by greater attention being devoted to their survival.

Infant mortality rates have declined substantially in every country in our sample (table 2.3). China's accomplishment is especially noteworthy: whereas 19.5 percent of all children born died in their first year of life during 1950–54, only 3.2 percent died during 1985–89.[9] No other country in the sample managed such a large decline. In the 1985–89 period, a number of countries still had high infant mortality rates. More than 9 percent of all children died in their first year of life in Bangladesh, India, Cambodia, Lao PDR, and Nepal. These countries are prime targets for intensified programs to lower infant mortality. Four of the five countries are in the high-fertility sample. The fifth, India, has a very high infant mortality rate relative to its life expectancy. This pattern may, in part, be due to the relatively poor care given to female children, but it also may indicate that child health programs in general are weak there.

At the other extreme are a number of countries—including China, the two Koreas, Malaysia, the Philippines, Sri Lanka, and Thailand—that have reduced the incidence of infant deaths to 5 percent or less. Malaysia and the Philippines aside, all these countries are in the low-fertility group.

Effects of Age and Sex Structures on Crude Birth and Death Rates

Besides fertility and mortality rates, the age and sex structures of populations also affect crude birth and death rates. Holding constant the average number of children ever born to women, crude birth rates are higher when the proportion of women of reproductive age in the population is greater. Holding constant life expectancy, crude death rates are generally higher in older populations—that is, populations with higher mean ages—than in younger populations.

*Table 2.3: Infant Mortality Rates in Selected Asian Countries, 1950–54 and 1985–89
(Deaths under the age of 1 per 1,000 Live Births)*

Country	1950-54	1985-89
Bangladesh	180	119
Bhutan	197	128
Cambodia	165	130
China	195	32
India	190	99
Indonesia	160	75
Japan	51	5
Korea, DPR	115	28
Korea, Rep. of	115	25
Lao, PDR	180	110
Malaysia	99	24
Mongolia	148	68
Myanmar	183	70
Nepal	197	128
Papua New Guinea	190	59
Philippines	100	45
Sri Lanka	91	28
Thailand	132	28
Vietnam	180	64
Country average[a]	157	70

a. Excludes data for Japan.
Source: United Nations 1990.

Cross-Country Differences in Age and Sex Structures

The age and sex structures of the eighteen countries in the sample differ markedly from one another because of different histories of population growth. The age pyramid for Bangladesh—characteristic of countries in the high-fertility group—shows the effects of prior rapid population growth in a high-mortality environment (figure 2.10). Each higher age group has significantly fewer people in it than in the age group below. The age pyramid for India (figure 2.11)—characteristic of countries in the medium-fertility group—is similar except that it does not collapse toward the middle axis as quickly as that for Bangladesh. This pattern arises, in part, because of slower recent population growth in India, and in part, because of India's lower mortality rates. The population pyramid for the Republic of Korea (figure 2.12)—characteristic of countries in the low-fertility group—is very different. The shorter bars toward the base of the pyramid show the effects of a recent rapid decrease in fertility.

How important are the differences in age structures shown in the figures? A rough indication can be obtained by starting with two 1990 age distributions, the Indian

Figure 2.10: Age Pyramid of Bangladesh, 1990

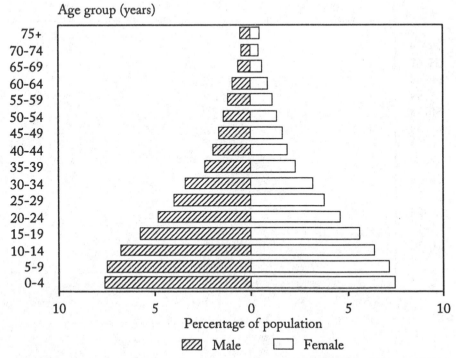

Source: Data from UN 1991b.

one (figure 2.11), the Korean one (figure 2.12), and projecting population growth for 1990–94, using standard World Bank projection assumptions about Indian fertility and mortality levels in that period as well as two age distributions for 1990, India's and the Republic of Korea's. With the Indian age distribution, the projections show a crude birth rate of 28.7, a crude death rate of 10.0, which imply a population growth rate of 1.87 percent a year (ignoring international migration). With the Korean age distribution, the projected crude birth rate was 32.2, the crude death rate was 11.2, resulting in population growth rate of 2.10 percent a year. The use of the Korean age structure thus produced a higher crude birth rate, a higher crude death rate, and a higher rate of population growth.

Many aspects of the age structure influence population growth. For ease of exposition, only two factors are considered here: (a) the proportion of women of reproductive age in the population, which influences crude birth rates; and (b) the median age of the population,[10] which influences crude death rates. The higher the proportion of women of reproductive age in the population, other things being constant, the higher will be the crude birth rate. In general, the higher the median

Figure 2.11: Age Pyramid of India, 1990

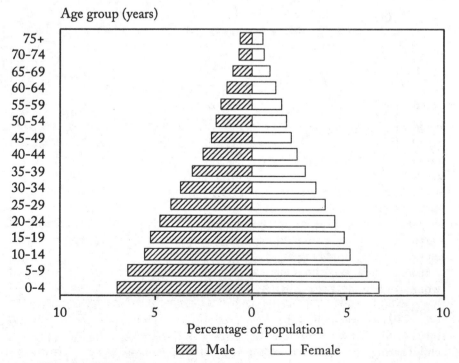

Age group (years)

Percentage of population

Male   Female

Source: Data from UN 1991b.

Figure 2.12: Age Pyramid of Korea, 1990

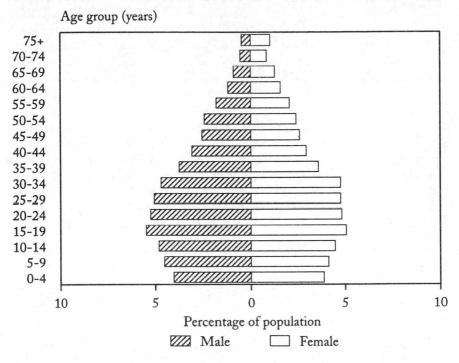

Age group (years)

Percentage of population

▨ Male   ☐ Female

Source: Data from UN 1991b.

age of the population, other things being constant, the higher the crude death rate will be. Korea had a higher proportion of reproductive age women in the population than India in 1990 (table 2.4), thus explaining the higher projected crude birth rate using Korea's age structure in the preceding calculation. But the median age in Korea was also higher, resulting in a higher projected crude death rate for India using Korea's age structure. The increase in the crude death rate was not sufficient to offset the increase in crude birth rate, however. On balance, therefore, the projections show a rise in India's projected population growth if it had Korea's age distribution in 1990.

In general, high-fertility countries in the sample have the lowest proportions of women of reproductive age in the population, and low-fertility countries have the highest proportions. The medium-fertility countries tend to have proportions which fall between the other two groups' data. The reason for the inverse relationship between the level of fertility and the proportion of women of childbearing age is clear from the population pyramids. Where fertility and population growth are relatively high, the proportion of the population below the

Table 2.4: Women of Reproductive Age as a Percentage of the Population, and Median Age of the Population in Selected Asian Countries, 1950 and 1990

Country	Women of reproductive age as percentage of the population[a]		Median age of the population[b]	
	1950	1990	1950	1990
Bangladesh	22.0	22.7	21.6	17.7
Cambodia	23.7	27.0	18.7	22.7
China	24.2	27.4	23.9	25.7
India	23.5	23.7	20.4	21.8
Indonesia	24.1	25.7	20.0	21.6
Japan	25.6	25.5	22.3	37.2
Korea, DPR	23.1	29.1	19.2	23.6
Korea, Rep. of	22.8	28.3	19.1	26.9
Lao PDR	23.7	22.8	18.9	18.2
Malaysia	22.2	25.0	19.8	20.9
Mongolia	23.6	23.9	19.0	19.1
Myanmar	24.9	25.1	21.8	20.9
Nepal	23.4	23.0	20.2	18.8
Papua New Guinea	23.0	23.4	20.3	19.2
Philippines	22.8	24.6	18.2	19.7
Sri Lanka	21.7	26.5	19.6	24.2
Thailand	23.6	27.0	18.4	22.9
Viet Nam	25.7	24.8	23.2	20.0
Country average[c]	23.4	25.3	20.1	21.4

a. In this table, the reproductive age range is 15–49 years.
b. The median age is the age which divides the population exactly in half.
c. Excludes data for Japan.
Source: United Nations 1991b.

age of fifteen tends to be high because more recent birth cohorts are considerably larger than those of the past. The result is a smaller proportion of females in the reproductive ages. Thus, Indonesia, whose population growth rate has fallen more rapidly than India's in the last two decades, has a higher proportion of women of reproductive age in its population, 25.7 percent compared with 23.7 percent in India. This difference is significant. If India had Indonesia's proportion of women of reproductive age, India's crude birth rate would increase by about 8 percent, and, assuming a constant crude death rate, its population growth rate would increase by around 0.2 percent a year.

As fertility declines, one early effect is an increase in the proportion of women of reproductive age in the population. That increase causes the crude birth rate to rise more than it otherwise would and slows the fall in the population growth rate. For a while, age structure effects reduce the influence of declines in fertility on the population growth rate. They explain why decreases in population growth rates are slow to materialize.

In general, high-fertility countries in the sample have lower median ages, and low-fertility countries, higher median ages. For example, the median age of the population of Bangladesh was only 17.7 years in 1990, and the median age of the Nepali population in that year was 18.8. In contrast, the median age of the Chinese population was 25.7 years in 1990 and the Republic of Korea's was 26.9. Higher median ages translate into higher crude death rates in the long run, other factors being constant. As fertility declines, populations grow older, and older populations eventually have higher crude death rates. In the short run, declining fertility also implies a decline in child deaths because of the reduced number of births. The result is to reduce the effect of higher median ages on the crude death rate.

Declining fertility has two main effects on the age structure: it increases the proportion of women of childbearing age, which tends to increase crude birth rates; and it raises the median age of the population, which tends to increase crude death rates. Generally, the first effect is more important than the second, and as the preceding Indian projections show, age structure effects have usually diminished the impact of falling fertility on population growth rates.

Some of the countries in the sample are still experiencing rising population growth rates. The effects in this case are just the opposite of those described above. The proportion of women of childbearing age decreases as does the mean age of the population. The result, generally, is a smaller rise in the population growth rate.

Age Structure Differences and the Crossover Phenomenon

Did age structure differences account for the crossover phenomenon noted earlier in figure 2.3, in which currently low-fertility countries experienced the fastest population growth in the 1950s, while those with currently high fertility had the slowest population growth, with the remaining countries occupying an intermediate position?

In 1950–54, crude birth rates in the high-, medium-, and low-fertility countries were almost identical. Do these nearly identical rates reflect similar levels of fertility, or were they an artifact of age and sex structure differences? The average total fertility rates in 1950–54 for the three groups were, in fact, nearly identical,[11] implying that differences in age/sex composition of populations are not an important factor in influencing crude birth rates in the early period. Crude death rates in 1950–54 were, on the other hand, quite different in the three groups of countries, but these differences were also not due to variations in the age/sex structure of the populations, as indicated by a comparison of two measures of the age/sex structure average dependency ratios[12] and median ages. The average dependency ratios for the low- and high-fertility groups were identical, 77.4 percent, while the average for the intermediate group was only slightly higher, at 79.1 percent. Similarly, the average median ages were nearly identical in the low- and high-fertility groups, at 20.0 and 19.9 respectively. In the intermediate group, the average was 20.6. Clearly, differences in crude death rates had little to do with age/sex structures differences. In the early period, therefore, differences in crude birth and death rates and population growth largely reflect differences in mortality and fertility rates rather than differences in age structures.

Distilling a Lesson from Asia's Demographic Past

As documented above, Asia's demographic past during the last forty years is characterized by diverse rates of population increase as well as mortality and fertility declines. Perhaps the most surprising aspect relates to the crossover phenomenon. Technically, the characteristics of the underlying demographic variables—crude birth and death rates, age/sex structures, as well as mortality and fertility conditions—accounted for this pattern. It is explained by the fact that the low-fertility countries in 1985–89 tended to be countries with relatively low mortality in the 1950s, whereas high-fertility countries in 1985–89 tended to be countries with comparatively high mortality in the 1950s.

This explanation begs further questions, however. Was it a coincidence that currently low-fertility countries had relatively low mortality in the early period? Or did a common factor influence both variables and their behavior over time? One possible interpretation of the crossover effect is that earlier mortality rates and later fertility rates are in fact connected by common forces acting through countries' *social capacity* for changing mortality and fertility conditions. Social capacity encompasses those characteristics of the social and economic organization of a country that enhance the capability of institutions, particularly the government, to provide social services to the population and that enhance the capacity of individuals to use those services appropriately. The social capacity of a country, then, depends, among other things, on the organizational efficiency of the government and the education of the population.

Both mortality rates and fertility rates are significantly influenced by a country's social capacity. To reduce mortality, governments or private institutions must provide medical facilities, trained staff, and pharmaceuticals, among other things, and the people must want to and be able to make use of that care. The sorts of institutional arrangements necessary for providing modern health care are similar to those needed to provide family planning services. Like health care, the provision of family planning services requires facilities, trained staff, and appropriate pharmaceuticals (mainly contraceptives). It also requires that people want to make use of family planning services and that those services are delivered in a way that enables people to use them effectively. Thus, it should come as no surprise that countries which, in the 1950s, showed themselves capable of organizing effective programs aimed at mortality reduction were also capable, in the 1970s and 1980s, of organizing effective family planning programs.

The relationship between social capacity and fertility decline is even more complex than sketched above. Greater social capacity has four possible effects on fertility: (a) it causes a decrease in mortality which acts to reduce the demand for children; (b) it leads to more rapid increases in education, particularly the education of women, which, in turn, leads to lower fertility; (c) it facilitates economic growth, which also helps reduce the demand for children; and (d) it results in a more efficient provision of family planning services and their more rapid adoption by the population. When greater social capacity is an important force for lowering fertility, the reduction in fertility tends to be more rapid because supply-side effects are reinforced by demand-side effects. When supply-side effects alone are the dominant force behind lowering fertility rates, the decline tends to move more slowly because the complementary demand-side effects are not as strong.

The Asian countries in the sample which reduced their fertility first were not a random subset, but rather the most socially capable. Social capacity is likely to increase over time as investments in institutional development and education bear fruit. Countries with medium and high fertility today are thus likely to have greater social capacity than they had in the past. Thus, in Asia, two offsetting forces are acting on fertility. Social capacity is generally increasing, but as some countries complete their transition from high to low fertility, those that remain behind are generally those with lower capacity. As a result, it is unlikely that, on average, the countries currently with intermediate and high fertility will follow the path of the Asian countries which have successfully reduced their fertility. Some of the countries with medium levels of fertility may well experience rapid fertility declines, particularly Malaysia[13] and Indonesia. Others may not, especially if social capacity is low. In those cases, family planning programs which concentrate only on supplying contraceptive supplies and services are likely to run into diminishing returns and declines in fertility, and population growth may be tepid. Countries with currently high or medium levels of fertility are generally countries of low social capability. Supply-side interventions have less scope for effectiveness in these instances, but those interventions may also suffer from diminishing returns in the future. If the social capacity of these countries does not substantially increase—notably through investments in broad-based education—sustained fertility decline and slower population growth may prove to be difficult and costly to attain.

Notes

1. For comparability across countries and over time, this chapter relies mainly on demographic data from the United Nations. Unless otherwise indicated, the 1985–89 figures are the United Nations medium variant projections.

2. The figure shows the unweighted country averages in population growth rates. The data for 1950–54 in the figure exclude the two Koreas, which were at war at that time; the data for 1970–74 and 1975–79 use growth rates for Cambodia which are linearly interpolated between the 1965–69 and the 1980–84 numbers, because of the high death rates in the 1970s due to civil unrest.

3. The high-fertility countries are those with total fertility rates above 4.5 in 1985–89. The medium-fertility countries had total fertility rates above 3.0 and less than or equal to 4.5. The low-fertility countries had total fertility rates of 3.0 or less. For the comparative purpose at hand, the data on the total fertility rate were taken from United Nations 1990. They do not coincide exactly with data from surveys, but have the advantage of being available for a large number of countries for comparable time periods.

4. These groups of countries will, in the remainder of the chapter, be referred to as low-fertility, medium-fertility, and high-fertility countries.

5. International immigration also plays a role, but for most of the countries in the sample and over most of the 1950–90 period, it was quantitatively unimportant.

6. As a digression, the flattening out of the crude death rates in the low- and medium-fertility countries provides a first glimpse into a factor which will grow in importance in the coming century: the increase in the mean age of many Asian populations. Population aging tends to increase crude death rates, while improvements in life expectancy tend to decrease them. The slow fall in the crude death rates in the low-fertility countries is due to the offsetting effects of population aging and life expectancy improvement. Even for countries in the medium-fertility group, the period of rapid declines in crude death rates is over. In the future, decreases in the crude birth rate will be translated almost directly into decreases in population growth because crude death rates will no longer be falling to any significant extent. In countries where the effects of population aging dominate, crude death rates are expected to increase in the future, making the task of slowing population growth even easier.

7. Whether or not below-replacement fertility will persist for substantial periods is an open issue. Below-replacement fertility is also found in Taiwan, Singapore, and Hong Kong, as well as in most industrial countries. To the extent that low fertility is the result of choices couples make in light of the perceived costs and benefits of childbearing, below-replacement fertility may persist, in the short-run, in Korea and other Asian countries, just as it has in most of the industrial world. In the longer run, the situation is unclear. Some countries could evolve institutions which promote childbearing. It is also possible that increases in incomes could, under some circumstances, result in higher fertility. On the other hand, prolonged periods of below-replacement fertility are also possible.

8. Figure 2.9 shows Bangladesh's total fertility declining from 7.02 births per woman in 1970–74 to 5.30 in 1985–89. These data came from United Nations 1990. More recent survey data suggest a considerably lower total fertility rate (see table 3.2).

9. Relative to its life expectancy, the infant mortality rate in China is nonetheless, as noted above, somewhat high. This is probably due mainly to the relatively poor care given to female children.

10. Fifty percent of the population is older than the median age and fifty percent is younger.

11. In the 1950–54 period, the two Koreas were at war. The average total fertility rate of the remaining three low-fertility countries is 6.1. The medium-fertility countries had an average total fertility rate of 6.2, as did the high-fertility countries. If we were to include the 1955–59 total fertility rates for the Koreas in the computation for the low-fertility countries, the average total fertility rate would be 6.0. Clearly, there was very little difference in the average total fertility rates across these groups of countries in the early 1950s.

12. The dependency ratio is defined as the number of people who are either in the age group 0–14 or 65 and above divided by the number of people in the 15–64 age group.

13. Malaysia is somewhat exceptional. It had a relatively low crude birth rate in the 1950s, indicating relatively high social capacity. The rate of economic growth in the 1980s has been relatively high, as might be expected of a country where social capacity had been relatively high for a number of decades. One reason that fertility was in the medium range was that, in the early 1980s, the government of Malaysia followed a pronatalist population policy. Thus, Malaysia used its social capacity to raise population growth rather than to lower it.

3

Contraceptive Prevalence, Fertility Levels, and Population Growth

POPULATION GROWTH RATES REFLECT the complex interaction of underlying demographic variables. In Asia, as elsewhere in the developing world, rising contraceptive prevalence rates are by far the most important factor behind falling fertility and population growth rates. Fertility levels and rates of population growth differ substantially, however, among countries with similar levels of contraceptive prevalence. This chapter provides an analytical framework for understanding the sources of these differences in fertility levels and population growth rates. We interpret the data for Asian countries using this framework and examine the cross-country comparison to shed light on the design of policies to influence demographic change.

Defining an Analytical Framework

In the absence of international migration, the percentage rate of population growth in a country in a particular year, PGR, is the difference between the crude birth rate, CBR, and the crude death rate, CDR, both divided by ten:[1]

$$PGR = \frac{CBR - CDR}{10} \tag{3.1}$$

Since population policy mainly works through the crude birth rate, it is important to consider, in greater detail, how that rate is determined.[2] For the purpose of this study, it can be expressed as:

$$CBR = 40 \cdot \omega \cdot TFR \cdot \left[\left(\frac{32}{3} \cdot \rho - \frac{27}{7} \right) - \left(\frac{\rho}{3} - \frac{1}{7} \right) \cdot MACB \right] \tag{3.2}$$

where
CBR is the crude birth rate;
ω is the fraction of the population who are women of reproductive age (15–49);
TFR is the total fertility rate, that is, the average number of children a woman has over her reproductive life span;

ρ is the fraction of the women of reproductive age who are in the 20–34 age group; and

MACB is the mean age at childbearing.[3]

Because equation (3.2) relies on a linearization of the age structure, it only approximates the true relationship. It nonetheless remains useful for examining the effect of changes in policy-sensitive variables on population growth.[4] The equation shows that the crude birth rate depends on the age/sex structure of the population through the two variables, the fraction of the population who are women of childbearing age, and the fraction of the women of childbearing age who are 20 to 34 years old.[5] Population policies affect the crude birth rate mainly through their effect on the total fertility rate, but they also affect it through the mean age at childbearing.

The total fertility rate—through which the major effects of policy work—is itself a function of other underlying variables. Bongaarts (1978) suggested the following decomposition of the total fertility rate into its proximate determinants:

$$TRF = C_m \cdot C_i \cdot C_c \cdot C_a \cdot 15.3 \qquad\qquad (3.3)$$

where

C_m, C_i, C_c, C_a are a set of indices, ranging between 0 and 1, that reflect the proportionate decreases from the maximum possible level of fertility (15.3 births per woman)[6] due, respectively, to marriage, the period of postpartum nonsusceptibility, contraception, and induced abortion. The period of postpartum nonsusceptibility is the interval after a birth during which a woman is protected against conception by noncontraceptive means. Prolonged breastfeeding delays the onset of ovulation and is the most important factor in determining the length of postpartum nonsusceptibility. Other factors that can influence the length of that interval include those dictated by social customs such as abstinence or spousal separation after childbirth.

Each of the indices in equation (3.3) can be expressed in easily understood parameters.[7] C_m depends on the proportion of women who ever marry and on the mean age at marriage. In Asia, marriage is nearly universal, so we concentrate below on the effects of differences in the mean age at marriage. C_i depends on the duration of breastfeeding and other factors discussed above. C_c reflects the influence of contraceptive prevalence and contraceptive efficiency, the latter being a function of the mix of contraceptive methods used in the population; and C_a depends on the marital abortion rate, the average number of abortions a woman experiences over her reproductive life span.

Making comparisons across countries and over time using equation (3.3) requires information on total fertility rates, marriage patterns (for C_m), the lengths of periods of postpartum nonsusceptibility (for C_i), contraceptive prevalence[8] and contraceptive efficiency rates[9] (for C_c), and abortion rates (for C_a). Many of these variables are unavailable for some countries or some periods, or both. Total fertility rates, contraceptive prevalence rates, and contraceptive efficiency rates based on the mix of contraceptive methods used, are the most frequently available data. Data on marriage patterns can, also, often be found. Information on postpartum nonsusceptibility is rarely available.[10]

The main advantages of this framework are (a) its simplicity, (b) its applicability to countries with fragmentary data, and (c) its usefulness in tracing the effects of policy-sensitive variables like the contraceptive prevalence rate on the total fertility rate, the crude birth rate, and the population growth rate. The main disadvantages are: (a) it is only an approximation to the true relationship between factors influencing population growth, and (b) the data available to implement it may be incomplete or inaccurate. Below, we use this framework to examine the differences in selected proximate determinants of fertility across Asian countries. Before we do that, however, it is instructive to discuss some simple examples.

The Sensitivity of the Total Fertility Rate and the Population Growth Rate to the Proximate Determinants: A Hypothetical Example

The purpose of this section is to show how the framework above works and to examine the sensitivity of the total fertility rate and the rate of population growth to changes in some of their determinants. This is done in the context of a set of scenarios. The column labeled "Baseline" in table 3.1 contains hypothetical data for the proximate determinants of relevance here, roughly reflecting the situation in South Asia around 1990. The scenarios show the sensitivity of the total fertility rate and the population growth rate to changes in some of their determinants.

In the baseline case, the contraceptive prevalence rate is 40 percent, the contraceptive effectiveness rate is 90 percent, the mean age at marriage is 20, the mean age at childbearing is 28.4, and the total marital abortion rate is 0. Using the framework presented here and the material in appendix A, those figures combine to produce a total fertility rate of 4.00. Following equation (3.2) this value for the total fertility rate, combined with the mean age at childbearing (28.4 years), and the age structure parameters, ω and ρ (25 percent and 50 percent respectively), produces a crude birth rate of 32.0. This crude birth rate, along with a crude death rate of 12.0, implies a population growth rate of 2.00 percent a year (see equation 3.1).[11]

In scenario 1, the contraceptive prevalence rate is increased from 40 percent to 50 percent, while all of the other factors influencing fertility are held constant. This causes the total fertility rate to fall from 4.00 to 3.36, the crude birth rate to fall from 32.0 to 26.9, and the rate of population growth to decrease from 2.00 to 1.49 percent a year. In scenario 2, the contraceptive prevalence rate is increased to 60 percent. This causes the rate of population growth to fall from 2.00 to 0.98 percent per year. In other words, each percentage point increase in the contraceptive prevalence rate reduces the population growth rate by about 0.05 percentage points per annum. In these scenarios, we increased the contraceptive prevalence rate

Table 3.1: *The Sensitivity of the Total Fertility Rate and the Population Growth Rate to Selected Determinants*

Variable	Acronym	Baseline	Scenarios[a] 1	2	3	4	5	6
Contraceptive prevalence rate (%)	CPR	40	*50*	*60*	40	*50*	40	40
Contraceptive effectiveness rate (%)	CER	90	90	90	90	90	*95*	90
Mean age at marriage (years)	MAM	20	20	20	20	*21*	20	20
Mean age at childbearing (years)	MACB	28.4	28.4	28.4	*27.4*	28.4	28.4	28.4
Total marital abortion rate (abortions per woman)	TMAR	0	0	0	0	0	0	*0.5*
Total fertility rate (births per woman)	TFR	4.00	3.36	2.73	4.00	3.12	3.86	3.72
Crude birth rate (births per 1,000 population)	CBR	32.0	26.9	21.8	33.0	25.0	30.9	29.8
Crude death rate (deaths per 1,000 population)	CDR	12.0	12.0	12.0	12.0	12.0	12.0	12.0
Population growth rate (% per year)	PGR	2.00	1.49	0.98	2.10	1.30	1.89	1.78

a. Underlined numbers indicate values different from those in the baseline situation.

Source: Authors' assumptions and calculations; see appendix A. The length of the period of postpartum nonsusceptibility is assumed to be equal to 15.7 months. The percent of the population who are women of reproductive age is assumed to be 0.25, and the fraction of those women who are in the age range 20 to 34 is assumed to be 0.5.

without changing either the mean age at marriage or the mean age at childbearing. This implies that the age pattern of contraceptive use remains the same.

Scenario 3 was designed to ascertain the importance of a change in the mean age at childbearing, holding all the proximate determinants of fertility and, therefore, the total fertility rate constant. Here we decreased the mean age at childbearing from 28.4 years old to 27.4 years old. The result was that the crude birth rate increased from 32.0 to 33.0 and the population growth rate increased from 2.00 to 2.10 percent a year. The equivalent effect could have been obtained by keeping everything at the baseline level and decreasing the contraceptive prevalence rate by 2 percentage points.

In scenario 4, we consider the case where an increase in contraceptive prevalence from 40 to 50 percent is associated with an increase in the mean age at marriage from 20 to 21. This combination reduces the rate of population growth from 2.00 to 1.30 percent a year. By comparing scenario 4 with scenario 1, we can see that the increase in the mean age at marriage alone causes the population growth rate to fall from 1.49 to 1.30 percent a year. The same effect on population growth could be obtained through an increase in the contraceptive prevalence rate from 50 to 54 percent, if the mean age at marriage is held constant at 20.

The effect of increasing the contraceptive effectiveness rate is shown in scenario 5. An increase from an average of 90 percent to 95 percent effective contraception causes the total fertility rate to fall from 4.00 to 3.86 and the population growth rate to decline from 2.00 to 1.89 percent a year. The final example concerns the demographic effects of induced abortions. If the total marital abortion rate increases from 0.0 to 0.5, the annual rate of population growth would slow from 2.00 percent per year to 1.78. A total marital abortion rate of 0.5 is substantial. Roughly speaking, it implies that for every two women who stay married throughout their reproductive span there will be, on average, one induced abortion. An increase in the contraceptive prevalence rate from 40 to 44 percent would have about the same effect as an increase of this magnitude in the rate of induced abortions.

The Proximate Determinants of
Fertility in Selected Asian Countries

Table 3.2 shows the total fertility rate, the mean age at marriage, the contraceptive prevalence rate, the contraceptive efficiency rate, the total marital abortion rate[12], and the mean age at childbearing for eleven Asian countries at various dates in the 1970s, 1980s, and 1990s. Across Asian countries, the dominant reason for the declines in total fertility rates during the past decades has been increases in contraceptive prevalence. In Bangladesh, for example, the prevalence rate rose from 6.5 percent in 1972–76 to 39.9 percent in 1990; in Thailand, it increased from 23.5 percent in 1972–76 to 65.5 percent in 1986. As we saw in table 3.1, increases in contraceptive prevalence rates of these orders would, by themselves, cause large decreases in total fertility rates and population growth rates. In addition, contraceptive efficiency has generally increased.

Table 3.2: Fertility Parameters in Selected Asian Countries, 1970–1993

Country	Period[a]	TFR	MAM	CPR	CER	TMAR	MACB
Bangladesh	1974–78	7.1	16.1	9.0	81.6	–	27.9
	1979–83	6.6	16.6	18.6	82.3	–	27.9
	1988	4.6	18.0	30.8	86.4	–	27.1
	1990	4.2	–	39.9	86.1	–	–
China	1982	2.9	22.6	70.6	92.2	0.6	25.9
	1984	2.4	22.9	74.0	93.7	0.6	26.2
	1988	2.5	22.1	75.0	94.0	0.8	26.0
	1990	2.3	–	87.2	–	–	–
	1991	2.2	–	89.4	–	–	–
	1992	2.0	22.5	83.4	–	–	–
	1993	2.0	–	–	–	–	–
India	1980	4.4	18.4	32.4	93.0	–	28.4
	1988	4.0	19.4	43.0	96.0	–	27.5
	1990	3.8	19.3	–	–	–	27.6
	1991	3.6	–	–	–	–	–
	1992–93	–	–	40.3	–	–	–
Indonesia	1972–76	4.5	19.3	20.0	84.7	–	28.3
	1983–87[b]	3.4	21.4	40.0	86.9	–	27.9
	1988–91	3.0	22.0	49.7	89.1	–	28.1
Korea, Rep. of	1970–74	3.4	23.3	37.0	84.0	0.6	28.8
	1975–79	2.6	23.9	50.7	87.4	0.7	27.6
	1985	1.5	24.6	65.5	90.9	2.1	26.4
Malaysia	1970–74	4.4	22.2	25.8	82.8	–	28.7
	1980–84	3.9	23.8	45.0	81.0	–	31.2
	1987	3.5	24.2	41.5	82.2	–	29.9
Nepal	1975	6.1	16.9	2.0	94.5	–	29.4
	1977–81	5.0	17.9	5.1	96.2	–	29.7
	1982–86	6.0	18.9	11.1	97.7	–	29.0
Philippines	1974–78	5.5	24.7	26.3	77.4	–	30.9
	1984–88	4.3	24.1	32.1	80.4	–	29.7
	1990–92	4.1	24.1	37.5	84.5	–	29.5
Sri Lanka	1971–75	3.2	25.3	30.0	83.7	–	30.2
	1978–82	3.3	24.1	48.3	83.8	–	29.5
	1983–87[c]	2.8	24.6	59.8	87.2	–	28.5
Thailand	1972–76	4.9	23.0	23.5	89.1	–	30.0
	1977–81	3.2	23.2	46.5	91.1	–	28.9
	1986	2.1	23.0	65.5	92.3	–	27.7
Viet Nam	1983–87	4.7	22.8	47.0	84.4	0.1	31.3

Note: The acronyms refer to measures defined as follows: TFR is the total fertility rate; MAM is the mean age at marriage for women; CPR is the contraceptive prevalence rate; CER is the contraceptive effectiveness rate; TMAR is the total marital abortion rate; MACB is the mean age at childbearing. See also table 3.1 and accompanying text.

a. Data for TFR and MACB refer to the period indicated. Data for the other variables are adjusted by interpolation of available data to match the indicated period.

b. Data for 1972–76 (Indonesia) refer to Java-Bali; however, data for other years refer to all Indonesia.

c. Data exclude northern and eastern parts of the country.

Source: Based on sources listed in section (b) in the references.

It is interesting to notice in table 3.2 that similar contraceptive prevalence rates are consistent with quite different total fertility rates. India in 1988 had a contraceptive prevalence rate of 43.0 and a total fertility rate of 4.0. Indonesia in 1983–87 had a lower rate of contraceptive prevalence but also a much lower total fertility rate, 3.4. Contraceptive efficiency was higher in India than in Indonesia, so this factor could not have accounted for India's higher total fertility rate. The mean age at marriage and the mean age at childbearing are similar between the two countries, so differences in these factors also could not have accounted for India's higher total fertility rate. We can therefore deduce that the difference in total fertility rates is due to factors that influence fertility but are not included in the table, such as the duration and intensity of breastfeeding. As can be seen from this example, these omitted factors can have a substantial impact on total fertility rates.

Increases in the mean age at marriage over time are the norm in table 3.2. For each country in the table, the increase in mean age between the earliest and latest year of observation is typically between one and two years. Where decreases are observed they are in countries where either the mean age at marriage was already high at the earliest observation, or, as in the case of China, the decrease is relatively small. In general, the data show that the mean age at childbearing has been decreasing over time, even though the mean age at marriage has been increasing. This usually occurs where contraceptive use is concentrated among relatively older women who wish to terminate their childbearing.

Based on very scanty data, it appears that a significant number of abortions within marriage were performed in China and in the Republic of Korea. It is certainly possible that the frequency of abortion was significant elsewhere as well.

Bangladesh

The total fertility rate fell rapidly during the 1980s, from about 6.6 in the 1979–83 period to about 4.2 in 1990. During that period the mean age at marriage rose from 16.6 to 18.0 (in 1988), and the contraceptive prevalence rate rose from 18.6 to 39.9. These figures mix data from a number of different surveys, and past survey data from Bangladesh have tended to overstate recent fertility declines. One way of testing the plausibility of these observations is to see whether they are consistent with our analytical framework.

We make two tests of the Bangladeshi data, both using 1988 as a base year. In the first, we hold all other proximate determinants of fertility constant at their 1988 levels and compute the implied effects of an increase in contraceptive prevalence from 30.8 to 39.9 as well as a decrease in contraceptive efficiency from 86.4 to 86.1. The computed fall in the total fertility rate is from 4.6 to 4.1, as compared to an observed fall from 4.6 to 4.2. The observed fall is almost exactly what we would predict given the changes in the contraceptive prevalence rate and the contraceptive efficiency rate. In the second test, we go back in time, from 1988 to 1974–78, and compute what the total fertility rate would have been if all other proximate determinants had remained constant at their 1988 levels, except the marriage rates, the contraceptive prevalence rate, and the contraceptive efficiency rate. The analytic framework predicts a total fertility rate of 6.7, as compared to the observed rate of 7.1. These figures are reasonably close, especially given the possible errors in measurement and the likelihood that other proximate determinants changed over time. Overall, it appears that the Bangladeshi data are plausible, given the analytic framework and that the rapid fertility decline in Bangladesh during the late 1970s and 1980s actually occurred.[13]

China

The data in table 3.2 cover the years 1982, 1984, 1988, and 1990 through 1993. A longer time series can be found in table A6.1 (appendix C). The one-child family policy began in 1979, when the total fertility rate was 2.75. In the prior decade, China also had an active population control policy, but the consequences of noncompliance were not as great as they subsequently became. The total fertility rate fell from 2.75 in 1979 to 2.24 in 1980, the first year in which the one-child family policy was fully in force. Subsequently, the total fertility rate rose to 2.86 in 1982, the first year shown in the table. As policy tightened and loosened, the total fertility rate rose and fell. In 1993, after the latest round of tightening, the total fertility rate stood at 2.0. In the early 1990s, the contraceptive prevalence rate was around 85 percent, with some variation due to policy changes, and probably observation errors as well. In the late 1980s, China had the lowest mean age at childbearing of all the countries in the table.

A number of scholars have raised the question of whether China could allow its residents more flexibility about the number of births they had if the government required that those births occur later in the wife's reproductive span.[14] The distinction here is between births forgone and births deferred. Deferring births to later in the reproductive span, or in other words, increasing the mean age at childbearing, reduces population growth, even if those women eventually have the same number of children they would otherwise have had. A policy which reduces the mean age at childbearing works against itself, in the sense that it has a higher rate of population growth for any given total fertility rate (see equation 3.2).

We can use the analytic framework above to get a rough feel for the possible quantitative importance of an "older mother" policy. Let us begin with the situation as it was in China around 1990, when the total fertility rate was 2.3, and assume that the mean age at childbearing remained at 26.0. Given China's crude death rate, roughly 7.3 and the demographic parameters in equation (3.2),[15] the analytic framework predicts a population growth rate of 1.39 percent per year. If everything else in equation (3.2) stays the same but the mean age at childbearing is increased from 26.0 to 30.0, the rate of population growth would fall from 1.39 to 1.16 percent a year. If the mean age at childbearing had remained the same, the same reduction in population growth could have been obtained from a decrease in the total fertility rate from 2.3 to 2.05, which is, roughly speaking, what actually occurred between 1990 and 1993. This example indicates that a "later mother" policy could indeed reduce population growth without reducing the average number of children that women have. In the Chinese case, increasing the mean age at childbearing by 4 years would allow women to have an average of 0.25 more births without increasing the rate of population growth.

India

From 1980 to 1988, the total fertility rate in India fell from 4.4 births per woman to 4.0, while the mean age at marriage rose from 18.4 years to 19.4 and the contraceptive prevalence rate rose from 32.4 to 43.0 percent. Between 1988 and 1991, the total fertility rate fell from 4.0 to 3.6 and the mean age at marriage remained roughly constant. The speed of the decline in India's total fertility rate increased significantly over the 1980s. On average, the total fertility rate fell by 0.05 birth per year between 1980 and 1988, and by more than twice as fast, 0.13 births per year, between 1988 and 1991. In stark contrast, the contraceptive prevalence rate in India actually fell from 43.0 percent in 1988 to 40.3 percent in 1992–93. In brief, the rise in contraceptive prevalence from 32.4 to 43.0 percent was associated with a 0.4 decline in the total fertility rate, but the recent decrease in contraceptive prevalence from 43.0 to 40.3 seems to be associated with an even more rapid fall in the total fertility rate.

On their face, the time series of Indian total fertility rates and contraceptive prevalence rates are inconsistent with one another. One possible reason for this could be that some of the figures are inaccurate. Of utmost concern to us here is the decline in the contraceptive prevalence rate. Could it just be an artifact of the data? The basic conclusion that there was a significant slowdown in the spread of contraceptive use or an actual decline is supported by two independent sorts of data. Survey data, from ORG (1990) and International Institute for Population Studies (1994) show the decline in use seen in table 3.2. This decline is due almost entirely to a reduction in the use of temporary methods of contraception. Rates of use of sterilization are almost identical in the two surveys, at around 30 to 31 percent of currently married women of childbearing age. Government of India service statistics on sterilization also show little trend during this period (see ORG (1990, p. 84) and IIPS (1994, p. 46)).

The Indian time series data on contraception and fertility are difficult to reconcile and it is advisable to use them with caution. They point both to a recent speed-up in the rate of decline of fertility and a recent decrease in the use of contraception. Understanding what has really happened is likely to aid in family planning policy formulation, since if India is experiencing reduced fertility because of factors not associated with contraceptive use, it would be important for policymakers to determine what those factors are.

Indonesia

Of the three observations in Indonesia, the first, for 1972–76, covers only Java and Bali; the next two—for 1983–87 and 1988–91—are national in scope. Since family planning was more advanced in Java and Bali than in the country as a whole in 1972–76, the change in fertility between the first two observations understates the rate of demographic change in Indonesia at that time. By 1988–91, the total fertility rate in Indonesia had already fallen to 3.0 births per woman, and the contraceptive prevalence rate had risen to 49.7 percent. The decline in fertility has been aided by a consistent rise in the age at marriage and in the contraceptive efficiency rate over the interval of observation.

The family planning program in Indonesia stands out in Asia as one which does not emphasize sterilization. Of the 49.7 percent of the currently married women of reproductive age who were using contraception in 1991, only 3.3 percent were using sterilization. The three main types of contraceptives used were the pill, IUD, and injections. (The Indonesian family planning program has also been a leader in providing contraceptive injections.)

Republic of Korea

There are three observations, going from a total fertility rate of 3.4 births per woman in 1970–74 (identical to Indonesia's rate in 1983–87), to 2.6 in 1975–79, and to 1.5 in 1985. This dramatic fall was caused by a number of factors, some of which were offsetting. The most important reason for the decline was the increase in contraceptive prevalence rates, from 37.0 percent in 1970–74 to 65.5 percent in 1985. Most striking about the data, however, is the increase in the total marital abortion rate, which rose from 0.6 abortions per woman in the earliest period, to 0.7 in the middle one, to 2.1 in 1985. As far as we can ascertain, in the mid-1980s the Republic of Korea had the highest total marital abortion rate in the Asia Region by a sizable margin. There is evidence to suggest that the sex selection of offspring was an important force in producing the high abortion rate (Ahn 1990). Recently, abortion for the purpose of sex selection has been made illegal in the country.

We can use the analytic framework to ascertain how important Korea's high abortion rate was to lowering its fertility. Suppose that in 1985, the Republic of Korea had a total marital abortion rate 0.8 (the value for China in 1988) instead of 2.1, and that all other fertility determinants remained at their 1985 levels. In that case, the total fertility rate would have been 1.9 instead of 1.5, and the rate of population growth would have increased between 0.3 and 0.4 percent from a level that was initially slightly less than 1 percent per year.

Malaysia

This is one of the most demographically interesting countries in the sample because in the mid-1980s, the Malaysian government[16] changed its policy from one encouraging family planning to one encouraging couples to have more children. Before the change in policy, the total fertility rate in Malaysia fell from 4.4 births per woman in 1970–74 to 3.9 in 1980–84. After the policy change, it fell to 3.5 births per woman in 1987. We cannot conclude from this observation that the government's policy change had little effect, because the total fertility rate could have fallen much faster, as it did in neighboring Thailand. The contraceptive prevalence rate rose very rapidly, from 25.8 percent in 1970–74 to 45.0 percent in 1980–84. Not only did this rapid rise come to a halt after the policy change, but the contraceptive prevalence rate actually fell. In 1987 it was 41.5 percent. We cannot be certain, at this point, whether or not this indicates a real decline in contraceptive use or an error in measurement.

Nepal

There are two observations, 1975 and 1982–86. The total fertility rate was 6.1 births per woman in 1975 and 6.0 in 1982–86, hardly budging in nearly a decade. Nevertheless, the contraceptive prevalence rate increased substantially, from 2.0 percent in 1975 to 11.1 percent in 1982–86. Two other factors also changed in ways that should have reduced the total fertility rate: the contraceptive efficiency rate rose from 94.5 to 97.7 percent, and the mean age at marriage rose by 2 years, from 16.9 years to 18.9. These data may well be inaccurate. If accurate, they indicate that some other proximate determinants, such as the extent of breastfeeding, were changing rapidly enough to offset the increase in total fertility.

Philippines

There are three observations, for 1974–78, 1984–88, and 1990–92. The total fertility rate fell from 5.5 in 1974–78, to 4.3 in 1984–88, and to 4.1 in 1990–92. The contraceptive prevalence rate appears to have risen consistently over the period, from 26.3 percent in 1974–78 to 37.5 percent in 1990–92. The relatively low level of contraceptive efficiency is due to the comparatively high proportion of couples who use traditional methods of contraception. In 1993, when contraceptive prevalence was 40.0, 38 percent of those who used contraception used "traditional methods."

At this point, we broaden our analytic framework by calculating what we call the *analytic birth interval measure (ABIM)*, using data on the mean age at childbearing, the mean age at marriage, and the total fertility rate.[17] This measure approximates the average interval between live births. For the Philippines, the interval is relatively low for the country's level of fertility. Comparable values of the birth interval measure are also observed in three other settings: China in the early 1980s, when the total fertility rate was around 2.4 births per woman; the Republic of Korea in 1985, when the total fertility rate was 1.5; and Sri Lanka in 1983–87, when the total fertility rate was 2.8. In all three settings, the total fertility rate was relatively low. None of the countries in the table with a total fertility rate anywhere near that of the Philippines also had such a low analytic birth interval.

Recently the family planning program in the Philippines has begun to stress the health benefits of contraception for mothers and children. This emphasis is clearly appropriate, given the cross-country comparisons. The unique combination of relatively high fertility and quite low birth intervals puts women and children more at risk in the Philippines than in any other country in the table.

Sri Lanka

The data refer to 1971–75, 1978–82, and 1983–87. The 1983–87 observation does not cover the same territory as the earlier two because civil unrest caused the omission of some of the northern and eastern provinces. The total fertility rate in Sri Lanka actually rose from 3.2 births per woman in 1971–75 to 3.3 in 1978–82. It then fell to 2.8 births per woman in 1983–87. The rise from 3.2 births per woman to 3.3 is somewhat surprising in view of the very large contemporaneous increase in the contraceptive prevalence rate, from 30.0 percent in 1971–75 to 48.3 percent in 1978–82. Even in the Asia region, where large increases in contraceptive prevalence over short time periods are now commonplace, a rise in contraceptive prevalence of 18.3 percentage points over a seven-year period is still noteworthy.

Sri Lanka historically has had one of the highest mean ages at marriage in Asia: Its mean age at marriage of 25.3 years in 1971–75 is the highest recorded in the table. The mean age at marriage of 24.6 years in 1983–87 is tied with the 1985 observation for the Republic of Korea as the highest in the 1980s. High ages at marriage are an important reason Sri Lanka's total fertility rates are relatively low.

Thailand

As with the Republic of Korea, the available observations span a period when fertility was high to a period when fertility reached replacement level. The total fertility rate fell from 4.9 births per woman in 1972–76, to 3.2 in 1977–81, to 2.1 in 1986. The reason fertility fell is almost classic in its simplicity. Far and away, the dominant reason was that the contraceptive prevalence rate rose dramatically and the other determinants had no offsetting effects. The contraceptive efficiency rate rose slightly during the period of observation, from 89.1 percent at the initial observation to 92.3 percent at the last observation, but that rise is not large enough to have caused a substantial decline in the total fertility rate. In addition, the mean age at marriage remained essentially constant.

Viet Nam

There is only one observation, 1983–87, but comparisons with Indonesia are noteworthy. Viet Nam's contraceptive prevalence rate was 47.0 percent, higher than the 40.0 percent observed for Indonesia in 1983–87. Yet its total fertility rate (4.7 births per woman) was considerably higher than Indonesia's (3.4 births per woman). In Viet Nam the contraceptive effectiveness rate was 84.4 percent, comparable to the rate of 86.9 percent in Indonesia. The mean age at marriage is higher in Viet Nam than in Indonesia, 22.8 years compared with 21.4 years in Indonesia. This factor, by itself, would have reduced Viet Nam's total fertility rate to lower than Indonesia's. Even the total marital abortion rate may be higher in Viet Nam than in Indonesia. If the data are accurate, Viet Nam's comparatively high total fertility rate must have been caused by some excluded factor, such as a relatively short period of breastfeeding.

Conclusions

Fertility and population growth are influenced by the rate of contraceptive prevalence and the mix of contraceptive methods used. They are also influenced by marriage patterns, the timing of births, and a host of other factors such as the effects of breastfeeding practices, coital frequency, social customs relating to abstinence, and the efficiency with which specific methods are used, among many other factors.

These underlying determinants of fertility and population growth have varied considerably both over time for particular countries and across countries. In the mid-1980s India, Indonesia, Malaysia, the Philippines, and Viet Nam all had roughly comparable contraceptive prevalence rates. In India it was 42.8 percent in 1987, in Indonesia 40.0 percent in 1983–87, in Malaysia 41.5 percent in 1987, in the Philippines 43.5 percent in 1984–88, and 47.0 percent in Viet Nam in 1983–87. Yet if one looks at total fertility rates (and, by inference, population growth rates), the picture is vastly different. Indonesia has the lowest total fertility rate, 3.4 births per woman; followed closely by Malaysia at 3.5. India has a much higher total fertility rate, 4.1 births per woman; the Philippines has a rate which is higher yet, 4.3; and Viet Nam has the highest rate of all, 4.7.

Although increases in contraceptive prevalence were the main reason for the observed decreases in fertility, the comparison among the five countries underscores the possible variation in total fertility rates, even when rates of contraceptive prevalence are comparable. People can and do influence their fertility in many ways, some of which can offset or complement the fertility-reducing effects of increases in contraceptive use.

To some extent, these other factors have received less attention as contraceptive use in policy design, in part because their importance in determining fertility and population growth has not been adequately recognized.[18] In order to translate more of the effect of increasing contraceptive prevalence into falling fertility and population growth, policy makers may wish to consider a greater variety of program variables in addition to contraceptive prevalence and method mix. The benefits of breastfeeding may need to be emphasized in some situations, while in others, effective use of contraception might need to be stressed.

Notes

1. Division by 10 is necessary because the *CBR (CDR)* is, by convention, defined as the number of births (deaths) divided by the population and multiplied by 1,000.

2. In this volume, we do not deal with population policies that focus on influencing crude death rates or immigration rates. See the *World Development Report 1993* (World Bank 1993) for a comprehensive statement on health care policies.

3. For example, if a woman had three children at ages 26, 29, and 32, her mean age at childbearing would be 29. To calculate this variable in a population, age-specific fertility rates are used to weight the ages at which mothers give birth to their children. This makes the MACB independent of the age structure of the population.

4. Actual data were used to test the accuracy of equation (3.2) for a number of Asian countries. The results suggest that it is a good approximation.

5. The age group 20–34 is used here to maximize the accuracy of the linearization. The age range is sufficiently large to reduce errors from age misreporting, and it also spans the ages of highest fertility.

6. Bongaarts and Potter (1983) used the 15.3 figure in their empirical work, but stress that its value is best considered to range between 13 and 17.

7. See appendix A for an elaboration of the structure of relationships involved.

8. The contraceptive prevalence rate (CPR) is the fraction of the number of currently married women 15 to 49 who are using some form of contraception at a given date. The denominator of the CPR includes women who are currently pregnant and seeking to become pregnant as well as women, who for physiological reasons, cannot bear any (more) children.

9. The contraceptive efficiency rate is determined by weighting the contraceptive methods used by a set of efficiency weights. Sterilization is given a weight of 1.0 and traditional methods 0.7. Other methods are given intermediate weights.

10. An approximation to the length of the period of nonsusceptibility can be obtained by translating survey data on the duration of breastfeeding into a measure of the length of the period of postpartum amenorrhea (see, for example, Bongaarts and Potter 1973, p. 25). This approximation, however, is so rough and is available, in comparable form, for so few countries that we do not present it below.

11. The population growth rate depends on the proportion of women in the reproductive age range and the fraction of those women who are 20 to 34 years old. Holding all fertility and mortality determinants constant, those proportions would change over time, and so would the population growth rate. Thus, the 2 percent rate of population growth given here should be interpreted as the current or short-run rate of population growth.

12. The total marital abortion rate is only shown in those cases where we have reliable data.

13. Phillips and others (1994) also finds these data to be consistent using other tests.

14. See, for example, Coale and others (1992); Bongaarts and Greenhalgh (1985); and Zeng and Vaupel (1989).

15. The crude death rate and the demographic parameters are computed from data in Bos and others (1994), p. 180.

16. The data for Malaysia in table 4.2 refer to peninsular Malaysia. Sabah and Sarawak are excluded. For economy of expression, when we speak of Malaysia below, we are referring to peninsular Malaysia.

17. The analytic birth interval measure, *ABIM*, is computed from the formula:

$$ABIM = \frac{2 \cdot (MACB - MAM - 2)}{TFR - 1}$$

where *MACB* is the mean age at childbearing, *MAM* is the mean age at marriage for women, and *TFR* is the total fertility rate. In the numerator the term *(MACB - MAM - 2)* measures the length of time from the first birth— assumed to occur two years after marriage—to the mean age at childbearing. If intervals between live births were constant in length, then half of the children would be born in *(MACB - MAM - 2)* years. The average number of such birth intervals is *TFR - 1*. Since half that number of intervals must fit into the period between the first birth and the mean age at childbearing, *ABIM* can be expressed using the formula above. This measure is appropriate for comparative purposes, but should not be used when survey data on individuals are available.

18. An exception to this rule, Moreno and Goldman (1991) shows that contraceptive failure rates for given methods vary substantially across countries. Their study includes Indonesia, Sri Lanka, and Thailand, in addition to 13 other developing countries in Latin America and North Africa. The first-year probability of a contraceptive failure for someone using the pill is 2.7 percent in Indonesia, 7.2 percent in Sri Lanka, and 2.8 percent in Thailand. For all methods, excluding sterilization, the first-year failure rate in Sri Lanka is 10.6 percent, more than 4 times as high as the rate in Thailand.

4

Expenditure, Finance, and Public-Private Roles in Family Planning

PUBLICLY SUPPORTED FAMILY PLANNING PROGRAMS exist in virtually all Asian countries today. This chapter documents selected aspects of this investment, including countries' aggregate spending on the programs, patterns of resource allocation among program inputs, and the relative roles of domestic versus external funding. It also considers the role of private providers of family planning services and the extent that public programs rely on user charges as a source of finance.

Levels and Trends in Aggregate Public Spending

Table 4.1 shows reported government spending on family planning programs across Asian countries. Expenditures are shown as a share of total public health expenditures, and as a share of gross national product (GNP). Although obviously related, the two indicators provide different perspectives on levels of spending. The first shows the size of family planning services relative to total government-supported health interventions; the second provides a measure of the "fiscal effort" made by the public sector to provide family planning services. In compiling data for the first indicator, care was taken to ensure that the denominator includes both health and family planning expenditures. In some countries, budget documents show health and family planning expenditure as separate line items, in which case the data would be added; in other countries, the health budget includes family planning, so this adjustment is redundant. The data reflect aggregate public spending irrespective of source of finance, and no attempt is made here to standardize for differences in the components included under reported family planning spending. These refinements are addressed in a later section of this chapter. With regard to the second indicator, aggregate spending converted via exchange rates into a single currency unit (say, US$) could also have been used for comparisons across countries. It is not employed here, however, because of domestic price differences in family planning commodities and services. Even if spending is expressed in purchasing power parity (PPP) currency units rather than exchange rate currency units, the comparisons are often flawed because PPP conversion rates are based on the prices of broad baskets of goods and services rather than on those for family planning commodities and services.

Table 4.1: Aggregate Public Expenditure on Family Planning Programs in Selected Asian Countries, 1985 and 1989

Country	As percentage of public health expenditure		As percentage of gross national product	
	1985	1989	1985	1989
Bangladesh	35.8	38.1	0.31	0.37
China	8.0	8.0	0.09	0.07
India	12.4	13.2	0.16	0.17
Indonesia	16.0	19.6	0.12	0.13
Korea, Rep. of	7.2	2.2	0.04	0.02
Malaysia	1.8	1.5	0.03	0.02
Nepal	14.0	11.0	0.16	0.16
Philippines	11.9	14.5[a]	0.05	0.03[a]
Sri Lanka	0.8	-	0.01	-
Thailand	4.1	4.1	0.04	0.03
Viet Nam	10.3	5.4	0.06	0.05

a. Data refer to 1988.
Source: See tables A4.1 and A4.2 in appendix C.

Because program design and activities differ widely, the data provide only a rough perspective on the differences across countries. The Republic of Korea, Malaysia, Thailand, and Sri Lanka, for example, show relatively low levels of spending mainly because family planning services are integrated with other health services, particularly maternal and child health care. For these countries, family planning expenditure in 1989 was no higher than 5 percent of total health spending and no more than 0.04 percent of GNP. Between 1985 and 1989, spending levels remained relatively stable. The data for these countries probably understate the amount actually spent because items of spending that are shared with other health services, particularly personnel costs, are commonly not attributed to the family planning program.

Among the remaining countries, Bangladesh has by far the largest allocations for family planning, both as a share of overall health spending and of the GNP. Over one-third of the health budget is spent on the country's family planning program. The amount is equivalent to 0.37 percent of the country's GNP. Dedicated programs of family planning also exist in India, Indonesia, and Nepal, but expenditure levels in 1989 are much more modest: 13 percent of public health spending in India, 20 percent in

Indonesia, and 11 percent in Nepal, corresponding to between 0.13 percent to 0.17 percent of GNP. It is likely that large expenditures are unavoidable during initial phases of the family planning, even if they mean tradeoffs against other components of health spending. Over the longer term, however, the need may arise to rationalize the pattern of allocation between the family planning program and other health services, particularly if overall health expenditures (which are low in Bangladesh relative to other Asian countries) do not increase.

Other interesting patterns and trends in expenditure also emerge from table 4.1. In China, for example, reported expenditures are relatively modest, at 8 percent of health spending and 0.07 percent of GNP.[1] By the latter indicator, China's expenditure is less than half India's. The "fiscal effort" in China is not necessarily weaker, however, because the cost of financial incentives is excluded. The social infrastructure of China is also unique, permitting a degree of government influence over client behavior that may not normally be possible in other settings (Greenhalgh 1990; see also chapter 6 for more details). The reported expenditures nonetheless reflect the resources needed to support the provision of widely available services.

In the Philippines, public spending on family planning services declined sharply as a share of overall health expenditures between 1985 and 1988. The reason is that while family planning allocations declined moderately between these dates (coinciding with growing uncertainty about the role of the Commission on Population [POPCOM] as a service delivery agency), health allocations actually doubled.[2] As a share of GNP, expenditures declined from 0.05 to 0.03 percent, comparable to spending levels in such countries as the Republic of Korea, Malaysia, and Thailand, where fertility rates are much lower. The comparisons suggest that higher allocations for family planning services in the Philippines may be warranted if fertility reduction is a policy goal. In Viet Nam, expenditure on family planning is also modest relative to GNP, again suggesting that increased allocation may be appropriate to promote family planning. As in the Philippines, the decline in the family planning spending as a share of public health expenditure results mainly from a rapidly increasing denominator rather than a declining numerator. The Republic of Korea shows a similar decline in resource allocation to family planning programs, but the cut reflects a deliberate redirection of spending coinciding with the decline of fertility to replacement level in the 1980s.

Public Spending on Selected Components of Family Planning Services

Although data on aggregated expenditures on family planning are useful for broad comparisons, they are limited in that substantial variation exists in program design and accounting procedures. In some countries, maternal and child health is included under family planning programs, while in others they are excluded. Perhaps the most important source of ambiguity relates to staff costs, which often represent the lion's share of overall costs. In some systems, the agency for family planning is administratively responsible for certain categories of health personnel whose salaries are reported as family planning expenditure even if they do not allocate all their time to provide such services. In other countries following a different administrative structure, all health staff, including those providing family planning, are paid through the health ministry, and their costs are therefore not reflected in reported expenditures on family planning. Even if no administrative differences exist, allocating the share of staff costs to family planning services would still be difficult. In almost all settings, health personnel, including those designated as family planning personnel, provide a range of health services besides family planning, and the pattern of time use across different services is rarely documented (see Chernichovsky and others 1991 for an exception).[3]

Because the foregoing difficulties are not easily resolved without microlevel data, no attempt is made here to obtain a complete documentation of spending differences across countries. Instead, in keeping with the study's focus on aggregate and broad variation, available data on spending were assembled for four important components of spending that can be closely and more or less unambiguously identified with family planning programs: contraceptive supplies, staff training in delivery of family planning services; information-education-communication activities; and incentive payments to acceptors and providers of family planning.[4] In settings where responsibility for expenditures lies with more than one agency, the data reflect the sum of their separate spending.

For comparative purposes, the expenditure data can be expressed meaningfully in relation to the number of married women of reproductive age (MWRA), since they constitute the main target population for family planning programs. Furthermore, the resulting expenditure per target population can be expressed in absolute terms (here, US$) or relative to the country's per capita GNP. The relevant data appear in table 4.2, showing aggregate expenditure on the four components of family planning programs as well as the distribution of expenditure across them. Because contraceptives are internationally traded, expenditure on these are expressed in dollars; the other components—training, IEC, and incentives—are more meaningfully expressed in relation to per capita GNP.

Spending on the four components of family planning programs varies widely across countries. Bangladesh is still far ahead of other countries, at 0.41 percent of per capita GNP per MWRA. Nepal also has relatively high levels of spending on those four components, while India, Indonesia, and Thailand have comparable levels of expenditure per woman—between 0.10 to 0.19 percent of per capita GNP. In the Republic of Korea, Sri Lanka and Viet Nam, expenditure in the four categories per target woman is significantly less, at between 0.06 and 0.09 percent of per capita GNP, but spending levels are even lower in Malaysia and the Philippines, averaging only 0.03 percent of per capita GNP. In Malaysia, official support for family planning is relatively muted. In the Philippines fertility is considerably higher than in the Republic of Korea or Malaysia, and the comparison here reinforces the case for increased spending.

The distribution of total spending across the four components shows some interesting features. In countries with modest to moderate levels of spending on

Table 4.2: *Annual Public Spending on Contraceptives, Family Planning–Related Training, IEC, and Incentives, Asian Countries, Most Recent Year*

Country	Expenditure per MWRA[a]			Distribution of spending on all four components (percentage)[b,c]				Year
	On contraceptives (US$)	On training, IEC & incentives	On all four components[b]	Contraceptives	Training	IEC	Incentives	
		(percentage of per capita GNP)						
Bangladesh	0.57	0.11	0.41	74	9	4	14	1990
China[d]	0.11	–	–	–	–	–	–	1990
India	0.18	0.14	0.19	28	5	7	60	1990
Indonesia	0.44	0.06	0.16	63	18	20	0	1989
Korea, Rep. of[e]	3.21	0.02	0.09	73	1	14	12	1989
Malaysia	0.49	0.00	0.03	88	4	8	0	1990
Nepal	0.22	0.15	0.30	49	8	13	30	1990
Philippines	0.09	0.01	0.03	65	13	21	1	1986
Sri Larka	0.25	0.01	0.07	82	9	3	6	1990
Thailand	1.06	0.02	0.10	82	10	7	0	1989
Viet Nam	0.02	0.04	0.06	34	29	37	0	1990

a. MWRA refers to married women of reproductive age (15–44).

b. The four components of expenditure are contraceptive commodities; training; information–education–communication (IEC) activities; and incentives. Incentives refers to payment (in cash and in kind) made to acceptors of family planning (usually sterilization and IUD insertion), and incentives paid to service providers, including doctors, nurses, midwives, and other personnel. In India and Bangladesh, the bulk of expenditure on incentives is paid to clients rather than providers, while the opposite is true in the Philippines.

c. Row figures may not add up to 100% owing to rounding errors; as noted in the text, spending on these four components represents only part of total public spending on family planning.

d. See chapter 6 for details on allocations in China's program. Because it is the only compulsory program, the pattern of spending may not lend itself easily to cross-country comparisons here.

e. In Republic of Korea, financial assistance is given to a number of low-income acceptors of sterilization, and free medical services for the preschool children of acceptors of sterilization if sterilized after one child. These subsidies have been declining steadily since 1986, with the sharpest drop occurring between 1989 and 1990. Subsidies in 1990 were only 34% of what they were in 1989.

Source: See table A4.3 in appendix C.

those components, the bulk of expenditure is allocated to contraceptive supplies. The striking exception is India, where allocations for incentives to acceptors of sterilization far exceed any other category. The result is that whereas overall spending in the four categories is comparable to Indonesia's, India's public spending on contraceptives per target woman averages US$0.18 per woman, compared with US$0.44 per woman in Indonesia and US$1.06 per woman in Thailand. These data offer a striking confirmation of the often-cited criticism that India's program places excessive stress on sterilization services, to the exclusion of other methods that might be more attractive to younger and lower-parity women (World Bank 1991a; World Bank, India–1989). Evidence in chapter 6 suggests that this pattern of resource allocation has had an adverse effect on the delivery of nonsterilization services in India.

Although Nepal and Bangladesh spend more than other Asian countries on the four family planning-related components, their patterns of allocation differ quite substantially, with Nepal devoting a significant share of resources to incentive payments. This pattern, coupled with its more modest overall expenditure, leads to a much lower level of spending on contraceptives in Nepal than in Bangladesh. As in India, this result reduces the system's capacity to attract younger women with yet-to-be-completed childbearing, leading some observers (for example, Tuladhar 1989) to argue for the abolition of incentive payments to acceptors of sterilization. In Bangladesh, a similar incentive arrangement operates, but because overall spending is exceptionally high, spending on contraceptive supplies remains relatively high compared to other countries in the region. If resources for the family planning program (which currently absorbs nearly 40 percent of all public health spending) should fall, the cut is likely to be absorbed through declines in spending on contraceptive supplies rather than on incentive payments, given that these are much more difficult to withdraw once they have been instituted. Although the prospect of reduced fiscal support for family planning services is not imminent, it may not be possible to sustain indefinitely the current scale of unusually large spending, and policymakers may need to explore options—including abolition of the incentive payments or a sharper targeting to selected populations—to avoid the pitfalls encountered in India and Nepal.

Among the countries with moderate or little spending on the four components, the Republic of Korea is the only one with a pattern of spending skewed away from contraceptive supplies, reflecting the predominance of sterilization in method mix. Instead, expenditure on IEC and incentive payments absorb significant shares, 14 percent and 12 percent respectively. Incentive payments are explicitly targeted toward low-income families. In the Philippines, the pattern of allocation favors contraceptive supplies, but because overall spending is relatively modest, the actual resources available for contraceptive inputs are extremely low, averaging US$0.09 per woman. This level of spending is only about a third as high as in Sri Lanka. Expenditure on contraceptives is even lower in Viet Nam, at US$0.02 per woman, owing to modest overall spending (see table 4.1) as well as an allocation skewed toward other inputs.

Domestic and External Sources of Funding for Programs

Domestic resources and foreign funds are the two main sources of finance that support public spending on family planning programs. Although donor funds represent a small share of aggregate development aid—about 2 percent during the 1980s according to data in World Bank 1991c and United Nations Fund for Population Activities (UNFPA) 1991—their importance within countries varies widely. In China, the Republic of Korea, and Malaysia, foreign funds account for a modest share of spending, averaging about 5 percent. In China, the small share of foreign funds perhaps reflects the government's commitment to population control as a policy priority. In the Republic of Korea, the scope for foreign financing is limited because replacement fertility has already been reached. In Malaysia, the country's relatively high income has enabled it to minimize reliance on foreign funds, thereby permitting greater domestic control over what is potentially a highly sensitive area of social policy.

Among the remaining countries, foreign aid accounts for very substantial shares of total public spending: in Bangladesh, 60 percent; Indonesia, 46 percent; Nepal, 35 percent; and the Philippines, 44 percent (table 4.3). Except in Nepal, where a sharp drop since 1985 is recorded, the shares of foreign funds have remained relatively stable between 1985 and 1989.[5] Relative poverty, juxtaposed against still high fertility rates, appears to be a common rationale for foreign involvement in these countries. Some believe that this arrangement hinders the development of domestically acceptable programs, as often expressed, for example, in the Philippine context (World Bank, Philippines–1991). Although this concern is valid, the experience of countries such as Indonesia shows that a successful balance can be achieved between local program development and external involvement.

India's reliance on foreign funds for its family planning program is relatively modest for a low-income country, possibly due to the size of the program relative to international funds available for family planning activities. Nevertheless, it is interesting to note the fall in foreign share from 21 percent in 1985 to 13 percent by 1989.

Thailand follows a similar decline in foreign-funding share, but the decline is much steeper, from 39 percent in 1985 to 17 percent in 1989, dropping to only 2 percent in 1990. The decline reflects a redirection of donor funding as fertility approached replacement level. In light of the shift in donor funding, the government has begun to adopt cost recovery policies for publicly provided family planning services. If the Thai experience is any guide, countries on the road to lower fertility (such as Indonesia) can similarly expect an eventual drying up of foreign support. While this prospect appears inevitable, it does not seem to occur before quite low levels of fertility have been reached. In some respects this slow shift is fortuitous, since the decline in foreign funds often calls for the mobilization of private domestic resources through user fees for public services or greater reliance on private providers—both difficult processes. Making this transition from previously free or subsidized services—or even more demanding,

Table 4.3: External Funding for Family Planning Programs as Percentage of Total Public Spending on Family Planning Programs, Asian Countries, 1985 and 1989

Country	1985	1989
Bangladesh	63.5	60.1
China	5.0	5.8[a]
India[b]	21.2	13.2
Indonesia	37.1	45.8
Korea, Rep. of	5.0	4.1
Malaysia	4.4	5.5
Nepal	69.3	35.2
Philippines	48.4	44.0
Thailand	38.9[c]	17.3[d]
Viet Nam	5.7	16.6[d]

Note: Total public spending on family planning programs includes government spending and external financing channeled through the government. External financing channeled through nongovernmental organizations is not included.

a. An estimate of 2% was given in a United Nations Fund for Population Activities (UNFPA) report (dated 3/15/89) to the Governing Council of the United Nations Development Programme on a proposed UNFPA population program for China.

b. First column refers to data for 1985–86.

c. Reflects average for period 1982–86.

d. Data for 1990 show a decrease to 2% in Thailand, and an increase to 20.6% in Viet Nam.

Source: Data for Viet Nam are from World Bank (Viet Nam–1991); data for the remaining countries are from sources cited in table A4.4.

from services provided with incentives (as in Bangladesh, India, and Nepal)—is difficult, requiring careful assessment of its impact on demand for contraception. It is thus not surprising that in both Thailand and Indonesia, studies of this nature are already under way (Ashakul 1989; University Research Corporation 1991).[6]

Viet Nam alone shows a rising trend in the share of donor funding of family planning programs, from 6 percent in 1985 to 17 percent in 1989, and to 21 percent in 1990. This increase—coinciding with the gradual opening of the country to outsiders—may continue because the scope for external assistance is substantial. The government is keen to lower fertility, but public funds are extremely tight, a constraint that may already have led to a sharp deterioration in public health services in general (World Bank, Viet Nam–1992).

Public-Private Roles in Family Planning

Given projected increases in contraceptive users and constrained public budgets and donor resources, some observers (for example, Gillespie and others 1989; Cross and others 1991; Lewis and Kenny 1988; Tsui and Donaldson 1987) consider an expanded role for private providers essential if demand is to be fully met at quality levels desired by clients.[7] Beyond budgetary considerations, possible gaps in the effectiveness and efficiency of service delivery also motivate interest in this issue.

The "private" sector encompasses a variety of providers, including nongovernmental or private voluntary organizations (NGOs); private practitioners, clinics, and hospitals; commercial outlets such as pharmacies, drugstores, and other shops (which sometimes also serve as outlets for subsidized contraceptive commodities, as in contraceptive social marketing schemes); quasi-public clinics of social security or insurance schemes; and employer-financed services. The extent of private financing varies widely across providers. NGOs sometimes charge user fees for their services, but the bulk of their income derives from such sources as foreign donor contributions, government grants and subsidies, and private philanthropy.[8] The other private providers are, by definition, less dependent on grants and subsidies, but among them commercial providers have the potential to offer more fiscal relief than quasi-public clinics and employer-sponsored services because, in most Asian countries, the latter typically cater to a limited clientele. Their coverage tends to be small because (a) social security and insurance plans are not well developed; and (b) relatively few companies are large enough to afford comprehensive employee benefits,[9] and only a modest share of the work force is employed by such companies.

In almost all Asian countries, the overwhelming majority of users (75 percent) rely on the government as a source of contraceptive service or supply—1.7 times the rate in Latin America and 1.2 times the rate in Africa (table 4.4). The comparison to Africa is surprising, since the more developed state of private enterprise in Asia might lead one to expect the private share to be larger in Asia than in Africa.

Within Asia, women in Malaysia and the Republic of Korea are among the least dependent on the government for contraceptive service or supply. In Malaysia, the outcome is, in some ways, not surprising because official support for family planning has been less aggressive than elsewhere.[10] The experience in Malaysia and the Republic of Korea suggests that in socially and economically developed settings—where the demand for contraception exists and private markets function—the private sector can play a large role in service delivery. In such countries as Thailand and possibly also Indonesia, the potential for private sector activity thus appears to be relatively untapped, given that conditions for private sector activity are generally quite favorable. In these countries, the stress on government activity, including heavy subsidization of services, may have crowded out the private sector (Cross and others 1991),[11] resulting in possible efficiency losses in light of Schultz's recent study (1989) using Thai data which showed that the marginal effect of private services on fertility behavior is substantially greater than that of public sector services.

Table 4.4: *Contraceptive Prevalence Rates and Percentage Distribution of Currently Contracepting Married Women according to Source of Service or Supply, Selected Asian Countries and World Regions*

Country/Region	Contraceptive prevalence rate (percentage)[a]	Distribution of women by source of contraceptive service (percentage)							Year
		Government sources	Nongovernment sources			Other[b] sources	All sources		
			NGO	Commercial	All				
Bangladesh[c]	28	69.0	2.0	25.2	27.2	3.8	100		1989
India	40	81.2	–	–	18.8	–	100		1986–87
Indonesia	44	83.6	–	12.3	12.3	4.1	100		1987
Korea, Rep. of[d]	70	60.8	–	36.3	36.3	3.0	100		1988
Malaysia	33	51.7	3.0	38.3	41.3	6.9	100		1989
Nepal[e]	15	73.9	20.4	2.7	23.1	2.9	100		1981
Philippines	21	68.2	–	–	26.4	5.4	100		1988
Sri Lanka	41	87.6	0.1	10.2	10.3	2.1	100		1987
Thailand	63	83.6	0.8	14.8	15.6	0.8	100		1987
Viet Nam	38	93.0	–	3.1	3.1	3.9	100		1988
Asia[f]	39	75.3	3.5[h]	17.9	21.4	3.7	100		–
Latin America[g]	38	44.4	12.1	40.4	52.5	3.1	100		1985–89
Sub-Saharan Africa[i]	10	65.3	12.2	16.0	28.1	6.4	100		1986–89

a. Reflect data for modern methods of contraception; data for Nepal refer to 1986, as reported in UNFPA Nepal–1989; for the remaining countries, they refer to year indicated in last column. Data differ from those in table 3.2 because of differences in methods included, services, and dates.

b. Includes family, friends, neighbors, and unspecified sources; for Republic of Korea, "other" category includes insurance–financed sources.

c. The commercial sector includes shops and doctors' clinics, with the former playing a predominant role. Under contraceptive social marketing schemes, government–subsidized commodities are made available to the public through existing commercial outlets.

d. "Government" means government–supported; services may be provided by private providers who are reimbursed by the government.

e. Data on contraceptive prevalence rate refer to 1986; data on distribution of women by source of contraceptive supply refer to 1981.

f. Arithmetic average of all the Asian countries listed here.

g. Data reflect arithmetic average for 10 countries: Brazil, Bolivia, Dominican Republic, Trinidad, Colombia, Mexico, Peru, Ecuador, Guatemala, and El Salvador. Modern methods only.

h. Calculated as the difference between all nongovernmental sources and commercial sources.

i. Data reflect arithmetic average for 11 countries: Senegal, Togo, Ghana, Ondo state (Nigeria), Liberia, Uganda, Kenya, Botswana, Zimbabwe, Burundi, and Mali. Row does not sum to 100% due to rounding errors. Modern methods only.

Source: Cross and others 1991 for Indonesia, Thailand, Sri Lanka, Latin America, and Sub–Saharan Africa; Lewis and Kenny 1988 for Nepal; India 1989c; Viet Nam 1990a; Philippines 1988; Mun and others 1989 for Republic of Korea; tabulation from 1989 Bangladesh Contraceptive Prevalence Survey; and tabulation from 1988–89 Second Malaysia Family Life Survey.

In the Philippines, where private sector involvement in social sector activities is usually more developed, its role in the delivery of family planning services appears to be somewhat modest. Given that private enterprise is pervasive in this country, this result may indicate relatively weak demand for contraception, reflecting in part conflicting public messages regarding the safety and social acceptability of family planning. As argued in a recent World Bank study (World Bank, Philippines–1991), raising contraceptive prevalence would require a concerted effort to remove misconceptions about the side effects of contraception, and to overcome religious reservations about its practice.

In Bangladesh, the commercial private sector serves an unexpectedly large proportion of contraceptive users.[12] Under contraceptive social marketing schemes (CSM), publicly subsidized pills and condoms are supplied to the public through shops that normally carry other goods and services. The survey data do not permit a distinction between clients who purchased supplies under the CSM arrangement and those who paid unsubsidized prices. Because of the aggregate volume of supplies channeled through CSM, most clients are believed to be in the former group. The Bangladeshi data suggest that while people in a low-income country may not be able to afford commercially priced contraceptives, some degree of willingness to pay nonetheless exists and can be tapped. The experience indicates there is scope even in low-income contexts for commercial providers to play an important role in satisfying expressed demand for contraception.

Differences in public-private division of service provision by type of contraceptive method are also noteworthy. Because clinical methods[13] are more demanding in equipment and staff inputs (characteristics that have obvious implications for start-up capital costs), private providers might be expected to shy away from this market. This expectation is borne out by the data in table 4.5 showing the source distribution of clinical and nonclinical contraceptive users. For Asia as a whole, over 85 percent of users rely on the government for clinical services compared to 55 percent in the nonclinical group. These percentages are 1.6 times and 1.8 times the corresponding percentages in Latin America. The relatively large gap for nonclinical methods between Asia and Latin America is surprising, providing yet another indication of the possibility that the public sector has been crowding out private providers.

Within Asia, Malaysia has a far lower share of clinical method clients using government services than its neighbors, averaging only 58 percent compared to over 85 percent in all the other countries. In the Republic of Korea, where one might expect comparable patterns, the government share of clinical clients is unexpectedly sizable at 83 percent, reflecting a policy of targeting subsidies to such methods. The picture is much more varied for nonclinical methods, with the government share of users ranging from an extreme low of 7 percent in the Republic of Korea to over 75 percent in Indonesia and Thailand. The shares in the latter two countries are larger even than those in countries with much lower incomes, notably Bangladesh, where one might expect private markets to be less well developed. In India, the public sector share of nonclinical clients is relatively modest at 45 percent. Given the stress on

Table 4.5: *Percent Distribution of Currently Married Women Using Clinical and Nonclinical Contraception by Source of Service or Supply, Selected Asian Countries and World Regions, 1980s*

Country/Region	Percentage using clinical methods[a]	Clinical methods[b]			Nonclinical methods[b]		
		Government sources	Nongovernment sources[c]		Government sources	Nongovernment sources[c]	
			Commercial	All		Commercial	All
Bangladesh	43	89.3	5.4	8.5	50.7	43.0	43.9
India	79	90.5	–	9.5	44.8	–	55.2
Indonesia	38	89.7	9.2	9.2	75.1	14.2	14.2
Korea, Rep. of	72	82.7	13.0	13.0	7.2	91.8	91.8
Malaysia	35	57.6	39.0	40.0	48.6	22.2	26.4
Nepal	78	84.2	0.0	15.8	49.9	6.4	45.3
Philippines	41	71.2	–	27.0	64.0	–	25.7
Sri Lanka	51	96.7	3.1	3.1	69.5	24.2	24.5
Thailand	52	92.9	7.0	7.1	75.5	21.6	23.0
Viet Nam	87	97.7	0.1	0.1	61.1	23.3	23.3
Asia	58	85.3	–	13.3	54.6	–	37.3
Latin America	43	53.6	28.9	44.4	29.6	54.9	63.8
Sub-Saharan Africa	12	73.6	8.9	19.7	58.2	24.4	38.1

a. Clinical methods include IUD and sterilization (male or female). For Viet Nam, menstrual regulation and abortion are also included, while for India, the data include only sterilization.

b. Government and nongovernment sources add up to less than 100% due to omission of the share of "other" sources, which include family, friends, and unspecified source.

c. The difference between the "Commercial" and "All" columns represents the share of NGOs.

Source: See table 4.4. Data in column 1 are from UNFPA 1989 for Nepal; World Bank (Indonesia–1990); and Janowitz and others 1990 (appendix table 1) for Sri Lanka and Thailand; and averages for Latin America and Sub–Saharan Africa in column 1 for the same countries as in table 4.4.

sterilization in the government's family planning program, it is not surprisingly that clients who are motivated enough to practice contraception but prefer temporary methods must seek private services.

Taken together, the data suggest there is scope for expanding the role of private providers, particularly for nonclinical methods of contraception, and in countries where public programs are mature and contraceptive use is well established. But heavy subsidization of public services makes it difficult for private providers to compete for clients, even if price is only one factor affecting clients' choice of contraceptive source. In addition, government regulation—such as price controls, restrictions on contraceptive advertising, and prescription requirements—often can reduce the viability of private services. To tilt the balance toward private provision, governments can, at a minimum, change the pricing of public services and lift overly restrictive regulations on private providers. Additional measures can include subsidized loans to cover the start-up costs of private family planning services, cutting taxes on contraceptive imports, investing in generic promotion of family planning to increase demand, and providing training to potential private sector agents (such as doctors, nurses, midwives, as well as pharmacists and other shop owners).

Indonesia's Blue Circle campaign is an example of government intervention to promote private sector activity (Population Information Program 1991; World Bank, Indonesia–1990). Recognizing the government's limited capacity to serve all users—particularly at convenience and quality levels clients desire—the campaign was launched to tap people's willingness to pay for better services. Its target population initially was the 8.4 million middle-income couples in Indonesia's 301 cities who make up 9 percent of the population. With continued buoyant economic growth and rising incomes, the authorities hope the Blue Circle strategy will boost the private sector share of users from slightly over 10 percent at present to 40 to 50 percent by 2000. The specific goal is perhaps optimistic because of bottlenecks in the supply of health personnel and still low incomes in rural areas. Nonetheless, moving in that direction has the potential of enabling the government to improve the targeting of subsidized services to priority segments of the population.

The scheme involves several major components: (a) providing training, equipment, and supplies to doctors and midwives for their private practice;[14] (b) multimedia publicity, advertising the availability of higher-quality private services; (c) introduction of subsidized family planning products under the Blue Circle logo; technical assistance to NGOs; and support to the organized business sector. Getting private doctors and nurses involved was the main plank in the strategy, and the provision of training was essential in this regard. The bigger challenge, however, was overcoming Ministry of Health reservations about allowing doctors and midwives to stock family planning drugs in their offices. With this obstacle removed, convenience to clients was greatly boosted because the availability of drugs at providers' offices eliminated unnecessary trips between the drugstore (where prescriptions for drugs are filled) and providers' offices. As an added convenience the Ministry of Health also agreed to let pill users holding Blue Circle membership cards assign one person to collect resupplies on behalf of neighborhood groups of users instead of going individually to the drugstore. Users with no side effect complaints can renew their prescriptions indefinitely.

It is perhaps still too early to judge the fiscal effect of this campaign. Nonetheless, the response of private providers has been enthusiastic, and they are attracting their own clientele. The example of the Blue Circle campaign illustrates government's potential catalytic role in stimulating private sector activity in the provision of family planning services. In the Indonesian context, the specific interventions involved modifying restrictive regulations, subsidizing training, and investing in publicity—all of which are activities with a strong public goods element.

User Contribution for Public Sector Services

Because the public sector is a predominant provider of services in Asian countries and is likely to continue playing a substantial role—even in countries where private sector activity is growing—users' contribution for public services is another policy option to ease the fiscal burden of providing family planning services and improve the commercial viability of private providers. Ashakul (1989), for example, shows that increased charges for public sector pills and sterilization can save public spending on family planning services in Thailand by 25 percent without lowering contraceptive prevalence. He argues that the savings could be redirected to address new health problems that are emerging with the country's demographic transition.

The option of user fees does not necessarily entail recovering all costs.[15] Even if costs are not fully recovered, user fees can relieve the fiscal burden of public services, directly by lowering subsidies per user in the public sector; and indirectly by narrowing the price gap between public and private services, thereby making it more feasible for private providers to compete for clients. Where overstretched subsidies result in poor services—inadequate and unreliable drug supplies, long waiting times, and so on—user fees can also help to mobilize the resources needed for improvement, with the possible effect of boosting demand rather than dampening it, particularly if consumers perceive free services or commodities to be of poor quality (Lewis 1986 and 1987).[16]

Against the potential benefits, there are nonetheless valid concerns about the possible adverse effect of user fees on demand and equity. To what extent can fees be raised or subsidies reduced without thwarting the goal of expanding contraceptive use? How would these changes affect poor people's access to family planning? These questions are difficult to answer in the abstract, so it is useful to begin by documenting current fee levels in our sample of countries as well as the responsiveness of contraceptive demand to prices at those fees. Available evidence on these parameters is provided below.

Current Fee Policies

According to reported data on official policies,[17] public family planning services in most Asian countries are generally free of charge for most methods (table 4.6). For sterilization, public programs in Bangladesh, India, the Republic of Korea, Nepal, and Sri Lanka not only provide free services but also make cash and in-kind payments to acceptors, usually immediately upon acceptance.[18]

From an economic perspective, method-related payments are analytically similar to charges because both interventions affect the cost of contraception facing potential users. Payments are nonetheless distinctive because they go beyond what governments normally do to encourage the consumption of other social services such as education and health. In these sectors, free services/commodities are probably the most that governments offer; for education, this may be supplemented by scholar-

Table 4.6: Official Pricing Policies for Public Family Planning Services in Selected Countries, circa 1987

Country	User fees charged	Offered free of charge[a]	Offered with payment to client
Bangladesh	–	O,C,J,D,S	St.,I
China	–	All	–
Hong Kong	All	–	–
India	Ab.	C,O	St.,I
Indonesia	–	I,O,C,J	–
Korea, Rep. of	I,O,C	Ab.[b], St.	St.[b]
Malaysia	I,O,C, St.	D,S	–
Mongolia	–	All	–
Nepal	–	O,C,J,D,S	St.,I
Pakistan	O,C,S	–	St.
Philippines	–	All	–
Sri Lanka	O,C	I,J	St.
Thailand	J	O,C,I,St.[c]	–
Viet Nam	–	All	–

Ab = abortion; J = injectables; O = oral pills; C = condoms; St = Sterilization; I = IUD; D = Diaphragm; and S = spermicide.

a. At public clinics or facilities.

b. For low–income women only.

c. Officially free, but clinics usually charge small fees.

Source. Ross and Isaacs 1988 for Indonesia and Thailand; Ross and others 1988 for the remaining countries.

ships for deserving pupils from poor families. In contrast, rapid population growth is viewed by some governments as so serious a threat to national well-being that free services with client payments are considered a necessary response.[19]

In the Asian countries where payments are made, there are two arrangements, one involving one-time payments, and the other involving continuing child-support subsidies. In China and the Republic of Korea, the incentives for small families include both types of payments. As detailed in chapter 6, continuing subsidies predominate in China's scheme and are available only to single-child couples.[20] In the Republic of Korea, payments are targeted to low-income couples, with a relatively large one-time bonus for single-child acceptors of sterilization, amounting to 9 percent of per capita GNP (table 4.7). With the persistence of below-replacement fertility in the country, the government has recently taken steps to phase out incentive payments.

In the other countries, payments are offered to acceptors of sterilization and IUD without regard to the number of children. The rates of payment for sterilization invariably exceed those for IUD. During 1989–91, they ranged from 5 percent of per capita GNP in Bangladesh to about 3 percent of per capita GNP in India, Nepal, and Sri Lanka. In none of these countries are payments targeted by income group, but beginning in 1991, payments in Nepal are being limited to 60 of the country's 75 districts. In India and Bangladesh, the rates have been adjusted periodically to keep up with inflation; in Sri Lanka, however, payments have remained fixed since 1980, and their value relative to per capita GNP has declined correspondingly over time.

In practice, actual charges and payments sometimes deviate from official schedules: where client payments are offered, budgetary appropriations for this purpose are based on projected targets of acceptors, and when the actual demand exceeds targets, funds may be unavailable to pay the extra acceptors; where local autonomy is permitted, clinics may charge fees even though services are officially free. Evidence on de facto fees and payments for public sector family planning services is available from survey data for a few Asian countries (table 4.8).

In most of countries, large proportions, though by no means all, of the users of public family planning receive services free of charge. Pill users in Sri Lanka are the exceptions, with only 4 percent receiving free services; this modest share is consistent with reported pricing policies. In Nepal and Thailand, the proportion of pill users obtaining free services is large—69 percent and 59 percent respectively—though not as large as one might expect based on reported pricing policies. Malaysia's profile is interesting because although fees are reportedly charged, a sizable proportion of clients in fact obtained services free of charge: about half for pills and condoms and 15 percent for injectables; and 13 percent for IUDs. These shares are generally lower than those for the other countries in the sample. Comparison between Indonesia and India is also noteworthy: both countries provide free services to over 80 percent of IUD clients; among the other methods, however, the Indonesian program puts more emphasis on free pills and condoms than on injectables and sterilization, whereas the Indian program emphasizes sterilization (provided free or with incentives) over free pills and condoms.[21]

Table 4.7: Schedule of Payment to Acceptors of Sterilization and IUD in Bangladesh, India, Republic of Korea, Nepal, and Sri Lanka (percentage of per capita GNP)

Country	Year	Target population	One-time payment per client		Annual child-support subsidies[b]
			Sterilization[a]	IUD	
Bangladesh[c]	1991	None	5.2	0.3	0.0
India[c]	1989	None	2.8	0.2	0.0
Korea, Rep. of	1989	Low-income: 1 Child	9.0	0.0	2.0
		2 Children	3.0	0.0	4.0
Nepal[c]	1991	60 of country's 75 districts	2.6	0.1	0.0
Sri Lanka	1991	None	3.4	0.0	0.0

a. Rates for tubectomies; vasectomy clients are paid at slightly different rates.

b. The estimates for Republic of Korea are based on average annual medical expenses per child aged 0–6 years reported in Korea National Federation of Medical Insurance (KNFMI) 1988. Child-support subsidies are available until an eligible child reaches age 6.

c. Includes cash and in-kind payments for sterilization acceptors. See appendix table A4.5 for breakdown and size of payments in local currency. In-kind payments are not made to IUD acceptors.

Source: See appendix table A4.5.

Table 4.8: *Percentage of Clients of Public Family Planning Services Who Receive Services Free of Charge, and Prices Charged to Paying Public Sector Clients, Selected Asian Countries*

Country	Survey Year	Percentage receiving services free of charge					Average price charged to paying clients for a year's contraceptive protection[a] (as percentage of per capita GNP)				
		Pill	Condom	Injectable	IUD	Sterilization	Pill	Condom	Injectable	IUD	Sterilization[b]
India	1986–87	51	30	–	82	94[c]	–	–	–	–	–
Indonesia	1987	85	95	34	86	40	0.42	0.37[d]	0.84	0.32	0.64
Malaysia[e]	1988–89	53	49	15	13	–	0.30	0.37	0.33	0.04	0.02
Nepal[f]	1986	69	–	–	–	–	1.22	–	–	–	–
Sri Lanka	1987	4	–	–	–	–	0.16	–	–	–	–
Thailand	1987	59	–	–	–	–	0.26	–	–	–	–
	1984	–	–	–	–	–	0.28	–	0.78	0.12	0.14

– means data not available.

a. A year's protection calculated with the following assumptions: 13 pill cycles per year; 100 condoms per year; 2.5 years use-duration for IUDs; 3-month protection per injection. For sterilization, length of protection is the difference between age 45 and the average age at sterilization in the population. Note that for Thailand, data for 1984 from Ashakul 1989 are already reported in price per month's protection, and are converted to annual prices by simple multiplication.

b. For female sterilization.

c. Includes 67.2% who received the service with incentive payment, and 17.7% who received it free of charge.

d. There is some uncertainty on the price of condoms because the survey questionnaire did not specifically solicit information on how many condoms the reported price refers to. In Indonesia packets come with 3 condoms or 12; the latter number is assumed for this calculation because the other number implies a prohibitively high price for a year's protection, more than 10 times the price of, for example, pills.

e. Data on 'percent receiving services free of charge' reflect the share of contraceptive users who live in communities where government-sponsored free services are available.

f. The available survey data do not permit identification of public and private sources, but as almost all providers fall into the government or NGO category (which in Nepal is heavily subsidized by the government), the data do provide a rough picture of the extent of free provision.

Source: India 1989c; 1987 National Indonesia Contraceptive Prevalence Survey; 1987 Thailand Demographic and Health Survey, and Ashakul 1989 for 1984 data for Thailand; 1986 Nepal Contraceptive Prevalence Survey; 1988–89 Second Malaysia Family Life Survey.

Moving toward the Indonesian pattern might be one approach for the Indian program to lessen its heavy bias toward sterilization.

Among the relatively few users who do pay for public sector services, the rates of payment are modest in all the countries for which data exist, averaging less than 1 percent of per capita GNP for a year's protection across the main contraceptive methods.[22] Differences across methods are interesting: in Indonesia, charges are higher for injectables and sterilization than for pills and IUDs; in Malaysia, charges are very low for IUDs and sterilization compared to charges for pills and condoms; in Thailand, the pattern is similar to that in Malaysia, with lower charges for IUDs and sterilization than for pills. The structure of pricing across methods obviously reflects differences of emphasis in public sector programs. A case can nonetheless be made for avoiding extreme price gaps among methods to reduce distortion in method choice. On this criterion, the structure of charges in all three countries may need to be rationalized.

Price Elasticities of Demand for Contraception

Beyond price levels and structures, the design of pricing policies also needs to take account of demand elasticities.[23] The available evidence is scanty, partly because price data have, until recently, been lacking in demographic surveys. Lewis's 1986 survey uncovered 13 separate studies based on data from 8 developing countries, 5 in Asia. Some of the studies report the results of experiments in which selected populations are offered contraceptives (usually pills and condoms) at several prices (Brazil, Colombia, Egypt, Taiwan [China], and the Republic of Korea); others track the before-and-after patterns of contraceptive use in localities where prices have been decreased for sterilization and pills (the Republic of Korea, Taiwan [China], and Thailand), and where client payments for sterilization were introduced (Sri Lanka). At the time of the Lewis survey, only one study—for the Philippines—used multiple regression techniques to assess the effect of price changes on contraceptive use.

Several conclusions emerge from these early studies. First, demand is not very different for free and low- or moderately-priced contraceptives; for example, in the Republic of Korea, there was no difference in prevalence in localities where pills and condoms were free and where they were priced at US$0.21 per cycle and US$0.21 per 6 condoms. Second, demand becomes more price-responsive as prices rise; in Taiwan (China), for example, while prevalence did not change when pill prices rose from zero to US$0.13, it dropped by half when prices reached US$0.25. Third, large price changes have big effects on demand; for example, when the government dropped sterilization fees from US$20 to zero in the Republic of Korea in the early 1980s, the number of acceptors in one locality increased from 10 to 170 per month; and in Sri Lanka, the introduction of incentive payments to male acceptors of sterilization—Rs. 100 from January to October 1980, and Rs. 500 after October 1980—led to an increase in vasectomies in the study area, from 250 before January 1980, to 400 from January to October, to 1,669 in October (the last figure may reflect in part postponed vasectomies in anticipation of the increase in incentive payment). Fourth, poor people are more price-responsive than people with higher incomes; in Brazil, for example, free pills offered in rural Piaui attracted 50 to 100 percent of rural users away from private providers, but shifted only 2 percent of users in urban Piaui.

Since the Lewis survey, at least four new studies (Schwartz and others 1989; Ashakul 1989; Ciszewski and Harvey 1991; and Molyneaux and Diman 1991), have appeared in the literature, with results generally consistent with the foregoing findings. Ciszewski and Harvey differ in methodology from the other studies. The authors report the effect of recent increases in Bangladesh in the prices of subsidized pills and condoms sold in commercial outlets through a social market-ing program. Partly to keep pace with inflation, program managers raised prices by 60 percent in 1990. The result was a 46 percent drop in the program's condom sales and a 17 percent drop in pill sales in the twelve months following the price rise compared to the preceding twelve months. The authors estimate that about 15 to 20 percent of condom users switched to other, cheaper brands, with a net decrease in overall condom use. About half a million customers from the lowest-income groups were estimated to have been lost. Although worsening economic condi-tions may have played a role, the authors attribute the sharp drop in sales mainly to the price increases. Large price increases clearly do affect demand, and their effect appears to be particularly strong among the poor.

The other three studies use survey data to derive price elasticities of demand for various contraceptive services and commodities (table 4.9). Schwartz and others report estimates for the Philippines (1978), Jamaica (1984), and Thailand (1984). Ashakul also uses 1984 data for Thailand, but from a different survey. Because separate regressions were run for urban and rural populations and for public and private sector sources of commodities and services, Ashakul's paper offers price elasticity estimates at various contraceptive prices.[24] Molyneaux and Diman's study is based on Indonesian data for 1987.

In all the studies the demand for contraceptives is highly inelastic in the price ranges of the analyses, meaning that a 1 percent price increase would cause much less than a 1 percent decline in use probabilities.[25] The results for Indonesia shed additional insights, showing that if the price rises for one contraceptive method, users would switch to other methods. Because of such substitution, "own" price elasticities (that is, the responsiveness of demand for a given contraceptive to a change in its own price) tend, in absolute value, to exceed the elasticities associated with a simultaneous change in the prices of all contraceptives. The results also suggest that a simultaneous change in the prices of all the major methods would reduce overall use probabilities, but by only a modest amount—about 0.12 percent following a 1 percent increase in the prices of the major contraceptive methods.

For Thailand, the findings from Schwartz and others (1989) and Ashakul (1989) can be merged to show an interesting pattern (figure 4.1). The plot of estimated elasticities against price yields a surprisingly smooth downward sloping function, without much distinction among the various contraceptive methods. Because methods differ in aspects other than price,[26] one might have expected

Table 4.9: Price Elasticities at Various Sample Mean Prices for a Year's Contraceptive Protection in the Philippines, Jamaica, Thailand, and Indonesia[a]

| Method | Philippines 1978[b] | | Jamaica 1984[b] | | Thailand 1984[b] | | | | Indonesia 1987 | | |
| | | | | | Schwartz and others | | Ashakul | | Elasticities | | |
	Elasticity	Mean price	Elasticity	Mean price	Elasticity	Mean price	Elasticity	Mean price	Own price	All prices[c]	Mean price
Condom	-0.15	0.24	-1.09	2.46	-0.56	3.10	-0.25	–	–	–	–
Injection	–	–	-0.79	1.80	-0.16	0.83	-0.29	1.26	-0.49	-0.05	1.06
							-0.25	1.04			
							-0.12	0.52			
Pill	-0.00	0.11	-0.07	0.56	-0.10	0.74	-0.23	1.11	-0.11	-0.02	0.21
							-0.09	0.36			
							-0.04	0.19			
IUD	0.01	0.02	–	–	-0.10	0.43	-0.04	0.16	0.14	-0.03	0.12
							-0.02	0.08			
Sterilization	–	–	–	–	-0.02	0.22	-0.05	0.18	–	–	–
							-0.02	0.10			
All major methods	–	–	–	–	–	–	–	–	–	-0.12[d]	–

– means data not available.

a. Mean prices are in units of per capita GNP, which was US$510 for the Philippines in 1978, US$1,150 for Jamaica in 1984, US$860 for Thailand in 1984, and US$450 for Indonesia in 1987.

b. Elasticities are own price elasticities, reflecting the responsiveness of use probabilities of a given contraceptive to changes in its own price.

c. Reflects the percentage change in use probability if the prices of all major contraceptive methods simultaneously rise by 1%.

d. Reflects the percentage change in overall use probability if the prices of all the major contraceptive methods simultaneously rise by 1%.

Source: Data for Philippines, Jamaica, and Thailand are calculated from Schwartz and others 1989, text tables 5.1–5.2 and appendix tables A5.4–A5.6; additional data for Thailand are from Ashakul 1989, tables 1–3; data for Indonesia are from Molyneaux and Diman 1991, tables 1–4. For Thailand, see also appendix table A4.6 in appendix C.

differences in users' willingness to pay for different products and services, and therefore, in estimated elasticities. This expectation is not borne out by the Thai data, possibly because current prices are relatively modest for all the methods (except condoms, which are supplied mainly by private providers in Thailand), mostly below 1 percent of per capita GNP for a year's protection. At higher prices, elasticities at given prices might well differ across methods, but no data are currently available to shed light on this issue.

Although the results in figure 4.1 are specific to Thailand, a middle-income country with a per capita GNP of US$860 in 1984, they nonetheless yield some parameters to identify situations where increased fees for public family planning services might be worth considering. As a cautious first step toward assessing the potential for increased user contributions for public family planning programs, one might focus on services or commodities where user contributions are currently smaller than 1 percent of per capita GNP for a year's contraceptive protection. This yardstick—arguably conservative because demand elasticities are still very inelastic at such prices—obviously offers no more than a starting point for considering cost recovery policies. The precise design of those policies will require in-depth analysis and experimentation in each setting for which they are intended.

Figure 4.1: Elasticity of Demand for Contraceptives with Respect to their Cost, Thailand 1984

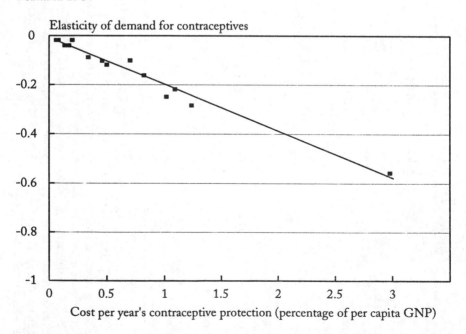

The need for and design of targeted cost recovery deserves especially close attention. Equity considerations aside, differences in the elasticities of demand among income groups would also call for differentiated cost recovery policies if their potentially adverse effects on contraceptive prevalence rates are to be minimized. There is unfortunately little empirical evidence on these differences. Of the studies cited above, for example, only Molyneaux and Diman's offer estimates of price elasticities by socioeconomic group. Their results show that low-income women would need protection from price increases if contraceptive use rates among them are to be maintained. When faced with higher prices, such women tend to stop contracepting rather than switch to other methods; in contrast, women from higher-income groups switch methods rather than stop contracepting. Indirect support for differentiating among income groups is also provided by the Thai data shown in figure 4.1: the downward sloping relationship suggests that people with lower incomes—and therefore facing higher contraceptive prices relative to their incomes—would tend to be more sensitive to price increases.[27]

Notes

1. More details about China's expenditure on family planning are provided in chapter 6. They are not shown here because China's data must be understood in the context of its unique family planning program, as discussed in that chapter.

2. The family planning program underwent important administrative reorganization in the late 1980s. Prior to 1989, the delivery of family planning services was shared between POPCOM and the Ministry of Health (MOH). After reorganization in 1989, service delivery is consolidated under the Ministry of Health, while POPCOM was assigned the task of policy formulation concerning population issues, broadly defined. Expenditure through POPCOM prior to 1989 reflects the bulk of expenditure on family planning because the agency also procured contraceptive supplies for the Ministry of Health and was responsible for other program inputs such as information-education–communication activities and training. MOH's expenditure in the past consisted mainly of personnel costs of doctors and paramedics, but since these staff also perform other duties, it is not possible to obtain a breakdown of these costs across the various programs.

3. Staff costs for family planning are perhaps most accurately reflected in budget accounts under contract arrangements between the government and private providers, as in Korea and Thailand for sterilization services. The amount reimbursed, sometimes called "subsidies," compensate for the cost of services, notably that of staff input. Such contracting-out arrangements are not widespread in Asia.

4. Incentive payments to acceptors—also called compensation in some countries (for example, India)—include cash payments as well as payments in kind (such as food and clothing). Incentive payments to providers refer to bonuses paid to individual providers (including doctors, nurses, motivators, etc.) on a per case basis. In some countries, reimbursement for service provision is made to designated non-government-sector providers, as in the Republic of Korea and Thailand, but because these payments are intended to cover the cost of service provision, they are not treated as incentives here.

5. In Nepal the sharp drop in the share of donor funding arises from a 70 to 80 percent rise in domestic spending between 1985 and 1989, against a constant level of external funding during the two years.

6. If the transition is considered difficult in these relatively advanced demographic contexts, it can only be expected to be harder in less developed situations. The need for a period of experimentation and assessment of cost-recovery policies should be recognized in the context of recent arguments in favor of shifting donor funds away from Asia toward other world regions where the need for donor funding is perceived to be greater (Sinding 1991).

7. See apendix B for a framework to analyze alternative policy options to enhance the private sector's role in family planning.

8. For example, during 1986–89, the Family Planning Association of Nepal derived over 80 percent of its income from international donors, over 10 percent from the government, and reported no income from user charges. In Malaysia, for

the period 1987–88, the Federation of Family Planning Associations also reported about 80 percent of income from foreign donors and over 10 percent of income from the government; revenue from user fees accounted for about 2 percent of income.

9. In large corporations employee benefits often include health services for workers and their families, as well as education benefits for workers' children. These services may be offered through on-site health clinics or on contract with outside providers. When workers are eligible for maternity and child-related benefits, companies often find it in their interest to sponsor family planning services because lower fertility reduces the costs of workers' benefit claims, particularly for children's education.

10. On the other hand, government involvement in the social sectors—health and education—is exceptionally strong in Malaysia compared to other Asian countries, so it is curious that a similar pattern does not hold for family planning services.

11. Private providers remain in operation only if they can recover costs and earn a profit. In settings where government services are highly subsidized, private services become less competitive, losing clients to the public sector. Some clients may of course continue to choose private sector services because of differences in other aspects of service delivery—including better quality in terms of such features as greater privacy, courtesy, cleanliness, and general ambience of clinics. Crowding out nevertheless remains an outcome, since the private sector share of clients is smaller than it otherwise might have been.

12. In Nepal, the nongovernment sector share of clients is comparable to that in Bangladesh. Most of the private sector providers, however, are nongovernmental organizations rather than commercial sector entrepreneurs. NGOs in Nepal involved in family planning receive a large part of their funding from the government and provide commodities and services at little or no cost to the public. For example, during 1986–89, the Family Planning Association of Nepal reported no income from the sale of commodities to clients (personal communication from staff at the World Bank's resident mission in Kathmandu).

13. Clinical methods include sterilization and IUD; nonclinical methods include pill, condom, and other resupply methods.

14. Most doctors and nurses in Indonesia are public sector employees who run their own private practices in the afternoons when public facilities are normally closed. Until recently, this arrangement was permitted only for doctors, but recently the restriction on midwives has been lifted (Population Information Program 1991, p. 33).

15. Indeed, as will be seen below, in countries where users are currently paid to accept family planning, the "user fee" option may merely involve a reduction in the rate of payment, rather than the imposition of a positive price.

16. Lewis (1987) reports the relationship between the demand for four types of contraceptives and their prices in the Philippines. The demand curves for sterilization, IUDs, and condoms have the usual downward slope, but at low prices, the curve for condoms bends backward. This pattern implies that at those prices, the demand

for condoms would rise rather than fall as prices rise because higher prices are also associated with better quality products.

17. The data are based on the reports of knowledgeable experts canvassed in a survey conducted by the Population Council on behalf of the UNFPA. The results are reported in Ross and others (1988) and are currently being updated with data from a new round of the survey.

18. In Bangladesh, India, and Nepal, payment is also made to providers and recruiters on a per case basis. These payments can have an indirect effect on demand for contraception through possible pressure from providers and recruiters. They are nonetheless ignored here because the focus is on the direct price to users of contraception.

19. The use of client payments raises important ethical issues (Chomitz and Birdsall 1991; Ross and Isaacs 1988), but which are beyond the scope of this paper to address. Judgment depends importantly on subjective ethical standards. Whereas some view payments as inherently coercive, others consider them essential to promote freedom of choice by removing the financial barriers to contraception. Client payments in India, for example, are called "compensation," the idea being that they compensate clients for time lost from work after sterilization and help to cover the cost of transportation and incidentals. The size of the payments is obviously a key issue: a small payment that merely replaces out-of-pocket expenses may be seen as a reasonable arrangement, but a large payment may be viewed as having a coercive effect. Moreover, because payments are usually fixed in amount, they affect low-income people to a greater degree than people with higher incomes.

20. Banister and Harbaugh (1991) estimates that payments to each eligible one-child couple in 1991 included a one-time bonus valued at 2.8 percent of per capita GNP and annual child-support subsidies valued at 5.2 percent of per capita GNP.

21. Interestingly, note that although the Indian program in theory offers payments to all sterilization clients, according to survey data for 1986–87, only two-thirds actually received the payment. About 18 percent received sterilization free of charge, while the remaining 6 percent actually paid to be sterilized.

22. The exception is Nepal where charges for pills average 1.22 percent of per capita GNP. Because Nepal's data do not differentiate between government and NGO sources of services, this proportion is not strictly comparable to the data for the other countries.

23. In this section, we deal with elasticities of the demand for contraceptives with respect to their purchase price. The full price of acquiring a year's worth of contraceptive protection is the sum of the purchase price of the contraceptives and the time cost of acquiring them. Where the purchase price is nearly zero, it may be but a small portion of the full price of contraceptives. In general, the full-price elasticity of demand for contraceptives will be larger in absolute magnitude than the purchase-price elasticity of demand. We do not include the time cost of acquiring contraceptives here because we know of no comparable data across Asian countries.

24. See appendix table A5.7. The results in Ashakul (1989) are generally consistent with the results reported by Schwartz and others (1989). For example,

the elasticity for injection from Schwartz and others is -0.16 at a mean price of 0.83 percent of per capita GNP; this value lies between Ashakul's estimate of -0.25 and -0.12 at mean prices of 1.04 percent and 0.52 percent of per capita GNP. Similar patterns can be found in the estimates for pill and IUD. For sterilization, however, Schwartz and others reports an elasticity of -0.02 at a mean price of 0.22 percent of per capita GNP, but this estimate is the same as Ashakul's estimate at less than half that mean price. Nonetheless, since both estimates are very low, the discrepancies are probably not serious.

25. Elasticities are usually calculated at the sample mean price of the contraceptive in question.

26. See World Bank 1992 for a nice summary of the use characteristics of the major contraceptive methods.

27. Further indirect evidence is provided by studies on the demand for general health services. Gertler, Locay, and Sanderson (1987) (based on Peruvian data), for example, shows that elasticities of demand are much higher among low-income groups than among high-income groups.

5

Delivery of Family Planning Services

As with financing arrangements, countries also vary widely in the delivery of family planning services. This chapter documents selected aspects of service delivery in Asian countries. The emphasis is on the public sector, in part because data on private activities are scanty, but perhaps more important, because the public sector is open to direct government intervention to improve the efficiency and equity of service delivery.

Institutional Modes

Publicly supported family planning services are organized under different institutional arrangements, with varying degrees of integration with the provision of health services.[1] In dedicated or vertical programs, most program functions are coordinated and implemented through an independent, autonomous structure. In integrated programs, family planning is offered as part of a range of other health services, usually under the overall purview of the health ministry.

Vertical programs are considered administratively simpler than integrated programs (Srikantan 1982), and they can focus specifically on demographic goals. Such programs are often an expression of the government's political commitment to reduce fertility. Their autonomy gives them the visibility to lobby for continued public support as well as the facility and authority to coordinate activities across government ministries and other entities. Integrated programs lack the sharp focus on demographic goals but can potentially offer services that are more acceptable and convenient to clients. The costs of service delivery are possibly lower because personnel, facilities, equipment, and other resources are shared with other health services.

Each institutional structure has unique advantages (Simmons and Philips 1987), and countries in Asia, as elsewhere, have chosen various structures to suit local conditions. Most programs in Asian countries began with vertical structures, but few are still organized as autonomous entities today. Of those which continue to retain a strong element of autonomy, clinical family planning services are nonetheless provided through existing health facilities. In China, for example, such services are contracted with health ministry facilities which are reimbursed by the family planning program for the cost of the services. Similarly, in Indonesia, the National Family Planning Coordinating Board (BKKBN) is organized as a vertical program with primary responsibility in such areas as information-education-communication activities, staff training, and community-based distribution and outreach services. Most family planning services, however, are delivered via health ministry facilities and staff who also provide other basic health services.

Most programs in Asian countries have increased the degree of service integration over time, coordinating closely with maternal and child health programs. In the Philippines, for example, program responsibility has recently been consolidated under the Department of Health to stress the health benefits of family planning (World Bank, Philippines–1991). In India, maternal and child health services were added to the family planning program as early as 1977, although actual implementation has been slow, partly because of continuing problems with staffing and training. In some countries, changes in the health ministry have essentially produced integrated services. In Malaysia, for example, increasing numbers of the health ministry's facilities have added family planning services to their menu of general health services, as part of the government's long-term strategy for health development. The National Population and Family Development Board continues to operate as a dedicated family planning program, mostly in urban areas, but its share of new acceptors of contraception has been declining over time.

Types of Services

A strong clinical orientation has characterized the early delivery of family planning services in most of Asia. To a large extent, the nature of available contraceptive methods in the early years of program activity—primarily high-dose oral pills, intrauterine devices (IUDs), and sterilization—dictated on-site clinic services. At the same time, government regulation, which classified contraceptives as medicines, also confined their availability to clinics.

In Asia, outreach activity was a significant complement to clinic-based services in the early phases of program development. Such activity was organized to promote family planning and to sustain contraceptive use among the initial cohorts of acceptors. Outreach is usually implemented by fieldworkers dedicated to family planning. Often based at public health facilities, these workers are deployed to contact, motivate, and recruit couples eligible for family planning. They also attempt to locate acceptors who have discontinued contraceptive use to ascertain if there are problems using the method chosen. Where problems exist, the fieldworker is expected to encourage the user to revisit the source clinic or to refer her to another provider. Fieldworkers' close contact with clients provides clinic and administrative staff with important community and client feedback on the acceptability of services being delivered. Outreach activity has evolved over time, but close contact with clients, particularly those in rural areas, continues to be maintained, for example, through home-visiting workers.

In the 1970s and early 1980s, new initiatives extending beyond the conventional clinical network were launched in various Asian countries to improve service accessibility, particularly to rural households. Two programs of significance in this expansionist phase are community-based distribution (CBD) of contraceptives and contraceptive social marketing (CSM). In both arrangements, the delivery of contraceptive supplies is shifted from the exclusive domain of clinical personnel to that of trained nonclinical personnel. In a CBD system, individuals in a community are selected to serve as its agents to distribute oral, barrier, and spermicidal contraceptives. The family planning program assumes responsibility for getting supplies to CBD agents. In turn, these agents distribute supplies directly to households on a regular basis. For oral pills, they are trained to screen for contraindications in potential users. CBD systems currently operate in such Asian countries as Bangladesh, China, India, Indonesia, Nepal, Pakistan, Sri Lanka, Thailand, and Viet Nam.

CSM programs attempt to improve accessibility by taking advantage of existing networks of local pharmacies, dispensaries, or village shops to serve as distribution points for oral pills, condoms, and spermicide. Pharmacists and shop owners are registered with the CSM program and are also trained to counsel and dispense the products. They purchase their contraceptive commodities at subsidized prices and retail them at an average profit margin of 15 percent. The CSM program is responsible for stocking and restocking contraceptive supplies; it also carries out extensive advertising campaigns and provides participating stores with marketing materials at no cost. Most CSM programs in Asia began in the mid-1970s, including those in India, Indonesia, the Republic of Korea, Malaysia, Nepal, the Philippines, Sri Lanka, and Thailand.

More recently, there is renewed interest in expanding postpartum delivery of family planning services as yet another important delivery strategy (Thapa and others 1991). In part, this interest is motivated by the growing cohorts of young women of childbearing age who seek to space their births rather than limit them immediately. The postpartum period is a particularly suitable time for family planning counseling. Births delivered in hospitals or maternity centers bring mothers into direct contact with trained family planning personnel. National programs can also draw on traditional midwives—who can be properly trained—to offer family planning advice to mothers delivering at home. Strong postpartum programs currently operate in the Republic of Korea, Malaysia, Singapore, Sri Lanka, Thailand, Taiwan (China), and Viet Nam.

With the deliberate shift away from exclusive clinic-based services, family planning programs in Asia have increasingly diversified delivery strategies over the past fifteen years. The stress on particular strategies has varied over time and across countries, as suggested by the data in table 5.1. These data are drawn from results of the Population Council's 1982 and 1989 international surveys of family planning program effort.[2] Based on information supplied by respondents canvassed for each country, program activities were rated on a scale of 0 to 4, with 0 indicating a weak effort, and 4 a strong effort.[3] The 1982 and 1989 surveys used comparable questionnaires, so the scores from the two studies can be used to track changes over time.

In several countries—Cambodia, Lao People's Democratic Republic, Myanmar, and Papua New Guinea—family planning activities of all types are largely absent in both 1982 and 1989, as suggested by scores at or close to zero. For most

Table 5.1: Family Planning Delivery Systems in Selected Asian Countries, 1982 and 1989 (Lapham–Mauldin–Ross Scores on a 0 to 4 scale)

Country	Community-based distribution[a]		Contraceptive social marketing[b]		Postpartum program[c]		Home-visiting workers[d]	
	1982	1989	1982	1989	1982	1989	1982	1989
Bangladesh	3.0	3.0	4.0	4.0	0.2	1.6	3.4	2.9
Cambodia	0.0	0.0	0.0	0.0	0.0	0.0	0.0	0.0
China	4.0	4.0	0.0	0.0	4.0	2.7	4.0	3.5
India	0.0	0.0	3.4	2.5	0.7	2.2	3.3	2.2
Indonesia	4.0	3.2	0.0	2.2	2.7	2.1	2.5	2.3
Korea, Rep. of	0.8	3.6	3.2	0.0	2.0	2.0	3.5	2.1
Lao PDR	0.0	0.0	0.0	0.0	0.0	0.0	0.0	0.0
Malaysia	0.0	0.0	0.0	0.0	0.6	3.8	0.5	3.4
Myanmar	0.0	0.0	0.0	0.0	0.0	0.0	0.0	2.4
Nepal	1.0	2.7	2.0	3.5	0.1	0.1	1.2	1.4
Pakistan	1.2	2.4	0.0	2.0	0.4	0.2	1.0	0.1
Papua New Guinea	0.2	0.0	0.0	0.0	0.2	0.1	0.0	0.0
Philippines	3.2	2.8	0.0	0.0	0.6	1.0	3.3	2.0
Singapore	0.0	0.0	0.0	0.0	4.0	4.0	4.0	0.0
Sri Lanka	4.0	3.8	4.0	3.8	3.6	4.0	3.1	3.2
Taiwan (China)	0.0	0.0	0.0	4.0	3.5	4.0	4.0	3.5
Thailand	1.3	4.0	0.0	1.3	1.0	4.0	0.0	3.6
Viet Nam	2.0	4.0	0.0	2.0	1.2	3.5	2.0	1.4

Note: See text and related footnotes for explanation on how the scores are constructed in the Lapham–Mauldin–Ross surveys. A score of 0 suggests no activity or effort in indicated area; a score of 4 suggests strong effort.

a. Refers to a distribution system to provide contraceptives in areas not easily served by clinics or other service points.

b. Refers to a program of subsidized contraceptive sales through commercial outlets.

c. Refers to arrangements in which women who have recently delivered babies, either in hospitals or at home, are given family planning information by trained workers or fieldworkers.

d. Refers to workers whose primary task is to visit women in their homes to talk about family planning and child care.

Source: See text.

other Asian countries, the pattern is one of selected emphasis on the various delivery systems. In 1989, for example, CBD and CSM in Bangladesh are much more well developed than the postpartum program (PPP) or home visitation (HV); in Thailand, the stress is on CBD, PPP, and HV; and in Singapore, only PPP receives emphasis. Sri Lanka appears to be the only country with strong effort scores on all four delivery strategies. Over time, countries also appear to have shifted strategies. For example, India's CSM and HV scores declined between 1982 and 1989, but the PPP score rose; in the Republic of Korea, the CBD effort rose sharply while the CSM and HV scores dropped. In Viet Nam all the scores except for HV rose; the pattern is not surprising given that program development is at an early phase in that country.

The choice of delivery systems raises important questions about costs, effectiveness, and safety. Assessment of these issues is hampered, in part, by data constraints, and experience shows that evaluations tend to yield broad ranges of results, making it difficult to draw precise conclusions; for example, a couple-year of protection produced by CBD systems costs "anywhere between $5 to $152" (World Bank 1992). Part of the reason may be that CBD systems can be designed very differently—in the type and mix of material inputs, personnel, and even workers' task routines. Similarly, other systems can encompass a wide variety of inputs. Thus in assessing the various delivery strategies, it may be as important to focus on the specific inputs involved in each strategy and their effectiveness in different settings, as on the strategies themselves as a whole. Also, complementarities and possibly even some duplication among the various approaches should not be ignored. Analyses to sort out these interactions are at an early stage, and drawing firm conclusions about the cost-effectiveness of the various delivery systems would be premature.

The Quality of Services

In recent years, concern has been growing about the poor quality of family planning services, particularly the neglect of users' perspectives in their delivery (Jain 1989; Bruce 1990). Definitions of quality vary, but there is broad agreement that good-quality services should have at least the following three elements (World Bank 1992): (a) access to a range of methods; (b) adequate counseling and sensitivity to client concerns; and (c) technically competent providers operating by proper medical standards. Data from the Lapham-Mauldin-Ross family planning surveys can again be used to gauge countries' performance on these criteria of quality (table 5.2). For criterion (a), scores on availability and accessibility of contraceptive services can be used.[4] On criteria (b) and (c), scores on the training program and the supervision system serve as plausible measures. Clearly, though, having good training and supervision only enhances the probability of adequate counseling and competent service; they do not guarantee sensitivity to client concerns.[5] Because quality is, by nature, a subjective dimension, the data provide no more than indicative perspectives.

Table 5.2: *Aspects of the Quality of Family Planning Services in Selected Asian Countries, 1982 and 1989 (Lapham–Mauldin–Ross Scores on a 0 to 4 scale)*

Country	Availability & accessibility[a]		Training program[b]		Supervision system[c]	
	1982	1989	1982	1989	1982	1989
Bangladesh	2.7	3.1	1.6	3.1	0.5	1.0
Cambodia	0.0	0.0	0.0	2.3	0.0	2.0
China	3.8	4.0	3.0	3.7	3.0	2.0
India	2.3	3.5	2.2	2.6	1.0	1.3
Indonesia	2.3	2.7	4.0	4.0	2.0	3.5
Korea, Rep. of	4.0	4.0	3.2	3.5	2.0	4.0
Lao PDR	0.0	0.0	0.0	0.0	0.0	0.0
Malaysia	2.5	3.2	2.9	4.0	2.2	2.0
Myanmar	0.6	0.9	0.0	0.0	0.0	0.0
Nepal	1.2	1.8	1.3	3.5	0.4	1.5
Pakistan	1.5	1.1	1.4	2.9	0.5	0.7
Papua New Guinea	1.4	0.6	0.8	1.3	0.0	0.5
Philippines	2.5	2.3	2.8	3.3	1.0	1.5
Singapore	4.0	4.0	3.5	3.7	4.0	4.0
Sri Lanka	2.8	3.3	3.3	3.9	1.0	2.4
Taiwan (China)	4.0	4.0	4.0	4.0	4.0	4.0
Thailand	3.3	3.7	4.0	4.0	1.5	3.2
Viet Nam	1.7	3.1	3.5	3.3	1.0	2.0
Country average[d]	2.3	2.5	2.3	3.0	1.3	2.0

Note: A score of 0 suggests weak performance in the indicated area; a score of 4 suggests strong performance.
a. Scores indicate the availability and ease of access to contraceptives. They are the aggregate scores on each of six method groups, standardized on a 0–4 scale to facilitate reading of the table. The six method groups (each with a maximum score of 4) are male and female sterilization, pill (and injectables), condoms (and spermicides and diaphragms), IUDs, and abortion (and menstrual regulation).
b. Scores reflect how adequate the training program is for various categories of staff involved in the family planning program.
c. Scores reflect how adequate the system of supervision is at all staff levels.
d. Unweighted.
Source: See text.

On access, the average score for Asia as a whole improved slightly between 1982 and 1989. In Cambodia and Lao PDR, no effort appears to have been made during this seven-year period to broaden access, while in Pakistan and Papua New Guinea, the feeble effort that existed in 1982 actually became even weaker by 1989. Modest improvements occurred in several countries starting with relatively poor access in 1982, including Nepal and Myanmar. More significant gains are reported for Bangladesh, India, Malaysia, Sri Lanka, and Viet Nam.[6] In several countries— including China, Republic of Korea, Singapore, Taiwan (China), and Thailand, access was already good in 1982, and performance has been maintained or improved.

Regionwide, gains in scores for training rose from an average of 2.3 in 1982 to 3.0 in 1989. High performers include such countries as Bangladesh, Malaysia, and Nepal, where scores between the two periods have risen sharply. A few countries— China, Indonesia, Singapore, Sri Lanka, Taiwan (China), and Thailand—sustained the high scores that were already achieved in 1982. Modest gains were recorded in the other countries.

On supervision, Asia's average score improved from a relatively modest score of 1.3 in 1982 to 2.0 in 1989, still small relative to the averages for the other two indicators. Strong performers include Republic of Korea, Indonesia, Singapore, Taiwan (China), and Thailand, all with 1989 scores above 3.2. China is the only country in the sample registering a significant decline in the score between 1982 and 1989. For the remaining countries, the scores have either stayed relatively stable or improved slightly.

Other aspects of program quality besides access, personnel training, and staff supervision, are important too. There is growing recognition that good programs must also have the capacity to address reproductive health issues (World Bank 1993). The AIDS epidemic has made this need amply clear. Good-quality family planning programs can help to slow the epidemic as well as prevent the spread of other sexually-transmitted diseases (STDs). They can do so by providing appropriate counseling and advice about sexual behavior and contraceptive choice, as well as by offering a broad range of contraceptive methods. In addition, they can link up with screening programs for STDs and expand their capacity to give follow-up treatment in the event of positive diagnoses.

Little information exists on the extent to which family planning programs in Asian countries address reproductive health problems. Thus although the indicators of access, training, and supervision suggest overall improvements in program quality over time, they paint an incomplete picture. In most Asian countries, it is likely that scope remains for improving the services of family planning programs.

Density of Public Sector Delivery Infrastructure

Because of possible tradeoffs against quality, the density of delivery infrastructure is a concern in family planning programs.[7] Proximity to service outlets promotes the use of family planning by reducing the time and travel costs to users (Tsui and Ochoa 1989). But bringing services closer to users almost always requires more outlets, with concomitant increases in operating costs for the system as a whole.[8] The pressure on costs may constrain allocations for individual outlets, potentially lowering the range and quality of services that each can realistically provide. A possible tradeoff may thus arise between the density of outlets and the quality of services. The optimal choice between these attributes in a program depends on many factors, including overall resources, characteristics of the population, and the relative effect of proximity and quality on service utilization. In the absence of detailed data, a country's performance is obviously difficult to assess. Nonetheless, cross-country comparisons of the density of service outlets offers some useful insights.

Table 5.3 shows data on the number of women of reproductive age relative to the number of outlets for sterilization and other methods, and for commodity-based methods only. In some countries, particularly those where the health infrastructure is poorly developed, mobile camps are commonly organized to provide services en masse, and are often staffed by personnel based at the static facilities (such as health posts, health centers, and so on). For this reason, and because camps differ widely in their organization and scale, the data in the table are limited to counts of static facilities.[9] A distinction is made between facilities providing sterilization and other methods, and those offering only commodity-based methods, because the former are usually much more sophisticated in equipment and staffing profiles. The table also offers information on the density of resupply staff, usually the lowest level worker in the hierarchy of personnel.[10]

Bangladesh, Nepal, and Viet Nam stand out as having the lowest density of public facilities providing contraceptive services.[11] Because private sector infrastructure in these countries is not well developed, the sparseness of facilities may be an obstacle to service delivery, particularly in the poorer parts of the country, and expansion of the network of facilities may be warranted. In the meantime, these countries rely heavily on mobile camps and nonprofit organizations (NPOs) to serve large proportions of the population. Over the longer term, NPO facilities clearly remain a viable outlet option; in contrast, the heavy reliance on mobile camps may not be optimal, since the transitory nature of these camps makes client follow-up difficult and hampers the system's capacity to promote the spread of nonsterilization methods of contraception. Because of the logistics involved, camps may also be more costly than static facilities, particularly in heavily populated areas.

India, on the other hand, has a relatively dense network of public facilities. For sterilizations, its indicator is the lowest by a wide margin among the sample of nine countries considered here (excluding the Republic of Korea); for commodity-based methods, it ranked third lowest. The emphasis on sterilization in the government's family planning program comes through clearly in these data. Despite the relatively favorable comparison, India's government nonetheless plans to increase the density of facilities by lowering the ratio between primary health centers to population from 1:30,000 to 1:10,000. From a cross-country perspective, however, the current supply of facilities appears adequate, particularly compared to such countries as Indonesia and Sri Lanka. Thus, rather than continuing to enhance an already favorable infrastructure, it may be more

Table 5.3: Ratio of Married Women of Reproductive Age (MWRA) to Various Public Sector Outlets for Family Planning Services, Asian Countries, Late 1980s[a]

Country	MWRA per static facility providing			MWRA per resupply person[b]	Year
	Sterilization & other methods	Commodity-based methods only	Any method		
Bangladesh	40,185	5,950	5,182	862	1990
India	6,489	1,313	1,092	642	1989
Indonesia	15,475	1,666	1,504	122	1987
Korea, Rep. of	683[c]	1,214	437	–	1990
Malaysia	89,226	2,476	2,409	–	1990
Nepal	88,444	3,818	3,660	185	1989
Philippines	27,650	1,813	1,701	–	1990
Sri Lanka	20,748	3,102	2,698	–	1990
Thailand	13,950	1,066	990	249	1990
Viet Nam	9,900	8,910	4,689	8,910	1990

a. Married women of reproductive age are those between ages 15 and 44. Data exclude mobile facilities and camps.
b. Usually for pills and condoms.
c. Includes private clinics eligible for government reimbursement for services performed.
Source: See table A5.1 in appendix C.

appropriate at this juncture to focus on improving the performance of existing facilities, including ensuring adequate staff training and supplies of contraceptive commodities.

In the Republic of Korea and Thailand, public sector outlets appear to be ubiquitous. The Republic of Korea operates an arrangement whereby the government contracts with private sector institutions to perform sterilizations at an agreed rate of per case reimbursement. These private institutions are included in the data because from a financial perspective, the government remains responsible for the cost of providing service. In Thailand, the existing infrastructure compares very favorably with other countries—so favorably that some observers argue that the government has effectively crowded out private providers (Lewis and Kenny, 1988). In Viet Nam, facilities for commodity-based methods appear sparse compared with other Asian countries; in contrast, facilities for sterilization appear to be more well developed. Viet Nam thus possibly needs to increase the number of lower-level outlets for family planning services.

Targeting of Public Sector Services

To what extent are government services and subsidies for family planning targeted to rural populations and lower-income groups? The available data for selected countries offer some interesting perspectives (table 5.4). As expected, the government plays a markedly smaller role in urban rather than rural areas in Asian countries, as elsewhere. As a measure of the relative focus on rural areas, consider the urban-rural gaps in the public sector's share of clients. The larger gap for Asia, compared to those for Latin America and Africa, suggests relatively more emphasis on reaching rural populations in Asian countries.

The performance of individual Asian countries can be assessed by relating the rural-urban gap to the regional average (15.5 percentage points according to the table). Countries with a gap exceeding this size may be viewed as having an exceptional degree of emphasis on rural services. Malaysia and Thailand belong in this group, with gaps of 23 and 26 percentage points respectively, or 47 and 65 percent larger than the regional average. Bangladesh performs quite well in this regard, too, with an absolute gap of 19 percentage points. India and Sri Lanka are close to the regional average, while Indonesia, the Republic of Korea, Nepal, and the Philippines perform relatively poorly. In the Republic of Korea and Nepal, where sterilization is the predominant method, the result is probably linked to the more limited potential for private provision of this service in both urban and rural areas. This reasoning also applies, albeit to a lesser extent, in the Philippines. In Indonesia, where sterilizations are relatively rare, the modest gap in the government's share of clients in urban and rural areas contrasts sharply with Thailand's experience. Enhancing public services to rural areas in Indonesia may therefore warrant further attention.

A second dimension of targeting relates to the incidence of services that are heavily subsidized by the government. The available data are patchy, permitting only broad

Table 5.4: Government Share of Contraceptive Service or Supply Source in Urban and Rural Areas, Selected Asian Countries and World Regions (percentage)

Country/Region	Urban	Rural	Rural–urban gap	
			Absolute[a]	Deviation from regional avg.[b]
Bangladesh	56.6	75.6	19.0	22
India	74.3	91.7	17.4	12
Indonesia	71.7	84.3	12.6	−19
Korea, Rep. of	57.9	69.5	11.6	−25
Malaysia	42.9	65.8	22.9	47
Nepal	64.3	75.4	11.1	−29
Philippines	62.4	75.3	12.9	−17
Sri Lanka	75.8	89.9	14.1	−9
Thailand	62.7	88.3	25.6	65
Asia	65.7	81.3	15.6	–
Latin America	39.6	51.5	11.9	–
Sub-Saharan Africa	60.1	67.3	7.2	–

a. Reflects arithmetic difference between rural and urban percentages.

b. Reflects ratio of the absolute percentage difference between urban and rural shares to the average of this gap for all Asian countries in the sample; for example, the value for Bangladesh, 22%, is derived as [(19.0 - 15.6)/15.6] x 100.

Source: As in table 4.4.

categorization of users by education (table 5.5). Clients with no education are at the bottom of the socioeconomic hierarchy, so their share of free services reveals the extent to which those services benefit the lowest-income groups. The data are more complete on pill users, so the following discussion focuses on this method.

Direct comparisons across countries is problematic because countries differ widely in overall education profiles. For example, the share of beneficiaries of free services from the group with no education is largest in Nepal, but this result is more a reflection of Nepal's poor education profile than of the country's success in targeting free services to the most disadvantaged socioeconomic group of users. Cross-country comparisons therefore need to take account of differences in overall education profiles. Nepal aside, in all countries in the sample, the share of

Table 5.5: Users of Free Contraceptive Pills Supplied through Government Sources, Selected Asian Countries, Late 1980s

Country	Survey year	Percentage of public source clients receiving free pills	Percentage of free users with no education	1985 female adult illiteracy rate (percentage)
Indonesia[a]	1987	85	15	35
Malaysia	1988–89	53	11	34
Nepal	1987	69	78	88
Sri Lanka	1987	4	0	17
Thailand	1987	59	5	12

a. Similar data for Indonesia are available on users of condoms, IUDs, and acceptors of sterilization. The percentage of recipients of free services with no education was 12.7 percent for condoms, 18.6 percent for IUDs, and 13.0 percent for sterilization.

Source: As in table 4.8 for data in columns 3 and 4; and World Bank 1991c for data in column 5.

beneficiaries with no education falls far short of the share of the adult female population who are illiterate,[12] suggesting that free services benefit the most disadvantaged group proportionately less than other socioeconomic groups. This result is ironic because free services are often justified by the argument that charges would restrict poor people's access to services.

The data also offer an interesting insight on the tradeoffs between the coverage of free services and the extent to which they reach the poorest group in the population. Consider first Indonesia and Malaysia, countries with comparable levels of overall education. The share of beneficiaries of free services from the no-education group is slightly larger in Indonesia, but the spread of free services is also much greater in Indonesia, reaching 85 percent of the users of government services, compared to only 53 percent in Malaysia. Sri Lanka and Thailand are another pair of countries with comparable levels of overall education. In Thailand, the share of the no-education group is slightly larger, but the spread of free services is also much greater, reaching 59 percent of all users of government services, compared to only 4 percent in Sri Lanka.

Taken together, these results suggest that although generous coverage of free public services does increase the reach of such services to the lowest-income groups, their spread would have to be very extensive indeed for the poorest of the poor to benefit more. Merely supplying free services is thus, by and large, a very blunt instrument for reaching this group. Needed instead are special efforts at targeting, possibly complemented with interventions to lower desired family size.

Partnership with Nongovernment Providers

The effectiveness of the government's role in financing and delivering family planning services depends importantly on whether and how it mobilizes the private sector to complement its activities. The previous chapter highlights the financial aspects of the public-private partnership, showing that heavy subsidies, particularly where poorly targeted, can crowd out private providers. As indicated there, the private sector consists of several types of providers, with commercial providers depending least on government subsidies. The pricing of public sector services obviously affects the financial viability of private sector activities, but government-imposed rules and regulations—such as those stipulating who may prescribe contraceptives, who may import and supply them to the public, and so on—also matter. Often intended to protect public safety, these regulations can nonetheless be overly restrictive and thus stifle private sector activity. The design of the regulatory environment therefore becomes an important policy concern. Information is scarce, however, on the rules and regulations that countries have adopted, and systematic evaluation is largely absent on their effects on providers and operational outcomes. As a result, specific conclusions are not possible on the optimal design of regulatory regimes to strengthen the public-private partnership in service delivery.

Apart from commercial providers, nonprofit organizations (NPOs) are another nongovernment sector with an active role in family planning in many countries.[13] NPOs are privately run, but many are publicly subsidized. From a financing perspective, therefore, NPOs provide modest fiscal relief, but they may be more effective than government-run operations in reaching specific client groups or in performing specific functions, and therefore play an important role as partners with the government in service delivery. In countries where national bodies have been formed to oversee population matters (such as Nepal and Indonesia), the fact that NPOs are almost always represented reflects clear recognition of their contribution. Government officials generally consider the flexibility of NPO governance and program development important assets in supplementing, improving, and strengthening the nation's family planning program. The NPO-government relationship is thus often strongly symbiotic and mutually supportive.

Family planning associations (FPAs) are the most common NPOs involved in the delivery of contraceptive services. The largest coordinating body for FPAs in the Asia Region, and worldwide, is the International Planned Parenthood Federation (IPPF). FPAs exist in seventeen Asian countries, with the earliest two established in India (1947) and Singapore (1949) (table 5.6). The 1950s saw FPAs started in Bangladesh, Hong Kong, Indonesia, Malaysia, Nepal, Pakistan, Sri Lanka, and Taiwan (China). Many of the FPAs in these countries were founding members of the IPPF when it was formed in 1952. It is noteworthy that in fifteen Asian countries FPAs were established prior to the start of the official family planning program. FPA leadership has provided an important stimulus to the eventual public sponsorship of family planning services (Donaldson and Tsui

Table 5.6: *Selected Characteristics of Asian Family Planning Associations*

Country	Year FPA established	Target areas/populations	Clinic services	Model projects[a]	IEC	Training
Bangladesh	1953	Urban, youth, women		x	x	x
China	1980	-			x	
Hong Kong	1952	Youth, men, handicapped persons	x		x	x
India	1947	-	x[b]	x[c]	x	
Indonesia	1957	Youth, women		x[c,d]	x	
Korea, Rep. of	1961	-	x		x	
Lao PDR[e]	1969	-		x		
Malaysia	1958	Urban, youth, women		x[b,c]	x	x
Nepal	1958	Youth	x		x	
Pakistan	1953	Youth, women, trade unions		x	x	x
Papua New Guinea	1974	Rural	x		x	
Philippines[f]	1969	Youth, women	x[c]		x	
Singapore	1949	Youth, disadvantaged groups		x[c]	x	
Sri Lanka	1953	Estates, industrial areas	x	x[c]	x	x
Taiwan (China)[g]	1954	-				
	1963	-				
Thailand	1970	Industrial area, women, youth		x[c]	x	x
Viet Nam	1979	-	x	x	x	x

a. Model projects are demonstration projects, often intended to test innovative programs of service delivery and outreach.
b. Sterilization.
c. Mothers' clubs.
d. Dissolved in 1975.
e. Participates in donor-funded integrated projects on family planning, parasitic control, and nutrition.
f. Early FPAs were formed in 1961 and 1965, and subsequently merged in 1969.
g. Two family planning associations were formed, one in 1954 and one in 1963. The more recent associations, the Planned Parenthood Association of the Republic of China, receives government subsidies and assists the Ministry of Health in distributing contraceptive supplies.
Source: Compiled from IPPF 1989.

1990). In funding arrangements, governments often contribute grants directly to the IPPF, which, in turn provides funding to the local affiliate. In addition to IPPF funding, FPAs also mobilize funds from the government as well as from users or other private contributors. Grants are generally the most important source of their income.

In the early decades of the family planning movement in Asia, FPAs were one of the few sources of family planning services. As national programs assumed this responsibility on a large scale, FPA activity has evolved to emphasize specific geographic areas, subpopulations, or tasks that are difficult or cumbersome for government programs to develop. Thus, FPAs are often involved in IEC (information-education-communications) activities, model project operations, training, and specialized clinic services. For example, generating demand for family planning services through IEC programs is a major activity of FPAs, one that public programs eschewed in their early years of operation. Because of their nongovernmental status, NPOs face fewer bureaucratic obstacles and have often been faster and more innovative than their government counterparts in their operations. For example, FPA projects have tested new and innovative delivery strategies—such as integrated services with other sectoral programs or clinical methods being delivered by specially trained nonmedical personnel. FPAs' flexibility also enables them to test new contraceptive technologies. The Sri Lanka Family Planning Association, for example, helped acquire clinic trial data for Norplant prior to 1991, when the method was approved for distribution through public clinics. Certainly, the introduction of sterilization services in public clinics, especially improved outpatient procedures, largely came through initial experimentation in FPA clinics.

Despite consensus about NPOs' role in service delivery, there have been few evaluations of the effect of their activities on contraceptive usage and fertility. Schultz (1989), based on Thai data from a household survey in 1980–81, appears to be the only study seriously addressing this issue. His findings suggest that at current levels of public spending on family planning services, additional spending would reduce fertility more if channeled through NPOs rather than through the clinic-based activities of the Ministry of Health. Expenditure on the public program was already relatively high (9 bahts per woman-year in 1975), and there are diminishing returns to additional spending. In contrast, NPO programs, with spending averaging only 0.6 bahts per woman, have not yet expanded sufficiently to encounter diminishing marginal returns. As a result, an additional baht would reduce fertility by 8.9 percent if spent through NPOs, compared to only a 2.4 percent reduction if spent through the public sector. Schultz notes that outlays for NPO activity are particularly effective outside municipal areas, where the commercial market for contraceptives is less well established.

Although Schultz's study is an isolated evaluation, it nonetheless suggests that government support for NPO activity can be efficient, particularly where the public program is already large. A similar result may well exist in other circumstances, but empirical evidence is lacking on which to draw conclusions. Also undocumented are the specific types of NPO activities that are particularly effective and the reasons for their effectiveness. Narrowing these knowledge gaps would help to identify ways in which government policies toward NPOs can enhance the public-private partnership in service delivery.

Notes

1. The sections on institutional modes, types of services, and quality of services draw on background materials kindly provided by Amy O. Tsui and Bates Buckner of the University of North Carolina.

2. The 1982 data were collected and compiled by Robert J. Lapham and W. Parker Mauldin, while the 1989 data were collected and compiled by W. Parker Mauldin and John Ross. For each of the 100-some developing countries included in the surveys, four types of respondents were canvassed: government officials directly involved in implementing family planning programs; donor personnel; citizens in the various countries who were knowledgeable about but not involved in policy or management of the programs; and knowledgeable foreigners.

3. The survey questionnaires solicited responses from knowledgeable respondents to thirty items grouped into four broad areas of program activities: policy and stage-setting activities; service and service-related activities; record keeping and evaluation; and availability and accessibility of fertility-control supplies and services.

4. For each country, the score for each of ten methods is determined according to the extent to which the population has "easy and ready access," which in the Lapham–Mauldin-Ross study (1990) means the recipient of services spends no more than about two hours per month to obtain supplies and services as well as spends no more than 1 percent of monthly wages to obtain a month's contraceptive supply.

5. The Lapham-Mauldin-Ross surveys (1990) also contain scores on the extent to which staff at all levels carry out assigned tasks. They are not included here because of partial overlap with the supervision scores.

6. The gains in India may be more apparent than real, however, particularly when compared against the score for Indonesia. The case study on India, reported later in chapter 7, suggests that in India, access is good mainly for sterilization.

7. In most Asian countries the infrastructure for family planning services is, by and large, the same as for the delivery of other health services. In some countries, such as the Philippines and Malaysia, the total number of health facilities exceeds the number offering family planning services because some facilities lack personnel with the appropriate training. The discrepancies are not large, however, so the data in table 5.3 provide a reasonably good picture of the infrastructure through which public family planning services are delivered.

8. Overall operating costs rise with number of outlets because of fixed costs at each service point and the limited scope for tapping economies of scale in a system with many outlets, each serving a small catchment population.

9. In some countries, data on actual counts of physical facilities are not as readily obtainable as one might expect since many of the facilities listed on paper may in fact be nonoperational for a variety of reasons, including lack of staff and drugs. To enhance comparability, care was taken on the data to include only operational facilities; thus in India, for example, the data exclude facilities without doctors or auxiliary nurse midwives; and in Nepal, the data reflect only facilities that actually provided services.

10. In India, for example, these would be the Village Health Guides who have been trained to provide rudimentary health and family planning services, and who are reportedly in position. They usually carry contraceptive supplies (pills and condoms) as part of their work kit. Such staff usually receive an honorarium for their work.

11. The low density of outlets may not necessarily hamper access where population densities are very high, as in Bangladesh (769 persons per square kilometer in 1990, compared to 253 in India, 130 in Nepal, and 196 in Viet Nam). Nepal's and Viet Nam's overall population densities are comparable to other Asian countries in the sample, so the sparseness of service outlets may be more of a constraint there.

12. The female adult illiteracy rate is taken as a rough proxy of the proportion of adult females with no education.

13. As explained in chapter 4, employer-financed and delivered services also belong in the private sector, but because of the limited size and scope of such services, they are not addressed in detail in this study. Regarding nonprofit organizations, a variety of names are used in referring to them, including NGOs (nongovernmental organizations), and PVOs (private voluntary organizations).

6

Selected Case Studies on Family Planning Programs

CLOSER EXAMINATION OF THE FAMILY PLANNING PROGRAMS in China, India, and Indonesia offers additional insights. Because ample documentation of these programs already exists in the literature, the discussion here focuses on data and findings not as yet fully documented elsewhere. For context, each country case study provides a brief description of program characteristics. Beyond that, the case studies are quite different from one another in methodology. Each one is designed to bring out points relevant not only to the particular country, but to other places in Asia as well.

China

In curbing population growth, the People's Republic of China (PRC) is widely viewed as a success story because it has achieved unusually low fertility for a poor country.[1] In the mid-1950s, Chinese women had on average over 6 births each (figure 6.1). By 1974, urban fertility had dropped below replacement level and has fluctuated between 1.1 and 1.8 to the end of our data series in 1987. In rural areas, fertility remained very high during the 1960s, but began a sharp decline, from 6.4 births per woman in 1970 to 3.0 by 1978. During the 1980s, rural fertility ranged between 2.5 and 3.3 births per woman.[2]

These trends reflect underlying changes in the proximate determinants of fertility, particularly increases in the mean age at first marriage, contraceptive prevalence, and abortion rates.[3] In China, marriage is nearly universal and childbearing outside marriage is rare, so the mean age at first marriage is an important predictor of fertility. It rose from 18.7 years in 1950 to 20.2 in 1970, reached a high of 23.1 years in 1979, and dropped to age 22.5 in 1992. During the 1970s, modern contraceptive practice became very widespread, when previously it was almost totally absent in the population. As of 1982, 70.6 percent of all married women aged 15 to 49 were using birth control techniques to prevent conception, with a high proportion of them relying on modern effective methods. By 1992, the contraceptive prevalence rate had risen to 83.4 percent, and the dominant forms of contraception were sterilization and the IUD. Increases in abortion also played a significant role in China's fertility decline. During the 1970s through 1978, there were about 5 million induced abortions a year in China. The number jumped to 8 million in 1979, grew still larger in the early 1980s, reaching a peak of 14 million

Figure 6.1: Total Fertility Rates in China, 1950-90

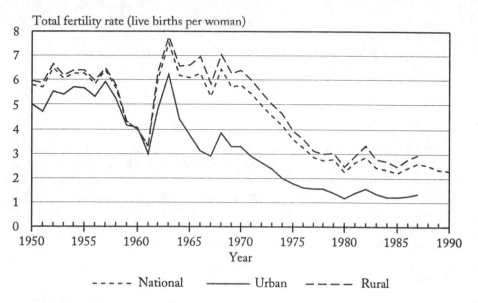

Source: Banister & Harbaugh, table 1.

in 1983. Since then the number of abortions continued to be large, between 9 million and 13 million a year.

China's family planning program, interacting with socioeconomic variables, has been credited with a key role in the country's demographic transition.[4] Its most publicized feature, and perhaps one of its most important, is that all couples are *required by law* to practice birth control. This provision—unique in the world so far as is known—admittedly weakens the relevance of China's program for other countries; governments elsewhere might find a compulsory policy objectionable on ethical or religious grounds, impracticable for lack of the social organization and controls required for implementation, or both. Nonetheless, other elements in the program, particularly relating to the practical task of service delivery and the mobilization of resources to finance it, offer potential insights to inform policy-making in other poor countries struggling to slow population growth. What then are the program's principal characteristics and inputs, and how have they affected Chinese fertility?

Overall Family Planning Goals and Policies

Observers of successful programs worldwide point to a government's commit-ment as a key ingredient. China's government is unusually firm in this respect, in large part because of concern that food supplies may not keep pace with population growth. For three decades under Communism, agricultural production—especially grain and key subsidiary foods—barely kept up with population growth. In addition a massive famine, caused mostly by poor agricultural policies, led to 30 million excess deaths. By 1977, per capita grain production was again at the level attained in 1957, but the per capita production of soybeans (for protein), edible vegetable oils (for fats), and other quality foods had seriously deteriorated. Population growth was partly responsible for this dilemma, but agricultural policies, which gave little incentive to produce above subsistence, share the blame.

Following the agricultural reforms initiated in 1978 (which remain in place today), food production has far outpaced population growth. Nonetheless, the government's population control policies are still based on the population-food impasse. Besides, problems in agricultural production, distribution, as well as storage remain, and prime agricultural land is still being lost to development, so the government continues to be concerned about maintaining per capita food supply as the population keeps on growing.[5]

China's antinatalist policies, implemented in earnest since about 1970, essentially aim to lower the birth rate and population growth each year as much as possible. The country's Constitution and Marriage Law (as revised in the early 1980s) mandates compulsory family planning, and provincial regulations, which have the force of law, specify in detail requirements for residents of each province. Under central government prodding, one province after another launched a campaign of "later, longer, fewer" in the early 1970s, requiring couples to marry at older ages, wait longer between births, and stop childbearing at a smaller completed family size than in the past. Government intervention has been so broad as to include regulations about the kind of birth control method women must use at each stage of life.

In 1979 the authorities adopted a one-child policy which they have attempted to implement ever since. This policy has been highly successful in the cities and urban towns, both because urban people are more amenable to having only one child than are rural people, and because government control over individuals is tighter in the urban areas. Rural people have resisted the one-child policy, and the government experimented with a two-child policy or a "one-and-a-half-child policy" for the rural areas in some provinces.[6] The latter policy imposes a one-child limit on couples with a first-born son, but allows a second birth to those with a first-born daughter. To give teeth to these regulations, mandatory sterilization was made an explicit nationwide policy in 1982 for most Han Chinese couples with two or more living children.[7] In 1983, abortion of all unauthorized births was adopted as another explicit nationwide policy. The one-child policy has gone through phases of loosening and tightening. As of this writing, the latest tightening began in 1991 and caused the total fertility rate to fall from 2.3 births per woman in 1990 to 2.0 in 1993. The spread of medical techniques that can determine the sex of a fetus has led to widespread sex-selective abortions. It is the current policy of the Chinese government that such testing be prohibited (China Population Information and Research Centre, 1993, p. 3).

Controls on reproductive behavior are feasible in practice because married women in China are monitored regularly by village, neighborhood, and workplace family planning personnel to ensure compliance with the regulations. Before conceiving a baby, couples are expected to secure official permission. According to China's fertility survey of 1988, the proportion of all births in the country that were "planned"—that is, authorized ahead of time—rose from 51 percent in 1980 to 58 percent in the first half of 1988. This increase was probably caused by a combination of factors: greater compulsion in the program, changed attitudes favoring small families, the rapid fertility decline among the minority population, and the relaxation of the one-child limit in most rural areas. In 1988, the proportion of births that were preapproved was 94 percent in cities, 57 percent in towns, and 52 percent in the countryside.

Expenditure on Family Planning Services

Achieving the fertility goals of the family planning program has required significant outlays of financial and other resources. China's data are, for various reasons, not directly comparable to other countries' data, but a careful accounting of the various costs involved nonetheless reveals some interesting insights.

Public spending on China's family planning program is reported in budget documents as "family planning operational expenses." As table 6.1 shows, this expenditure has averaged roughly 0.08 percent of GNP nationwide between 1978 and 1990. In per capita terms, spending has increased steadily, reaching twice its 1978 level by 1990.[8] Taking the reported data at face value, China's spending thus appears modest by Asian standards. For example, family planning expenditures in 1989 were 0.17 percent of GNP in India and 0.13 percent of GNP in Indonesia.

The reported "operational expenses" are only part of total outlays, however. A 1983 government regulation which provides perhaps the most detailed published statement on the subject stipulates that these expenses cover the costs of contraceptive supplies, birth control surgeries, office expenses, small instrument purchases for birth control service stations, and wages for full-time family planning cadres in villages and urban neighborhoods. Not included are (a) the costs of birth control surgeries for the staff of state-owned enterprises, and for military personnel and their dependents;[9] (b) wages and other expenses of family planning organizations at the county level and above;[10] (c) capital construction for family planning programs; (d) maternal and child health services; and (e) various financial incentives to single-child parents.

The reported operational costs of China's program thus underestimate the program's actual costs. As it turns out, financial incentives are a major component of costs, but for comparative purposes, consider first the costs of supplying family planning services (table 6.2). Summing up Banister's and Harbaugh's carefully

Table 6.1: Reported Operational Expenses of China's Family Planning Program, 1978–90

Year	Total (millions of current yuan)	Total expenses as percent of GNP	Per capita expenses in 1990 yuan
1978	198	0.06	0.6
1980	330	0.07	0.8
1981	389[a]	0.08	0.9
1982	446	0.09	0.9
1983	527[a]	0.09	1.0
1984	624[a]	0.09	1.0
1985	745	0.09	1.0
1986	803	0.08	1.0
1987	852	0.08	1.0
1988	1004	0.07	1.0
1989	1214[a]	0.08	1.2
1990	1380	0.08	1.2

a. Banister and Harbaugh 1991 notes that data are derived from reported increases from the previous year.

Source: Data for column 2 are from Banister and Harbaugh 1991, table 8; data for column 3 are calculated using GNP data from World Bank Economic and Social Database (BESD).

estimated costs of each major input to supply services gives total operational costs of 799 million yuan in 1985, 926 million yuan in 1985, and 1,295 million yuan in 1989. These sums—about 7 to 9 percent above reported expenses—represent 0.08 to 0.09 percent of GNP. Including the costs of maternal and child health services raises expenditures to around 0.10 percent of GNP. The bulk of operational expenditures are allocated mainly to support fieldwork and clinical services. Because of the program's emphasis on passive birth control methods, spending on contraceptive commodities claims only about 7 percent of total estimated spending. Spending on IEC activities takes less than 5 percent.

At 0.10 percent of GNP, China's spending on family planning services is still smaller than spending in other low-income Asian countries. Some may object that the comparison is invalid because volunteer input is significant in China's program. Adjusting the numbers for this item is difficult, however, because volunteer input is

Table 6.2: Estimated Operational Expenses and Their Allocation in China's Family Planning Program, 1985, 1987, and 1989

	1985	1987	1989
Estimated total operational expenses:[a]			
In millions of current yuan	799	926	1,295
As percentage of reported expenditure	107	109	107
As percentage of GNP	0.09	0.08	0.08
Percentage of total on:			
Administration	1.9	1.7	1.8
Family planning services			
(a) Nonclinical[b]	46.6	43.3	44.2
(b) Clinical[c]	34.4	39.7	36.0
Contraceptive commodities	7.0	7.3	5.5
IEC activities	5.4	4.6	3.3
Staff training	0.7	1.6	1.2
Research and evaluation	0.5	0.4	0.4
Equipment and building	3.5	1.3	7.6
All components	100.0	100.0	100.0

a. Expenditures on maternal and child health (MCH) services are not included. In 1987, such expenditures amounted to 133.04 million yuan, or about 14% of total operational expenses on family planning. Including MCH expenses in the family planning program would thus boost total operational expenses to 0.09% of GNP in that year.

b. Includes (a) the wages of full- and part-time family planning personnel; and (b) payments to workers who distribute contraceptives door to door.

c. Includes (a) estimated expenses of providing follow-up services to women who have undergone sterilization or had an IUD inserted; and (b) reimbursed fees for surgical birth control (that is, fees paid on behalf of clients to hospitals and other providers).

Source: Adapted from Banister and Harbaugh 1991, table 12; GNP data are from World Bank BESD database.

also present in the other countries' programs; and because the effectiveness of such input depends not only on the number of people reportedly involved, but also on the time, effort, and motivation they bring to the task. A second consideration is that prices for contraceptive commodities and wages for family planning personnel are kept artificially low in China—possibly because contraceptives are produced domestically and the wages of family planning fieldworkers and clinical service providers are tightly controlled. To the extent that these markets are much more competitive elsewhere, China's spending may be underestimated. Furthermore, China's highly-structured political and social order—which facilitates access to individual women in their homes—also helps to cap the costs of service delivery.

On the other hand, China's program is largely government-sponsored, with a negligible role for private sector provision. Thus the costs estimated represent the costs of supplying services to the entire nation. In other countries, there is more private provision and funding, and government spending covers a smaller portion of the population than in China. Making this adjustment, and taking account of the possibly greater inefficiencies of government provision, would counteract some of the price and cost biases discussed above. On balance, it thus seems reasonable to use the initial estimate of 0.10 percent of GNP as a benchmark for comparing countries' spending to supply family planning services.

Excluding incentive payments, Bangladesh's spending on family planning services was 0.36 percent of GNP in 1989; for India the corresponding figure is 0.14 percent; and for Nepal, it is 0.13 percent.[11] In Indonesia, where the family planning program does not involve incentive payments, the program cost the government 0.13 percent of GNP in 1989. Current spending on public family planning services in these four countries—but especially in Bangladesh—thus appear adequate in comparison to China's level of expenditure, even allowing for the possibility of higher costs in voluntary programs. Further increases in spending may therefore need especially careful judgment. On the other hand, in such countries as the Philippines and Viet Nam, where fertility is still considered high and current spending is modest, at 0.03 to 0.05 percent of GNP, the China benchmark provides a case for increased spending to deliver an adequate supply of services.

Financial Incentives and Penalties in China's Program

China uses a unique system of incentives and penalties to achieve the government's family planning goals. These interventions are different from simply supplying family planning services because they affect the stream of costs and benefits of children to parents, and are thus oriented to alter the demand for children.

Chinese couples who pledge to have only one child are rewarded with a one-time bonus as well as continuing subsidies for health and education that are paid well into the child's teenage years (table 6.3). The bonus varies from province to province and reportedly ranges between 30 to 50 yuan, just under 3 percent of per capita GNP in 1989. The regulations also stipulate that each single child should receive a health care allowance from birth to age 14 at the rate of 5 to 7 yuan a month (although payments as low as 2.5 yuan are reported in some areas). Single children also receive free education up to middle school. Together, the annual health and education subsidies per single child amount to over 5 percent of per capita GNP. Other benefits sometimes include preferential housing and better retirement terms for the parents (urban areas) and better land allocation (rural areas). In comparison to incentives in other countries' programs, these incentives are extremely generous.[12]

In aggregate, the cost of the single-child incentives amounted to 2 to 3 billion yuan annually in the second half of the 1980s (table 6.4), averaging about 0.24 percent of GNP. Spending on incentives was thus between 2.5 to 3 times as much as spending on the delivery of services. In resource allocation, the Chinese program is clearly

Table 6.3: Financial Incentives for Single-Child Families in China, 1989

		Payment per eligible couple[a]	
	Duration of payment	Yuan	As percentage of per capita GNP[b]
One-child contract bonus	One-time only	40	2.8
Annual health subsidy	Till child reaches age 14	60	4.2
Average annual education subsidy[c]	Nursery through middle school	15	1.0

Note: In some parts of China, single-child incentives are reinforced by other incentives, including sick leave for birth control surgery, bonus leaves for later marriage and delayed pregnancy, nutrition allowances after sterilization and abortion due to IUD failure. In Shanghai county, adjacent to the city of Shanghai, the value of these incentives in 1979–83 was about 16% that of the incentives listed in this table.

a. The rates of payment vary across localities in China. The numbers in this table reflect averages used in Banister and Harbaugh (1991) to compute aggregate expenses on incentives.

b. Per capita GNP in 1989 was 1,418 yuan in current prices according to World Bank BESD database.

c. Reflects average across grades from nursery through middle school.

Source: Banister and Harbaugh 1991, tables 12 and 18.

much more oriented toward lowering the demand for children—through parity-related incentives and disincentives, but not through spending on IEC—than on simply supplying family planning services to meet existing demand. Ensuring easily available and adequate services is undoubtedly needed, but the Chinese authorities apparently consider it necessary to go beyond a laissez-faire and largely reactive supply strategy to keep fertility down.

Besides parity-based subsidies, the family planning program in China also offers other incentives to recipients of birth control, including sick leave for birth control surgery, extended marriage and maternity leaves for late marriage and delayed pregnancy,[13] and nutritional allowances under certain circumstances.[14] In aggregate terms, however, the costs of these incentives are dwarfed by spending on the single-child incentives.[15]

China's family planning program also applies negative incentives to deter pregnancies and births. Aside from losing the one-child subsidies, couples who have unauthorized births can, depending on locality, expect penalties such as the following:

Table 6.4: Aggregate Expenditure on Financial Incentives for Single-Child Families in China, 1985, 1987, and 1989

	1985	1987	1989
Estimated total expenditure:			
In millions of current yuan	2,333	2,782	3,251
Ratio to total operational expenses	2.9	3.0	2.5
As percentage of GNP[a]	0.27	0.25	0.21
Percentage of total on:			
One-time contract bonus	2.2	2.6	1.3
Health subsidies	75.7	69.7	65.4
Education subsidies	22.1	27.7	33.3
All components	100.0	100.0	100.0

a. Combined operational and incentive expenses in China's family planning program thus sum to 0.37% of GNP in 1985, 0.33% of GNP in 1987, and 0.29% of GNP in 1989.

Source: Banister and Harbaugh(1991), table 12; data on GNP from World Bank BESD database.

- For one unauthorized child both parents are fined 10 percent of their wages for seven consecutive years; for two unauthorized children, the fine rises to 20 percent of the parents' wages for fourteen consecutive years.

- Violators of family planning policies employed in state organizations become ineligible for (a) day care or hardship subsidies; (b) pay increases or bonuses for three years; and (c) promotion.

- Women who have unauthorized children receive no maternity benefits; furthermore, the cumulative value of single-child incentives that were previously received must be returned. Sterilization is mandatory for couples with three children.

- Couples who are permitted to have a second child are denied all benefits of the single-child program beginning the month they obtain approval to have the second child.

Many more people in urban areas abide by the one-child policy than in rural areas. One reason is that resources for the promised benefits are better guaranteed in urban areas. Most urban residents are employed by state or collective enterprises, and they would incur known and significant costs to defy the one-child policy. In rural areas, the terms of the incentives are not clearly defined, and the resources to provide them are not guaranteed. Furthermore, the value of children, especially boys, significantly outweighs the value of the single-child incentives. Because wage employment is rare in rural areas, wage-related penalties are ineffective, prompting the authorities to impose outright monetary fines. Most of the rural population are vulnerable to the threat of official confiscation and are too poor to pay steep fines. Unauthorized births still occur, however, because the more prosperous peasants often are willing and able to pay significant sums to have unauthorized births; the poorest peasants have too few possessions of value for confiscation to be an effective deterrent.

Sources of Funding

In a 1989 meeting attended by family planning committees nationwide, Premier Li Peng noted that "It [is] better for each province and each unit to cope with its own expenditures [on family planning]. . . . expenditure occurring in the locality should be taken care of by the locality and expenditures occurring in the military should be taken care of by the military. As to how to cope with the problems, please discuss among yourselves and come up with your own solutions." Funding in China's family planning program is thus highly decentralized, with the central government's responsibility limited mostly to expenses for activities directly under its administration.[16]

With regard to operational expenses for family planning, provincial authorities typically decide on a target of per capita expenses for departments at lower administrative levels, using it as a basis for collecting the necessary funds. The mandated funds are levied through taxation on individuals or local enterprises and collected by local finance departments. In some localities, particularly rural areas, fines on people who have unauthorized births generate sufficient funds to cover all operational expenses for family planning in the area.[17] Because of decentralization, localities differ greatly in the amount of money raised, the method of resource mobilization, and the way the money is spent.

Incentives, by far the largest expense of China's program, are funded through a separate mechanism. According to the 1983 regulation on family planning financing, responsibility for expenses of the one-child health subsidies and contract awards is shared by the work units of eligible couples.[18] The cost of education subsidies is jointly shouldered by work units, the Ministry of Education, the Ministry of Social Welfare, and township and town committees.

In urban areas, where the main work units are state-owned and collective enterprises, the incentives are funded from enterprise welfare funds and retained profits, supplemented, when needed, from enterprise management fees. According to published accounts, enterprises' aggregate spending on single-child incentives accounts for about 3 percent of all personnel costs. Government and other similar organizations, including schools, draw their resources for incentives from the welfare funds of their staff. When funds are insufficient, money budgeted for the unit's administrative or operational expenses is sometimes used. Work units are also responsible for the cost of non-parity-based incentives, including birth-control-related sick leave and nutritional allowances as well as bonus leaves for late marriage and delayed pregnancy. In rural areas, incentives are funded from local public welfare funds. When such funds are inadequate, eligible couples may instead be allocated more contract farm land or enjoy a lower tax on the crops they grow. In selected hardship areas, the cost of incentives is equally borne by the central and local governments.[19]

Delivery of Services

China's family planning program is a team project, not only in financing but also in the delivery of services. The State Family Planning Commission leads the effort from the center,[20] concentrating on overall policy formulation and coordination, tracking progress toward the government's population goals, and setting general directions for family planning work in the provinces. Supporting its work are other central government agencies whose responsibilities are spelled out in a 1981 set of regulations, including the State Commissions for Planning, Science, Agriculture, and Nationality; the Ministries of Public Health, Chemical Industry, Culture, Education, Civil Administration, and Finance; and the Department of Public Security, and the State Bureau of Labor.[21] In addition, myriad actors at lower levels of government or administration also contribute to various aspects of service delivery, right down to peasant small groups, neighborhood small groups, and workshop or section teams.

Although all birth control methods are legal in China,[22] in practice the mix of allowable contraceptive methods is among the most restricted in Asia. In 1992, 93.6 percent of all Chinese couples who were contracepting were using either sterilization or the IUD.[23] The actual availability of services differs by locality, and the program relies on various mechanisms and channels of outreach. A network of family planning stations promotes family planning, performs contraceptive operations, and trains family planning workers. In 1990, there were 2,203 county-level family planning service stations and 25,345 stations at the township level, accounting, respectively, for 92 percent and 47 percent of the target number of stations to be established. Stations are available in about 90 percent of China's counties, 30 percent of towns, and a few villages. Because only 35 percent of the stations are fully equipped, however, clinical contraceptive services are still provided mainly in hospitals. Thus, active debate continues about the need for expansion, both to enhance the capability of existing stations, as well as to add to their number.

To make up for the inadequacy of physical facilities, the work of family planning cadres emphasizes grassroots outreach to clients, including door-to-door distribution of contraceptives.[24] In 1987, 147,000 full-time family planning cadres were employed, representing 0.1 percent of all state employees in the country. About 60 percent are "managerial cadres" at the grassroots level. Such workers are required to spend time interacting directly with individuals: one-fourth of the year for state family planning cadres, one-third of the year for provincial or prefectural cadres, and one-half of the year for county cadres. These workers are expected to go door to door talking and listening to people, both to obtain feedback as well as to promote the government's message on family planning. In addition to the full-time workers, about 1 million part-timers were reportedly employed in 1989.

Supervising the work of fieldworkers presents challenging problems in China as elsewhere. A well-structured hierarchy exists for this purpose, but interestingly, the authorities also rely on performance-related pay as an added mechanism. In most localities, government workers are paid on a floating wage scale, with a bonus component determined by work performance. Performance is assessed by comparing actual births against authorized births in a worker's assigned locality.[25] Acceptor targets, commonly used in other countries, are not relevant in the reward system. Moreover, achievement is checked against data from independent field surveys and censuses, rather than against reports from fieldworkers (which often paint an overly optimistic picture of field results). In most localities, the incentive arrangement helps to promote conscientious work, but their effectiveness tends to be weaker in the richer rural areas. Bonuses have a modest effect on performance in such places because cadres have other sources of income. In very poor areas, however, where wages and bonuses from family planning work often are workers' only source of income, cadres sometimes become desperate to reach their birth targets in order to qualify for the bonuses and resort to highly coercive measures to prevent unauthorized births.

China's family planning program also relies on services provided through the China Family Planning Association (CFPA), the only nongovernmental organization active in the program. CFPA is, in fact, led by government-paid, full-time family planning cadres who steer the organization to follow government policy. By July 1991, more than 600,000 CFPA branches in the country reportedly covered 90 percent of counties, 80 percent of towns, and 70 percent of villages in China; membership is estimated to be about 35 million. The association's work helps to supplement the government's outreach efforts, particularly in rural areas with inadequate numbers of personnel and family planning service stations.

Very recently, the government has moved still closer to tapping private contributions to support its effort in family planning. In 1986, a pilot project for retailing contraceptives was started in Beijing with the objectives of improving convenience to the public and eliminating waste in the program. It proved highly effective. Thus, beginning in May 1987, 132 drugstores in Beijing began selling contraceptive supplies and devices at manufacturer's price instead of providing them free. In November 1988, a government circular—issued jointly by the State Family Planning Commission; the Ministries of Finance, Chemical Industry, and Commerce; and the State Pharmaceutical Administration—instructed all contraceptive outlets to adopt a dual-track system offering supplies free of charge as well as at retail prices (understood to be about 15 percent above factory-listed prices). According to incomplete data, by the end of 1989, retail outlets for contraceptives included 5,548 drugstores, 2,195 hospitals, 1,802 cooperatives, as well as more than 3,000 other types of organizations, with a total estimated clientele of 8 percent of all current users. Not known, however, is the composition of paying clients relative to those who continue to obtain free supplies through these outlets.

Interventions and Their Effectiveness

China's compulsory family planning policies lead couples to have fewer children than they would have had in the absence of those policies. Although preferences generally exceed what the government allows, couples today might want two or three children instead of six or seven. In urban areas, most people comply with the government's one-child limit because of the very high cost of defiance in penalties and forgone benefits. In rural areas, frequent monitoring forces women to keep IUDs longer than they want, abort pregnancies they would like to carry to term, and be sterilized before they have the number of children they desire.

Experience shows, nonetheless, that there are limits to the ability of a pervasive, compulsory family planning program to further reduce fertility in a low-income context. Fertility dropped from 5.8 births per woman in 1970 to 2.8 births per woman only seven years later, but for the next thirteen years, it has fluctuated between 2.2 and 2.9 births per woman. The very rapid transition between 1970 and 1977 suggests that the Chinese people did not vigorously resist the shift from bearing six children to only three per couple. Since 1979 the government has introduced the one-child policy, expanded compulsory abortion and sterilization almost nationwide, included minority populations in the program of birth limitation, and constantly fine-tuned the program. Yet there has been no sustained decline in fertility, but only a roller-coaster pattern, with births per woman hitting a low point in 1980, peaking in 1982, dropping again to a nadir in 1985, peaking once more in 1987, and more recently declining again.

The fertility fluctuations since 1979 reflect an unstable tension between people's marriage or fertility aspirations and limitations on fertility set by the government. Popular resistance to the forced late marriage policy of the 1970s prompted the government to lower the required minimum ages at marriage in 1980. The fertility peak in 1981–82 was partly a surge in first births following the surge of marriages in 1980–81. The subsequent, slightly dampened, fertility peak centered on 1987 was in part the surge of second births from those same marriages. At the same time, marital fertility has been affected by a cycle of increasing government pressure (1979–83), followed by popular backlash (1983–84), followed, in turn, by a slight relaxation of the one-child policy and people's taking advantage of it to have more children (1986–87). As the authorities became aware that fertility was rising in 1986, they began an escalation in the degree of compulsion in the program that has continued to the present.

Economic, social, and political changes in China since the 1970s have had and will have mixed effects on fertility. China launched a program of economic reform in 1978. By 1984 most rural people's communes had been dismantled and cadres' control over the lives of villagers has correspondingly been weakening. At the same time, while agricultural liberalization proceeded, the perceived value of children to rural families may have increased because each child, especially a son, can be expected to provide labor to increase production on the farm or get a nonagricultural job to increase family income, and also provide family welfare support now that the former rural welfare system has been weakened. These changes, combined with greater internal migration under the reforms, are factors that may eventually cause fertility to rise.

Over the longer term, some important forces are making people more resistant to government orders. Widespread education and literacy, now accompanied by access to radio and especially television, are raising popular aspirations far higher and faster than the still hobbled, part-command part-market economy can deliver. The promise that stopping at one child will somehow raise societal, and therefore personal, prosperity faster is probably not very convincing to most Chinese citizens. They can see that households with several sons are still doing better economically than other households. To the extent that government control relaxes with the general trend toward economic liberalization, future fertility is likely to rise.

Potential Lessons from China's Experience

Numerous lessons can be drawn from China's family planning program. Some possible lessons would, however, be applicable only to countries attempting a compulsory approach. Most countries have voluntary family planning programs. What lessons can such countries learn from China?

In the early phase of fertility decline, the provision of widely available services had been an important element. As fertility reached relatively low levels, the government of China felt it necessary to supplement a supply-dominated strategy with more measures to influence the demand for children. If all the decline in total fertility from 1979 through 1993 were attributed to the influence of those additional demand-side factors, their effect would amount to a decline of 0.75 births per woman. It is interesting to note that China's total fertility rate took fifteen years to decline from 3 births per woman (around 1976–77) to 2 births per woman (1992). Bos and Bulatao (1990) show that for countries for which they had data, the same drop from comparable initial levels of fertility took an average of 14.4 years in the context of voluntary family planning policies. Thus the one-child policy which began in 1979, with its package of parity-related incentives and penalties as well as severe restrictions on the number of births, may be judged as having had a relatively limited effect on Chinese fertility. In the 1980s, economic conditions in China were not stagnant, but improving rapidly. Even so, replacement level fertility proved difficult to achieve. The lesson is that even in the best of circumstances, the type of demand-side interventions used in China is not a particularly effective instrument for achieving replacement fertility.

China has nonetheless shown that, even in a low-income country, human and financial resources can be tapped to carry out a strong, self-reliant program to deliver family planning services. The Chinese government spreads the burden of program costs by mandating that each level of government and each enterprise contribute certain numbers of staff or amounts of funds. It leaves to local governments the responsibility for decisions on the level of funds to be raised, the method of resource mobilization, and the allocation of resources. Other countries could similarly encourage decentralized involvement in the family planning effort by units below the central government level. But there must be a government with a will to promote family planning, the capacity for implementation, and the ability to engage a broad cross-section of the bureaucracy at all levels in the effort. A well-functioning, modern economy is not required—China is proof of that.

In China, a relatively modest level of expenditure for family planning service delivery—around 0.1 percent of GNP in China during the 1980s[26]—combined with human ingenuity and flexibility, went a long way toward achieving lower fertility. China's program is not static. When some aspects are not working to the government's liking, other creative solutions are tried, then publicized if they work. Often the new strategies involve organizational changes instead of more funds. In China, much of this creative leadership is directed toward overcoming popular resistance and replacing coercive policies that have ceased to be effective with new coercive tactics. Nonetheless, flexible leadership could also be applied to voluntary programs in other countries. Similarly, some of the strategies adopted to contain costs and reduce waste might also be relevant, including mobilizing volunteer input, using low-cost workers to promote family planning, linking bonuses to work performance, and experimenting with retail sales of contraceptives.

China's program is results-oriented and uses a variety of complementary approaches in service delivery to facilitate the achievement of low fertility. Since the 1950s all methods of birth control have been legal in the country. In contrast, many other countries have outlawed one or more methods, or have blocked popular access to particular techniques. It is not impossible to reduce fertility under such constraints, but it is more difficult than in countries like China where all methods are allowed. Contraceptive supplies and surgery are given to married couples free of charge and at reasonably convenient locations. The negative side effects of birth control operations are recognized as a potential threat to program success, and the authorities have, partly for this reason, moved to restrict which clinics may provide which operations. To maximize accessibility with minimum risk to users is a goal that family planning programs everywhere might find relevant. China's domestically financed system for providing contraceptives and surgery in a network accessible and often free to most people is a model applicable in other low-income settings.[27]

In China, as elsewhere, the physical infrastructure for service delivery is inadequate in number, and clinics are not always equipped to carry out the full range of family planning work. The authorities overcome this by emphasizing grassroots outreach, relying on door-to-door distribution of contraceptives in some areas, and requiring family planning workers to interact closely at the field level with women in the target population. Contacts at this level also provide the channels for reinforcing pro-family planning messages spread through the more impersonal mass media. The active efforts at bringing services and information to the population rather than waiting for women to visit a yet-to-be-fully-developed service infrastructure, or for messages communicated from a distance to take effect, is a model for other countries.

Experience in China also shows that a success-oriented program needs an effective method for measuring success. In China the success or failure of the program is not measured by counting "acceptors" of this or that contraceptive method, but by looking at actual fertility per woman and the actual birth rate. All these measures are imperfect. In China, as elsewhere, when it is family planning workers who are collecting and reporting the data that measure their own success, the result is that acceptors are overreported and births underreported. Chinese leaders learned in the early 1980s that such data are not reliable. Since 1982, they have carried out several fertility surveys and censuses of exceptional quality. Several times the results of these massive efforts have shown that fertility was higher than previously thought. Such reality checks are needed to monitor the program's actual performance.

The China model has many lessons of potential relevance in countries attempting to lower fertility through voluntary family planning programs. For these countries, compulsion is not an option. But for them the focus in China's program on results, grass roots outreach, and commitment to education and maternal and child health are features with potential relevance.

India

Launched in 1951, the Indian family planning program is the oldest in the world.[28] With the increasing incorporation of maternal and child health services in the 1970s, the program was renamed the family welfare program in 1977. In the early years, the program mounted large-scale information-education-communication campaigns to spread contraceptive knowledge and promote small family norms. Over time, the principal channel for delivering family planning services—a network of health facilities comprising primary health centers and subcenters at the lowest levels in the system—has gradually expanded with budget support from the central government, and today provides an impressively broad coverage of the population.[29] Other program interventions include intensive annual campaigns to recruit acceptors of sterilization as well as social marketing schemes to distribute condoms, and more recently, pills.

Aside from the above activities, which are run by the Family Welfare Department in the Ministry of Health, a number of other government agencies—including those overseeing postal services, defense, railways, and border roads—also operate family welfare programs. In the private sector, family planning services are offered by large manufacturing enterprises to their employees (as at, for example, Tata Steel, which started the earliest program of its kind), as well as by private commercial service providers and nongovernmental organizations. The latter play a relatively minor role, however, serving a very small, mainly urban, clientele.

Most observers agree that the family welfare program has contributed to fertility decline in India by raising contraceptive prevalence. Most also agree, however, that several major weaknesses have hampered the program's effectiveness.[30] Improving performance is thus a priority, particularly as the program matures and increasingly faces the challenge of reaching population groups that still favor large families. A first step in this task is to assess how the program operates currently. A substantial number of surveys and studies address this objective (such as Operations Research Group 1990); the results, by and large, are in agreement that the program is overly dominated by sterilization services and that services for temporary methods are inadequate for lack of supplies and trained personnel.[31]

Data from a recent survey of the National Sample Survey Organization (NSSO) corroborate past findings on the performance of the family welfare program but offer insights from slightly different perspectives.[32] Normally, NSSO's large annual surveys collect information on household consumption and other aspects of household behavior. In 1986–87, the core survey questionnaires were supplemented with a module on the use of social services. The data on family planning covered over 70,000 urban and rural households and reveal interesting patterns of financing and use of family planning services. Aside from providing an independent reading of program performance, the NSSO survey has the advantage of containing (a) very good consumption data which permit disaggregation of program outcomes across socioeconomic groups; and (b) more detailed information on aspects of use of family planning services and financing than are available elsewhere.

Patterns of User Finance

India's family welfare program offers payments to acceptors of sterilization and IUDs. The survey data indicate, however, striking deviations from the stated provisions (table 6.5). Users are classified into one of three groups in the survey: those who received the service with incentive (that is, "compensation payment," in the language of the Family Welfare Department), free, or on payment. Regrettably, no information is available on the size of the payments.

Two-thirds of the women sterilized during the year before the survey reported receiving payment. Thus, the popular impression of a blanket incentive system is somewhat inaccurate, since nearly a quarter of those sterilized report receiving the service merely free, and nearly a tenth actually paid for the service.

For IUDs, payments benefit less than a tenth of the clients, with the remaining clients evenly split between the "free" and "on payment" categories. The stipulated incentives for this method thus exist largely as a plan on paper. For the other contraceptive methods, incentive payments benefit a negligible share of users. Free services reach less than 30 percent of pill users and less than 20 percent of condom users. Correspondingly, the proportion who reported paying is large.

Table 6.5: Percentage of Users of Various Contraceptive Methods by Category of Service Received, India 1986–87

Method	With incentive	Free	On payment	All
Sterilization[a]	67.2	23.3	9.4	100.0
IUD	8.9	44.0	47.0	100.0
Pill	3.1	28.0	68.9	100.0
Condom	2.7	19.2	78.1	100.0
Other methods[b]	4.4	37.5	58.0	100.0

a. Respondents include only those sterilized during the year previous to the survey.
b. Includes diaphragm, spermicide, injection, and medically terminated pregnancy.
Source: India 1989c.

Further distinction is possible according to users' sources of service and place of residence (table 6.6).[33] Among acceptors of sterilizations at a government source, 71 percent of those in rural areas received incentive payments compared to only 56 percent in urban areas. A surprisingly large share of urban acceptors of this method— nearly 11 percent—actually paid for the service. In a program with an incentive arrangement, this phenomenon is puzzling at first sight. It is possible that paying clients received better or different services than clients receiving incentives; or that people are far more willing to pay for the services that are currently rendered than is generally assumed. The truth of these conjectures is not possible to confirm with the available data. Nonetheless, the existence of paying public sector clients, and the fact that in both urban and rural areas, sizable shares of clients received sterilizations free of charge, suggest that incentive payments could probably be targeted more sharply without affecting acceptance rates. The main issue is to identify specific client characteristics for effective targeting.

IUD clients at government facilities commonly received free services, rather than services with incentives, and a sizable share reported paying. For pills and condoms, paying clients at public sources of service are even more common. Again, these patterns suggest the surprising conclusion that people are in fact willing to pay for what has often been criticized as poor-quality services offered at public facilities.

Incidence of Payments to Acceptors of Sterilization

Incentive payments for sterilization are not insignificant at Rs. 145 per acceptor (Rs. 100 in cash and Rs. 45 in-kind; the total equals about 3 percent of per capita GNP in 1989). It is thus of interest to examine their incidence across population

Table 6.6: Percentage of Users of Various Contraceptive Methods by Category of Service Received, Rural and Urban India 1986–87

Method		From government sources			From other sources		All
		With incentive	Free	On payment	Free	On payment	
Sterilization	Rural	71.4	16.8	3.7	5.1	3.1	100.0
	Urban	55.9	20.3	10.7	7.1	5.9	100.0
	INDIA[a]	67.2	17.7	5.6	5.7	3.8	100.0
IUD	Rural	8.0	31.8	5.7	13.6	40.9	100.0
	Urban	11.7	32.9	18.5	7.2	29.7	100.0
	INDIA[a]	8.9	32.1	9.1	11.9	37.9	100.0
Pill	Rural	3.3	21.3	19.3	10.7	45.3	100.0
	Urban	2.3	12.4	26.8	5.0	53.5	100.0
	INDIA[a]	3.1	18.9	21.3	9.1	47.5	100.0
Condom	Rural	2.7	13.6	35.1	8.0	40.7	100.0
	Urban	2.7	8.1	33.2	5.0	51.1	100.0
	INDIA[a]	2.7	12.1	34.6	7.2	43.5	100.0
Other methods[b]	Rural	4.5	22.1	3.1	13.9	56.4	100.0
	Urban	4.2	31.5	9.4	10.4	44.5	100.0
	INDIA[a]	4.4	24.6	4.8	13.0	53.2	100.0

a. Weighted by rural-urban shares of population (73% and 27% respectively).
b. Includes diaphragm, spermicide, injection, and medically terminated pregnancy.
Source: India 1989c, tables 4.5R, 4.5U, and 4.7.

groups. Figure 6.2 shows the Gini-curve for rural and urban groups, with consumption fractiles arranged in ascending order on the horizontal axis, and the share of clients receiving incentive payments on the vertical axis. If beneficiaries come equally from all consumption fractiles, the relationship between consumption fractile and share of clients receiving payment would be a 45-degree line through the origin. But the data show Gini-curves that rise above this line, suggesting that beneficiaries in both rural and urban areas are concentrated in lower-income groups. This tendency is stronger, however, in urban than rural areas. For example, 45 percent of the beneficiaries in urban areas come from the bottom 20 percent of the population by consumption status, compared with 32 percent in rural areas.

As a mechanism for income transfer, incentive payments reach the desired population groups. But as shown below, this result arises because lower-income groups have poorer access to temporary contraceptive methods compared to higher-income groups. From a demographic perspective, it is noteworthy that the concentration of lower-income groups among sterilization clients may have an unforeseen adverse effect. Because such groups tend to value immediate income more highly than income spread over a longer period, the incentive scheme would encourage more closely spaced births than in situations where contraceptive choice is less heavily biased in favor of sterilizations. If not counteracted by declines in desired family size—which occur more slowly among lower-income groups—the shorten-

Figure 6.2: Distribution of Aggregate Incentive Payments for Family Planning, India 1986–87

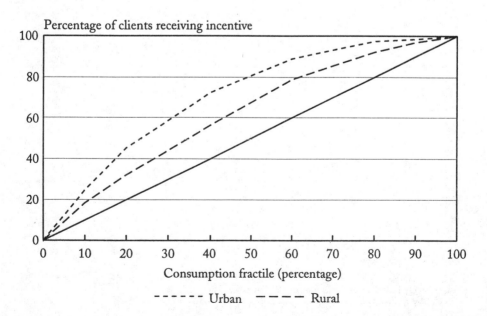

ing of birth intervals would cause the population to grow faster rather than slower. Indirect evidence suggests that, over time, birth intervals in India may indeed have shortened. Using readily available data on the mean age at childbearing, the mean age at marriage, and the total fertility rate, it is possible to compute an *analytic birth interval measure*[34] which serves as an adequate proxy for actual birth intervals for the purpose at hand. In India, that interval was 4.4 years in 1981, but by 1987 it had dropped to 4.1 years.

Availability of Nonsterilization Methods

A very large share of the resources in India's family planning program is used to finance incentive payments for sterilization. There is evidence that this pattern of allocation has compromised the availability of temporary methods. The National Sample Survey of 1986/7 gives information on the proportion of nonsterilized couples in the sample who sought various temporary methods of contraception, and the proportion who failed in their quest (table 6.7). The share of nonsterilized couples seeking any one of the methods appears, at first glance, to be relatively modest, reaching a high of only 10 percent, for condoms. Even so, the family planning program fails dismally: the share of seekers who did not obtain the desired service was 75 percent for IUDs, 67 percent for pills, and 41 percent for condoms. For all methods, services are markedly less available in rural than urban areas.

Relative to the contraceptive prevalence rate in India (43.0 percent in 1988), the share of nonsterilized couples seeking temporary methods is, in fact, large. To elaborate, since roughly one-third of eligible couples are sterilized, those who sought condoms account for 10 percent of the remaining two-thirds, or 6.7 percent of all eligible couples. Among these, 40.5 percent did not obtain the services. If they had,

Table 6.7: Seekers of Nonsterilization Methods of Contraception, India 1986–87

Method	Percentage of nonsterilized couples who sought service			Percentage of service seekers who did not receive service		
	Rural	*Urban*	*India*[b]	*Rural*	*Urban*	*India*[b]
IUD	4.8	5.6	5.0	81.8	55.7	74.7
Pill	5.5	6.3	5.7	72.7	52.2	67.1
Condom	8.5	14.2	10.0	47.0	23.0	40.5
Other methods[a]	4.5	3.9	4.3	87.7	84.4	86.8

a. Reflects arithmetic average for diaphragm, spermicide, injection, and medically terminated pregnancy.

b. Reflects average weighted by the rural-urban population shares (73% and 27% respectively based on World Bank, 1991d, table 31).

Source: Computed from statement 4.6 in India 1989c.

the contraceptive prevalence rate would have increased by 2.7 percentage points, raising India's contraceptive prevalence rate to 45.5 percent. If the same calculation were made for the other three categories in the table, India's contraceptive prevalence rate would have increased by about 10 percentage points, to 52.8 percent. Because people may have sought and not found more than one method, this result is probably overstated. Nonetheless, the magnitude of the effect of nonavailability of temporary methods appears significant.

The survey gives no information on whether unsuccessful seekers were looking for free services or were prepared to pay but services were not rendered. It is simply known that for all the temporary methods noted, about half of the failed seekers sought services at nongovernment facilities. Because the private sector is by nature responsive to consumer demand, the size of this group is indeed surprising. Because no distinction is made, however, between voluntary and commercial providers in the survey, conclusions are difficult to draw regarding the possible causes of nonsupply. What is clear is that both government and nongovernment providers are currently not fully geared to satisfy the demand for temporary contraception among Indian couples.

The poor supply of temporary contraception has a clear income bias in both rural and urban areas (table 6.8). The system fails to supply IUDs to between 80 and 90 percent of the seekers from the bottom 60 percent of the rural population by consumption level, compared to 66 percent of those in the second highest decile and 61 percent in the highest decile. Differences in availability across consumption groups is even larger for pills and condoms. The share of failed pill seekers in the lowest decile is 1.6 times that in the highest decile; for condoms, it is 2.5 times. In urban areas, the gaps among consumption fractiles are, if anything, wider still: the share of failed pill seekers in the lowest decile is more than twice that in the highest decile; for condoms, it is 3.3 times. The urban-rural differences are not surprising because the urban economy has more capacity to offer consumer choice, particularly to those who can pay.

Summary

Most observers agree that continued fertility decline in India depends critically on changes in both demand- and supply-side factors. In the past, the family welfare program has focused on the supply of family planning services as the chief means to reduce population growth. This focus was arguably appropriate and effective in earlier years, when the supply of services was still too small relative to the existing demand for family planning. But because socioeconomic and health conditions—particularly female education, labor market conditions, and children's health—have improved only slowly in India, the demand for children appears to have declined modestly (at a decrease of 0.05 children a year in desired family size between 1980 and 1988, compared with 0.09 children a year in Bangladesh between 1975 and 1988),[35] and the effectiveness of a supply-driven program inevitably levels off. Thus, without substantial changes in those conditions,

Table 6.8: Unsuccessful Seekers of Selected Family Planning Services as a Percentage of All Service Seekers by Consumption Fractile in Urban and Rural Areas, India 1986–87

Fractile group	Rural areas			Urban areas		
	IUD	Pill	Condom	IUD	Pill	Condom
0 – 10	81	75	57	76	76	46
10 – 20	88	80	58	74	69	34
20 – 40	86	84	58	63	56	25
40 – 60	87	72	49	54	47	20
60 – 80	79	69	40	46	45	17
80 – 90	66	58	30	40	45	17
90 – 100	61	48	23	38	33	14
All groups	82	73	47	56	52	23

Source: Computed from table 3 in India 1989c.

continued expansion of the program may not help reduce fertility to the same extent as it has in the past.

At the same time, the family welfare program itself suffers from serious inadequacies. The National Sample Survey results show that as the family welfare program is currently organized, the stress on sterilization is indeed excessive because it has severely compromised the system's capacity to supply temporary methods, particularly to lower-income populations. Because these methods appeal to younger women and are used to space births, their poor availability is a serious obstacle to slowing population growth. Changes in the way resources are allocated among program inputs and services delivered may thus be needed to enhance the program's effectiveness.

Indonesia

The last few decades witnessed rapid demographic changes in Indonesia, with population growth rates slowing during the 1980s in contrast to an accelerating pattern during the previous three decades (table 6.9). These trends reflect an important transformation of fertility behavior. Whereas Indonesian women exceeded five births each up until the mid-1970s, their fertility declined, on average, by about two children each by the late 1980s, with the decline being most rapid in Java-Bali. The effects of declining fertility in the 1980s was sufficiently large to offset those of contemporaneous mortality decline, resulting in the observed slowdown in overall population growth rates during that decade.

Institutional Context of Fertility Decline

Indonesia's fertility decline occurred in the context of a widespread public family planning program started in 1970 with the establishment of the National Family Planning Coordinating Board (BKKBN).[36] The program has, from its inception, enjoyed strong political support at the highest levels of government. Still in place and active today, it is deservedly identified by most observers as a central ingredient in Indonesia's demographic transition (Hull and Hatmadji 1990; World Bank, Indonesia–1990; World Bank, Indonesia–1991).

Family planning activities developed in phases under the overall coordination of BKKBN. They began with clinic-based services provided through the health ministry's maternal and child health program. It became apparent, however, that a more proactive approach was needed to extend the reach of services. Accordingly, beginning in 1970, fieldworkers were recruited in large numbers to motivate couples house to house, and in 1974, the Village Contraceptive Distribution Centers (VCDC) program was started. Organized and supervised by family planning fieldworkers with the help of volunteers, VCDC personnel supply oral pills, distribute condoms, offer contraceptive information, and supply simple medicines against side effects and health complications. To supplement clinic-based services, training programs were also mounted for mobile teams—consisting of para- and nonmedical personnel and medical staff—to bring family planning services, especially information-education-communication (IEC) activities, to villages without clinics. In addition, meetings (*posyandus*) were organized, usually on a monthly basis, by village heads with volunteer help and technical support from health clinic staff. The *posyandus* offered integrated maternal and child health services including family planning, targeted to pregnant women, lactating mothers, and families with young children.

With the support of the country's political leadership, BKKBN attracted broad-based involvement of other government bureaucracies in family planning activities.[37] The 1970s and 1980s thus saw aggressive expansion of BKKBN's family planning initiatives throughout the country. Contraceptive services and information, the core program activity, became widely available through a variety of delivery mechanisms. By the mid- to late-1980s, some 63,000 villages and 190,000 subvillages had a VCDC; over 8,000 public clinic service points, three-quarters of which came under the health ministry's jurisdiction, offered family planning services, with backup services available through hospitals; and about 200,000 *posyandus* had been established. In general, the public sector was the dominant force in service delivery, with a share of 80 percent of the country's contraceptive clientele in 1987. Beginning in 1986, however, the KB Mandari ("self-reliant") movement was launched to attract greater private involvement in service delivery and financing.

Indonesia's aggressive and well-organized family planning program undoubtedly played a role in bringing about fertility decline. But the last fifteen to twenty years in Indonesia also saw rapid and sharp socioeconomic transformation, marked by the spread of mass education, expanding job opportunities, and rising incomes and

Table 6.9: Selected Demographic Characteristics of Indonesia, Selected Years 1950–90

Population size		Annual growth rate of population		Total fertility rate			Infant mortality rate	
Year	(millions)	Period	(percentage a year)	Period	Indonesia	Java-Bali	Period	(per thousand live births)
					(births per woman)			
1950	78	1950–60	1.90	1967–71	5.6	5.4	1950–54	160
1960	94	1960–70	2.24	1971–75	5.2	4.9	1955–59	145
1970	118	1970–80	2.34	1976–79	4.7	4.2	1960–64	133
1980	148	1980–85	2.10	1981–84	4.1	3.7	1965–69	124
1985	165	1985–90	2.01	1983–87	3.4	3.2	1970–74	114
1990	178						1975–79	105
							1980–84	95
							1988	69

Source: World Bank (Indonesia–1990); supplemented by survey and census data on fertility cited in Gertler and Molyneaux 1994. Population size for 1990 is from Bos and Bulatao 1990.

standards of living—changes that have probably increased the demand for small families. There is thus also consensus among observers that demand-side effects were an added factor in Indonesia's demographic transition.

Assessing the Contribution of Demand and Supply Factors

How important were the demand-side factors relative to the effects of the family planning program? Such a question is not purely academic, for the answer is relevant to the design of public policies aimed at reducing fertility, not only for Indonesia, but also more generally in the context of developing countries at various stages of fertility decline.[38] The issue has attracted continuing debate in the literature, but conclusive answers have been elusive, owing to methodological and data constraints. At the heart of the debate has been the difficulty of accurately measuring the attributes of family planning programs and relating them to women's fertility behavior.

Several recent data sets for Indonesia permit creation of time series information on fertility, family planning program inputs, and economic development, offering a unique opportunity to assess the linkages among these variables, as detailed in the work of Gertler and Molyneaux (1994). Their analysis relied on:

- The 1987 National Indonesian Contraceptive Prevalence Survey (NICPS), which contains data on individual women's fertility and contraceptive use histories during the five years preceding the survey.[39] These data were disaggregated at quarterly intervals for a total of 21 periods, starting from the third quarter of 1982 through the fourth quarter of 1986.

- Contemporaneous *kecamatan*-level data[40] on public family planning inputs from BKKBN's service statistics.

- Wage data from the 1982 Social and Economic Survey (SUSENAS) and the 1986–87 Income and Employment Surveys (SAKERNAS).[41]

- Data on community variables from the 1983 and 1986 village infrastructure censuses (PODES) conducted by the Indonesian Central Bureau of Statistics.[42]

Aggregating the NICPS fertility and contraception data for women in the same *kecamatan*, and merging the result to data from the other surveys, produced the panel data set, with 378 community-level observations, used in Gertler and Molyneaux (1994).[43]

Analytical Framework, Methodological Issues, and Results

Gertler and Molyneaux (1994) relied on a proximate determinants framework in which fertility is decomposed into three main components—marriage, contraception, and fecundability.[44] In this framework, "fecundability"[45] is treated as a residual factor aggregating the effects of (a) omitted proximate determinants, such as marital disruption, the duration of postpartum amenorrhea, and induced abortion; and (b) variables thought to influence "natural fecundability," including the timing and frequency of coitus, duration of postpartum abstinence, and biological endowments.

The first set of results relates to the contribution of each of the three proximate determinants to fertility decline in Indonesia during 1982–87, the period covered by the 1987 NICPS. The monthly probability of births among married women aged 15–49 in the sample fell from 0.0101 in 1982 to 0.0076 in 1986, a contraction of 25 percent. In comparison, the total fertility rate fell by 17 percent over the 2.5-year period from midpoint of the 1981–84 period to the midpoint of the 1983–87 period. Increases in contraception proved to be the dominant factor, accounting for nearly 75 percent of the drop in fertility between 1982–86 (table 6.10). Changes in marriage patterns contributed about 18 percent, leaving only a modest 8 percent accounted for by changes in fecundability. These results are consistent with those of a more rigorous decomposition of fertility changes between 1976 and 1987, based on comparisons of the 1976 World Fertility Survey and the 1987 NICPS (Adioetomo, Kitting, and Taufik 1990).

The effect of family planning programmatic inputs and other factors on fertility can be assessed from their influence on the three proximate determinants identified above—contraception, marriage, and fecundability. Cross-sectional data are inappropriate for this analysis in the Indonesian context because the placement of family planning inputs is neither random nor uniform. After initial expansion of the program, BKKBN began carefully monitoring contraceptive prevalence at local levels. At the same time, provincial and district officials were given autonomy to tailor family planning inputs to local conditions as well as substantial professional incentives to increase contraceptive prevalence in their region. Officials at all levels developed targets and provided resources based on existing prevalence reports with an explicit strategy of recruiting new acceptors in regions with low

Table 6.10: Percentage Contribution of Various Proximate Determinants to Fertility Decline in Indonesia, 1982–87

Proximate determinant	Percentage contribution
Contraceptive use	74.9
Marriage	16.8
Fecundability[a]	8.3
All	100.0

a. Demographer's term that refers to the fertility of women in the absence of birth control
Source: Gertler and Molyneaux 1994, based on 1987 NICPS data.

contraceptive prevalence (BKKBN 1984). These arrangements imply that cross-sectional data would yield correlations that captured the combined influence of program placement and program effect. The usefulness of the results would correspondingly be limited.

To overcome this limitation, Gertler and Molyneaux (1994) used a combination of cross-section and time-series data in a fixed-effects model instead, following the method of Rosenzweig and Wolpin (1986). The essential characteristic of this approach is that *changes* in the dependent variable (fertility) are related to *changes* in the regressors (program inputs, economic conditions, and community endowments). One consequence is the elimination of possible mismeasurements which could have occurred if programs were systematically placed in especially favorable or unfavorable environments.

Because of the dominant effect of changes in contraceptive use as a proximate determinant of fertility decline and because of its central relevance in policy analysis, we focus on it here. Table 6.11 shows the total change in fertility predicted by the regression results of Gertler and Molyneaux (1994), disaggregated by the main factors influencing it. In the model, changes in contraceptive use between 1982 and 1986 would cause a decline in fertility of 17.8 percent.[46]

The effect of contraceptive change on fertility is decomposed into five sets of factors: (a) the age distribution of women, (b) the education profile of mothers, (c) the wages in the community for men and women, (d) family planning inputs, and (e) measures of community infrastructure. Changes in the educational profile of women accounted for about 54 percent of the fertility decline (working through changes in contraceptive use). Changes in wage rates accounted for another 36 percent. The remaining 10 percent was due to changes in the age distribution of women (5.3 percent), changes in family planning inputs (5.5 percent), and changes in the community infrastructure measures (-1.0 percent).

Interpretation of the Results

Taken at face value, these figures indicate that education and wage rates, that is, socioeconomic variables, played a much more important role in explaining the increase of contraceptive use in Indonesia during 1982–86 than did family planning program variables. This is a potentially important finding and needs careful interpretation and evaluation before application in policy formulation.

The results do not, in themselves, indicate that family planning inputs had little effect on contraceptive use and fertility. They show the combined effect of two influences: (a) the responsiveness of contraceptive use to changes in various factors, and (b) the size of the changes in those factors between 1982 and 1986. The small percentage contribution of increases in family planning inputs to the overall increase in contraceptive use could materialize if the changes in family planning inputs were relatively small. Changes in the family planning inputs, however, particularly in the density of family planning team visits and health clinics, increased substantially during the sample period (table 6.12). The implication is that contraceptive use and

Table 6.11: Predicted Fertility Change Due to the Effects of Various Factors on Contraception, Indonesia, 1982–86

Changes in factors influencing contraception	Predicted percentage change	Contribution to change (percentage)
Age distribution	−0.94	5.3
Mother's education	−9.66	54.4
Wages (for men and women)	−6.35	35.8
Family planning inputs[a]	−0.98	5.5
Community infrastructure[b]	0.17	−1.0
Total effect of contraceptive change on fertility	17.76	100.00

Note: Contraception is measured by percent ever married contracepting. Results are predicted from a fixed–effects proximate determinants logit model.

a. Refers to the combined effects of changes in (a) monthly family planning team visit per thousand population; (b) Village Contraceptive Distribution Centers per thousand population; (c) health clinics per thousand population; and (d) family planning fieldworkers per thousand population.

b. Refers to the combined effects of changes in (a) the number of primary schools per thousand population; (b) junior high schools per thousand population; (c) *desas* with paved roads per *kecamatan*; (d) *desas* with movie theaters per *kecamatan*.

Source: Calculated from Gertler and Molyneaux 1994.

fertility have indeed been relatively unresponsive to the changes in family planning inputs considered here during this period.[47]

It bears emphasizing that these results are based on a fixed-effects model which relates *changes* during 1982–86 in family planning inputs and the socioeconomic variables to *changes* in contraceptive use. During this period, the supply of family planning facilities and services was already very widespread in Indonesia, particularly in Java and Bali, the context of the analysis of Gertler and Molyneaux (1994). In this setting, it is possible for diminishing returns to set in and for contraceptive use differences to depend more on factors relating to the demand for small families than on variables relating to the supply of family planning services. This effect certainly does not mean that previous investments in family planning infrastructure and services were unimportant, only that *additional* investments of the same kind had limited effects. Furthermore, the results refer to the average situation. In places with sparse family planning inputs, increases in inputs could still have a large effect on contraceptive use and fertility.

It is nonetheless important to recognize that several other factors could account for the weak effect of the family planning variables observed in Gertler and Molyneaux (1994). One is the omission of variables that might have changed during the period of analysis. An example is changes in the private supply of contraceptive services. In the absence of this variable, the results measure the *net effect of public* family planning inputs; they do not permit one to conclude that the totality of family planning services (public *and* private) has a weak effect. It is possible, for example, that where public programs expanded most rapidly, private programs expanded least rapidly, because of crowding out. If this effect were important, the estimates of the effects of *public* family planning inputs would be smaller than it, in fact, is. But if the crowding-out argument were relevant, increased public investments in family planning have a relatively weak effect precisely because they substitute for increases in private services.

A second factor which might have contributed to the weak family planning effect arises from the combination of data sets. The data from the NICPS refer to women who live in particular villages and may not be representative of the entire *kecamatan*. Merging the data on fertility, contraceptive use, and education from particular villages with *kecamatan*-level data on other variables can, in certain circumstances, result in the underestimation of effects. The wage rate data, however, were observed at a higher level of aggregation than the family planning data (district versus subdistrict), and the wage rates were quite important while the family planning data

Table 6.12: Means and Percentage Changes in Selected Indicators of Family Planning Inputs and Socioeconomic Conditions in Sample Communities, Indonesia, 1982–86

| | Mean of variable | | Percentage change |
Socioeconomic conditions	1982	1986	1982–86
Share of women with no education (%)	0.263	0.209	−21
Female wage rates[a]	4.903	5.105	4
Male wage rates[a]	5.234	5.390	3
Monthly family planning team visits[b]	0.205	0.899	338
Village Contraceptive Distribution Centers[b]	0.387	0.529	37
Health Clinics[b]	0.015	0.046	209
Family planning fieldworkers[b]	0.116	0.074	−37

Note: The variables shown are measured in the same units as were used in Gertler, Molyneaux, and Tanok (1991) in their regression estimates.

a. Logarithm of hourly wages rates. Note that percent changes in these logarithms are not the same as percent changes in wage rates.

b. Measured in number per thousand population.

Source: Gertler and Molyneaux 1994.

were not. Thus, although it is possible that this sort of data problem could account for the weak effect of the family planning variables, there is no reason to believe that it would weaken the family planning effect more than the wage effect.

A third factor is the structure of the relationships built into the estimation model. It is assumed that there are no lags between the changes in family planning inputs and changes in contraceptive use and fertility. If these lags were important, the measured effects of the family planning inputs would be too small.

Finally, it is also important to recognize that Gertler and Molyneaux (1994) focused on only some of BKKBN's program inputs. Limitations in the data prevented analysis of the effect of contraceptive subsidies, for example, which are estimated to absorb 40 to 60 percent of BKKBN resources (Chernichovsky and others 1991, and World Bank, Indonesia–1990). Nonetheless, the study does include the bulk of BKKBN's noncontraceptive inputs, as well as those of volunteer organizations and the health ministry (which are not included in BKKBN budgets). The results of Gertler and Molyneaux (1994) thus do not suggest that *all* public family planning input had little effect, only those added in the form of the variables used in their analysis.

Policy Implications

What are the implications of these findings for policy analysis? In the mid-1980s Indonesia had already developed a dense system of infrastructure and family planning services. Although the supply of these inputs may have had a significant effect in the past, incremental investments seem to have had much less payoff. In other words, Indonesia had approached diminishing marginal returns by pursuing a policy that emphasized public supply interventions. Indonesian authorities apparently recognized this and, in 1986, they initiated an aggressive program to increase the participation of the private sector in service delivery while concentrating public investments in lagging areas. The findings in Gertler and Molyneaux (1994) provide strong support for this shift in strategy.

Notes

1. This discussion on China draws heavily on Banister and Harbaugh (1991), a background paper commissioned for this study. The authors are, respectively, chief and staff member of the China Branch, Center for International Research, U.S. Bureau of the Census. Their paper has far more information than can be presented here, and the interested reader is referred there for further details, including source citations.

2. According to the latest data available to us at this writing, the total fertility rate in 1987 averaged 1.36 in urban areas, and 2.94 in rural areas. Nationwide, the rate in 1993 was 2.00. See also appendix table A6.1 for trends in fertility since 1950.

3. To recall, the proximate determinants of fertility are the intermediate behavioral and biological factors through which social, economic, and environmental variables affect fertility. See chapter 3 above.

4. The importance of socioeconomic variables relative to family planning inputs is difficult to determine. One reason is that the program is not uniformly implemented throughout the country. For example, couples living in backward areas or from minority groups may be allowed two or three children, whereas those in more advanced parts of the country must stop at one child. Thus, a high correlation between fertility and socioeconomic variables does not imply that only such variables are responsible for the variation in fertility across localities.

5. As noted elsewhere, population momentum causes the population to increase in size for many years after fertility has declined to near-replacement levels.

6. In the late 1980s, only six provinces allowed all rural couples two children. Another sixteen provinces adopted a "one-and-a-half child" policy. At that time, seven provinces still had a strict one-child limit.

7. Han Chinese are the majority ethnic group in China, accounting for 92 percent of the whole population, according to the 1990 census.

8. The rise reflects the effect of real GNP growing faster than the population.

9. These costs are borne by the enterprises and the military.

10. Such organizations are designated as administrative organs, and their staff are classified as administrative personnel.

11. See appendix tables A4.1, A4.2, and A4.3 for the data on which these ratios are based.

12. For example, acceptors of sterilization receive only a one-time compensation equal to about 5 percent of per capita GNP in Bangladesh, and about 3 percent of per capita GNP in India. In the Republic of Korea, single-child low-income acceptors of sterilization receive a one-time payment of about 7 percent of per capita GNP, as well as a health subsidy—equivalent to about 2 percent of per capita GNP in value—that continues to be paid till the child reaches age 6. Low-income families who accept sterilization after two children receive a smaller incentive (see appendix table A4.5).

13. Under provisions of the Women's Protection Law of September 1988, women who comply with late marriage, later birth, and one-child policies could be eligible for paid maternity leave lasting between six months and three years.

14. Nutrional allowances are offered to acceptors of sterilization and IUD as well as to women who undergo an abortion after becoming pregnant while an IUD is in place.

15. In Shanghai county, for example, expenses for these incentives are about 16 percent of the expenses for the single-child incentives.

16. International donors also have a role in China's family planning program, but their financial contribution is relatively small. In the late 1980s, foreign assistance for family planning in China accounted for less than 1 percent of the program's total annual expenditures, as estimated by Banister and Harbaugh (1991). Supporting domestic production of contraceptives is a main component of donor activity in China's family planning program.

17. Banister and Harbaugh (1991, p. 114), gives the example of a county in Sichuan province where fines collected for excessive births funded 96 percent of the county's operational expenditure on family planning.

18. Couples with private businesses are to obtain their awards from a private business association fund pooled from contributions from private industry and commerce.

19. Hardship areas are independent administrative units where the annual per capita income is less than 50 yuan.

20. The State Family Planning Commission has direct oversight of seven public institutions engaged in research on population and information dissemination, and two social groups—China Family Planning Association and China Population Welfare Foundation—providing family planning services.

21. The responsibilities of each of these agencies are described in detail in Banister and Harbaugh (1991, appendix B). In brief, the State Planning Commission participates in formulating and communicating population policy as well as in supervising its implementation in the provinces. The State Science Commission takes charge of formulating policies and regulations to guide family planning research. The State Agriculture Commission ensures that rural economic policies support the government's family planning goals. The State Nationality Commission helps to stipulate population policy relating to China's minority populations. The Ministry of Public Health leads in setting conditions of pay and work for medical workers, planning and macroadministration of maternity and child health care as well as setting the technical standards for family planning services. The Ministry of Chemical Industry is charged with organizing the scientific research, manufacture, and supply of contraceptive pills and devices. The Ministry of Culture has responsibility for promoting artistic activities to spread the message of family planning. The Ministry of Education is charged with ensuring that courses on family planning and population-related subjects are included in the curriculum in schools, colleges, and universities. The Ministry of Civil Administration conducts propaganda regarding late marriage and birth control in the process of marriage registration, and provides relief to people disabled by birth control surgeries. The Ministry of Finance mobilizes and allocates funds to support family planning. The Public Security Department collects and provides the data from the

population registration system for birth planning and works with the judicial system to identify violators of the family planning regulations. The State Labor Bureau ensures that employment practices are consistent with the government's one-child policy.

22. As early as the 1950s, China lifted controls on abortion, sterilization, and the importation of birth control devices. Since then all methods of birth control have been legal.

23. This figure is from China Population Information and Research Centre (CPIRC) (1993c), p. 4.

24. Payment to workers making door-to-door contraceptive distribution accounted for about 8 percent of the program's total operational expenditures in 1989.

25. Incentive pay is also used for other workers. For example, managers and staff at contraceptive distribution centers are rewarded with year-end bonuses if they have guaranteed the timely delivery of commodities and saved on expenses.

26. In 1989, operational expenditure on family planning programs in Asian countries ranged from a high of 0.37 percent of GNP (in Bangladesh) to a low of 0.2 percent of GNP (in Malaysia).

27. The recent introduction of retail sales of contraceptives in China suggests that even in a low-income context, there is a segment of the population, particularly in urban areas, for whom free supplies are not an essential condition for contraceptive use.

28. The description of program origin and characteristics in this and the next paragraph draws on World Bank (1991a), to which the reader is referred for more details.

29. Fully functional primary health centers have the capacity, with adequate staff and supplies, to offer comprehensive health and family planning services, including sterilization and IUD insertions. They also support and supervise outreach services from the subcenters. In concept, subcenters are staffed by both male and female multipurpose workers, and are intended to offer rudimentary health, maternal and child health (MCH), and family planning services, but the latter activities are often hampered, particularly in the northern states, for lack of the female worker.

30. The main weaknesses are the program's overemphasis on sterilization; its focus on expansion at the cost of program operations, quality, and effectiveness; its overly centralized structure; and its lack of attention to demand-side factors (see World Bank 1991a for an elaboration).

31. The lack of supplies and trained personnel to offer temporary methods is corroborated by the early results from an evaluation launched in 1989 by the Family Welfare Department, which, in the first phase (August to October 1989), collected information from 2,637 households in 13 districts of 11 states; and 159 primary health centers and 179 subcenters in 15 states.

32. NSSO surveys are implemented by a large cadre of regular (mostly male) employees of the organization spread throughout the country. These fieldworkers are highly qualified (at least a bachelor's degree) and are trained and experienced in fieldwork. For most types of interviews with households, data accuracy is excellent.

For family planning, however, the data may be limited because (a) information was gathered from the male partner of eligible couples in most instances; and (b) the topic of interview is itself sensitive, and informants may not confide fully to others. To the extent that these limitations affect all groups more or less equally, intergroup comparisons should not be problematic. In passing, note that because the NSSO is not normally engaged in family planning activities, the survey offers a highly independent assessment of performance of the family planning program.

33. Distinction is possible only between government and "other" sources because no information is available to differentiate between voluntary and commercial providers.

34. The mathematical definition of this measure is shown in the discussion on the Philippines in chapter 3.

35. Because of data constraints and to ensure comparability over time and between countries, the rates of decline in desired family size are for women who still had no children at the time of the survey, most of whom would be young women at the start of their reproductive lives.

36. In the early 1950s, birth control had already been advocated by several community leaders, culminating in the formation of the Indonesia Planned Parenthood Association (IPPA) in 1957, which was subsequently affiliated with the International Planned Parenthood Federation. Although the association operated without the support of the then tacitly pronatalist government, it nonetheless managed to establish a network of family planning clinics by the 1960s. For more details on the historical origins of the BKKBN, see World Bank (Indonesia–1990).

37. As early as 1974–79, the family planning program was deliberately decentralized and integrated with other development activities. At each level of jurisdiction countrywide—involving 27 provinces, 300 regencies, 3,339 subdistricts, some 67,000 villages, and 240,000 subvillages—the governing authorities have been made accountable for family planning program activities as part of their responsibilities for development programs.

38. The following discussion draws on Gertler and Molyneaux (1994), a background paper commissioned for this study. The reader is referred there for details of their analysis and related literature citations.

39. The 1987 NICPS data were sampled to be representative of 93 percent of the Indonesian population.

40. *Kecamatans* (subdistricts) are the next higher level of administration from *desas* (villages). The data are available on a monthly basis but were aggregated in the analysis of Gertler and Molyneaux (1994) to quarters to match the time profile of the fertility and contraceptive data.

41. From these surveys it is possible to estimate hourly male and female regional wage rates adjusted for age and education. The results were interpolated to obtain the quarterly data needed to match the time profile of the fertility and contraceptive data.

42. As for the wage data, the infrastructure variables were interpolated to obtain the quarterly data needed to match the time profile of the fertility and contraceptive data.

43. Of the 400 community observations, 22 had to be eliminated because of missing codes.

44. See discussion in chapter 3 where a formal specification is provided.

45. This term is used by demographers to refer to fertility of women in the absence of birth control.

46. Table 6.11 is based on approximations which use the results of a fixed-effects logit estimation. (Logit estimation is used when the variable studied has a yes/no character. In this case, the yes/no variable refers to whether the woman is currently using contraception.) The decline in fertility computed from these approximations is 17.8 percent. Measuring the effect of contraceptive change alone without those approximations yields a change of 18.8 percent. Those approximations greatly simplify the calculation of the magnitudes of the influences of the factors which affect contraceptive change.

47. This conclusion is confirmed by the figures in Gertler and Molyneaux (1994), which show the derivatives of contraceptive use with respect to these variables.

7

Future Population Sizes of Asian Countries

THIS CHAPTER CONSIDERS THE POSSIBLE FUTURE courses of population growth in selected Asian countries. The discussion is motivated by two interrelated, but ultimately quite different, sets of policy concerns. First, we would like to know how much population growth Asian countries are likely to have to accommodate in the future. Second, we would like to ascertain the power of population policies to alter future population sizes.

The task of predicting future population growth accurately is an impossible one, given our current state of knowledge.[1] Population projections can nonetheless offer a useful guide. Accordingly, the latest available World Bank population projections for 2030 are presented below.[2] These projections assume that fertility in every country will eventually go to the replacement level and remain there. Future population sizes depend on the date at which replacement fertility occurs.[3] By varying this assumption it is possible to ascertain the potential effect of population policies on future population sizes.

World Bank Population Projections to the Year 2030

During 1990–2030, Asian countries are projected to experience considerable future population growth, with increases, in the aggregate, comparable in absolute magnitude to increases in the forty years between 1950 and 1990 (table 7.1). China added 579 million to its population between 1950 and 1990. In the subsequent forty years, it is projected to add another 367 million. India added 492 million people to its population from 1950 to 1990. By 2030, it is projected to add another 583 million. Overall, the eighteen countries in the table grew by 1.523 billion people between 1950 and 1990 and are projected to grow by 1.540 billion between 1990 and 2030.

In percentage terms, future increases in population are generally expected to be smaller than past increases (figure 7.1). For example, the population of Bangladesh, which grew by 163 percent between 1950 and 1990, is projected to grow by 74 percent during 1990 and 2030; the population of the Philippines grew by 193 percent during 1950–90 but is projected to increase by 98 percent in the next forty years. Overall, percentage increases in the sample are expected to be less than half as fast from 1990 to 2030 than they were from 1950 to 1990.[4] Nonetheless, future percentage increases between 1990 and 2030 remain considerable in a number of countries: 80 percent or above in Bhutan, Cambodia, Lao People's Democratic

Table 7.1: Standard World Bank Projections of Population Size of Selected Asian Countries in 2030

Country	Projected population, 2030 Absolute size (millions)	Projected population, 2030 Ratio to size in 1990[a]	Absolute increase in population size (millions) 1990–2030	Absolute increase in population size (millions) 1950–90
Bangladesh	191.1	1.74	81	68
Bhutan	3.2	2.25	2	1
Cambodia	16.4	1.90	8	4
China	1,500.6	1.32	367	579
India	1,432.2	1.69	583	492
Indonesia	274.7	1.54	96	99
Korea, DPR	34.7	1.60	13	12
Korea, Rep.	53.7	1.25	11	23
Lao PDR	10.9	2.64	7	2
Malaysia	32.0	1.80	14	12
Myanmar	76.7	1.83	34	24
Nepal	40.8	2.16	22	11
Pakistan	259.0	2.31	147	73
Papua New Guinea	7.6	1.96	4	2
Philippines	121.4	1.98	60	40
Sri Lanka	24.5	1.44	8	9
Thailand	83.3	1.48	27	36
Viet Nam	123.2	1.86	57	36
Asia[b]	4,286.1	1.56 (1.82)	1,540	1,523

a. Refer to table 2.1 for comparison with the corresponding ratio in the forty years to 1990.
b. Unweighted figures are in parentheses.
Source: Bos and others 1994 for 1990 and 2030 data under standard projections; United Nations 1991 for 1950 data.

Figure 7.1: Percentage Increase in Population Size in Selected Asian Countries, 1950–90 and 1990–2030

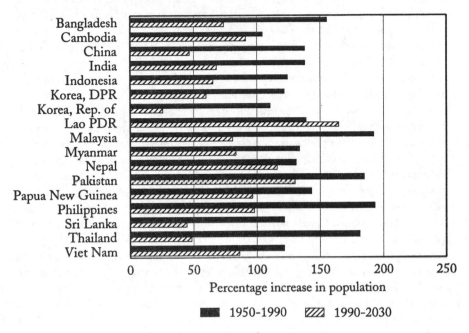

Percentage increase in population

■ 1950-1990   ▨ 1990-2030

Source: UN 1991 for 1950 data; Bos and others 1994 for 1990 and 2030 data.

Republic, Malaysia, Myanmar, Nepal, Pakistan, Papua New Guinea, the Philippines, and Viet Nam. Four countries are expected to have especially modest increases, both in relation to other countries and in relation to their own recent demographic past: the Republic of Korea, China, Sri Lanka and Thailand.

Some aspects of the World Bank projections appear, at first sight, somewhat puzzling. For example, the total fertility rate in Indonesia used in the projections for 1990–94 is 2.9, and it declines from there to replacement level fertility in 2005. In India, the total fertility rate used in the projection for 1990–94 is 3.7 and it declines to replacement level in 2010. What is the advantage gained by Indonesia, in the future, for having the lower total fertility rate and the earlier data of replacement level fertility? Not much, according to figure 7.1. Between 1990 and 2030, India's population is projected to grow 69 percent. During the same period, Indonesia's population is expected to grow by 54 percent. Over forty years, Indonesia's population growth will only be 15 percentage points lower than India's. The corresponding average rate of population growth in Indonesia during those four decades would be

1.1 percent a year, while India's would be 1.3 percent a year. The difference is a relatively small two-tenths of one percent a year.

Another puzzle in the data is the significant increase in Thailand's population even though the fertility level in the projections goes to replacement level in 1995 and stays there. The Thai population is anticipated to grow by 48 percent from 1990 to 2030, or at an average annual rate of 1.0 percent a year.

The foregoing patterns of future population growth illustrate the effect of what demographers call "population momentum." When a country experiences replacement level fertility, each generation produces exactly the number of children required to replace itself. In the long run, countries with replacement level fertility stop growing and achieve a stable population size. In the short run, populations with replacement level fertility continue to grow because of the relatively large fraction of the population in the childbearing ages. Replacing this large group requires more births than the deaths among the relatively small group of elderly people. Because births exceed deaths, the population continues to grow until the age structure reaches its stable configuration. The process through which population growth slows down and eventually stops is thus a long one, even after replacement fertility is achieved. In many Asian countries, zero population growth will not occur for more than half a century after replacement level fertility is reached.

A few hypothetical examples can help clarify how population momentum affects population growth. For simplicity, consider first two populations, A and B, of the same size in 1990. Population A, however, has a larger proportion of young people compared with population B (table 7.2). In both populations, everyone who is born lives to age 99; the sex-ratio is exactly half; and women ages 20–39 average three births each over their reproductive life span in 1990, but fertility drops to replacement level (two births each in this population) beginning in 2010. Under these assumptions, population A will increase by 36 percent by 2010, 50 percent by 2030, and 71 percent by 2050. Population B, which began with an older age structure, will increase much less—20 percent by 2010, 26 percent by 2030, 37 percent by 2050.[5]

Population momentum causes young populations to continue growing even if fertility falls immediately to replacement level. Consider, for example, population C in the table. Initially it is identical to population A except that fertility is already at replacement level in 1990. Population C will nonetheless grow by 21 percent by 2010, 36 percent by 2030, and 43 percent by 2050 (when it stabilizes at a size of 500). These examples illustrate the burden of young age structures on future population growth. It explains why fertility declines translate into slower population growth only after a long lag.

Population Momentum and Population Growth in Asia

In the early years of the next century, population momentum is likely to be the main source of population growth in Asian countries (table 7.3). Four countries in the table are expected to be at or below replacement fertility levels in 1995. Among the

Table 7.2: *Hypothetical Examples to Illustrate the Effect of Population Momentum on Population Growth*

Population	Assumptions about the total fertility rate	Age group	1990	2010	2030	2050
A	3 in 1990,	80 – 99	25	50	75	100
	dropping to	60 – 79	50	75	100	100
	2 from	40 – 59	75	100	100	150
	2010 onward	20 – 39	100	100	150	100
		0 – 19	100	150	100	150
		All groups[a]	350	475(36)	525(50)	600(71)
B	As in	80 – 99	50	65	75	80
	population A	60 – 79	65	75	80	80
		40 – 59	75	80	80	120
		20 – 39	80	80	120	80
		0 – 19	80	120	80	120
		All groups[a]	350	420(20)	435(26)	480(37)
C	2 from	80 – 99	25	50	75	100
	1990	60 – 79	50	75	100	100
	onward	40 – 59	75	100	100	100
		20 – 39	100	100	100	100
		0 – 19	100	100	100	100
		All groups[a]	350	425(21)	475(36)	500(43)

a. Figures in parentheses show percentage increases over the 1990 population.
Source: Authors' assumptions.

remaining countries, most would experience two-thirds or more of their expected population growth even if fertility fell to replacement level in 1995. Only two of the eighteen countries, Bhutan and Lao PDR, would experience less than half their expected population growth if they reach replacement level fertility in 1995. It is important not to interpret population momentum to mean that a certain amount of population growth is "inevitable." Some countries in the table, such as Sri Lanka, are quite close to replacement level fertility. It is possible that their fertility will fall below replacement level for a while and that their 2030 population could be lower than would be projected under the assumption of constant and immediate replacement level fertility.

The effects of population momentum can be clearly seen in figure 7.2. For each of the sample countries, figure 7.2 shows the projected percentage increase in population size between 1990 and 2030 under standard World Bank projections (dark bars), and the percentage increase that would occur over those four decades if

Table 7.3: Percentage of World Bank Projected Population Increase during 1990 to 2030 Due to Population Momentum, Selected Asian Countries

Country[a]	Percentage Population Increase
Bangladesh	84.4
Bhutan	39.3
Cambodia	70.7
India	79.6
Indonesia	94.9
Lao PDR	39.7
Malaysia	85.1
Myanmar	55.9
Nepal	53.7
Pakistan	58.1
Papua New Guinea	59.8
Philippines	69.4
Sri Lanka	98.3
Viet Nam	79.4
Asia[b]	76.4(69.2)

Note: The contribution of population momentum is calculated as the ratio of the percentage increase in population between 1990 and 2030 with replacement fertility in 1995, to the corresponding increase under standard World Bank projections.

a. Data for China, DPR Korea, Rep. of Korea and Thailand not shown because fertility in these countries was already at or below replacement level in 1995.

b. The averages exclude data for the four countries at or below replacement level fertility in 1995; the unweighted average is in parentheses.

Source: Bos and others 1994 for 1990 and 2030 data under standard projections; personal communication from Eduard Bos (September 23, 1994) for data on 2030 projections under the assumption that countries reach replacement level fertility in 1995. Except for the assumed date of replacement fertility, all other assumptions are identical in the two country specific projections.

replacement level fertility had been reached in 1995 and maintained at that level thereafter (light bars).

The comparisons are striking. For example, instead of growing by 74 percent from 1990 to 2030 under standard World Bank projections, the population of Bangladesh would grow by 62 percent if replacement level fertility began in 1995. In other words, of the 84 percent population growth expected in Bang-

Figure 7.2: Two Projections of Population Increase in Selected Asian Countries, 1990–2030

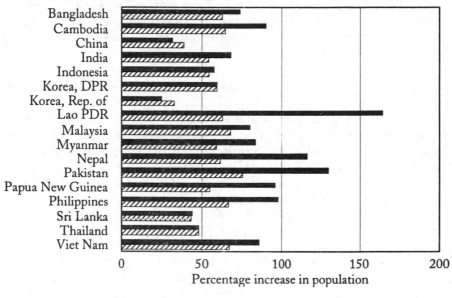

■ Standard projection ▨ Replacement fertility in 1995

Source: See table 7.3.

ladesh, 62 percent would occur even with replacement level fertility. This is the consequence of population momentum. The difference between 74 percent growth and 62 percent growth over forty years is the result of having above-replacement-level fertility. Thus, in Bangladesh, nearly 84 percent of the projected population growth between 1990 and 2030 would be due to population momentum.

Population momentum explains some of the cross-country puzzles in projected population growth noted earlier. For example, India, with a considerably higher total fertility rate than Indonesia, is projected to grow by 69 percent in the 1990–2030 period, while Indonesia is expected to grow by 54 percent. The reason that the differential in population growth is not larger is that Indonesia's population age structure embodies only slightly less population momentum than India's. With replacement level fertility from 1995 onward, Indonesia's population would grow by 51 percent from 1990 to 2030, and India's population would grow by 55 percent during that period. The effect of population momentum thus reduces the advantage that Indonesia gains from having a lower total fertility rate. Thailand, which the

World Bank projects as reaching replacement level fertility in 1995, has a population expected to grow by 48 percent from 1990 to 2030 nevertheless.

To summarize, future population growth is projected to be much slower than it was in the past in most Asian countries, although the absolute addition to the population in the 1990–2030 period is projected to be about the same as the absolute addition to the population during the 1950–90 period. With fertility falling toward replacement levels in the future, most of the population growth in Asia is projected to be due to population momentum caused by currently existing age structures.

The Assumptions behind World Bank Population Projections

World Bank population projections are based on assumptions concerning the future course of fertility, mortality, and net international migration rates.[6] Mortality projections are based on both anticipated changes in life expectancy at birth as well as the infant mortality rate, and are adjusted to take into account the effects of the AIDS epidemic.[7] International migration rates for Asian countries are, in general, assumed to be zero. A discussion of mortality and migration rate projections goes beyond the scope of this study. For the purposes here, the major assumptions utilized in the projections are forecasts of future fertility rates.[8]

Figure 7.3 shows the dates at which replacement level fertility occurs under World Bank population projections. The projections presume that China and the Republic of Korea already have below-replacement fertility in 1990. The Democratic People's Republic of Korea and Thailand are expected to achieve replacement level fertility in 1995 and maintain that level of fertility into the indefinite future. Sri Lanka is projected to reach replacement level fertility by 2000, Indonesia by 2005, Bangladesh, India, and Malaysia by 2010, and Viet Nam by 2015. Three countries are assumed to reach replacement level fertility by 2020: Cambodia, Myanmar, and the Philippines. Thus, by 2020, a little more than two decades from now, thirteen out of the eighteen sample countries are expected to experience replacement level fertility. Most of the countries expected to reach replacement level fertility after 2020 have comparatively small populations. The exception is Pakistan, whose population is expected to grow by 131 percent between 1990 and 2030.

The projections provide a modestly optimistic view of the future in the sense that lower fertility and population growth are expected. They assume that the period between now and 2015 will see a remarkable fertility decline in most Asian countries. By that time Bangladesh, China, India, and Viet Nam are all expected to have *completed* their fertility transitions and experience replacement level fertility.

To what extent will these projections materialize? Will India and Bangladesh, for example, reach replacement level fertility by 2010? Will China maintain at- or below-replacement-level fertility? These questions cannot be answered. The likelihood of reaching replacement level fertility on schedule depends crucially on myriad factors, including whether the countries will experience political stability, achieve continued economic growth, apply appropriate family planning policies

Figure 7.3: Date at which Replacement Fertility Is Reached Under World Bank Population Projections for Selected Asian Countries

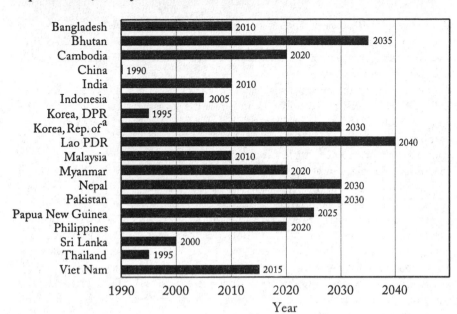

a. Fertility fell below replacement level before 1990 and is assumed to rise to that level again by 2030.
Source: Bos and others 1994.

with suitable levels of funding, and so on. To the extent that transitions to replacement fertility are slower than assumed, future population growth will be larger than the projections indicate. How much larger is the subject of next section.

Sensitivity of the Projections to Assumptions about the Replacement Fertility Date

A great deal of uncertainty is unavoidable in each population projection because the future paths of fertility, mortality, and immigration will be influenced by unforeseen factors. Projections appear to give a clear reading of the future, but our crystal ball is, in fact, quite cloudy. How murky are the projections? India, for example, is projected to have a population of 1.4 billion in 2030. How likely is it that its population in 2030 will turn out to be 1.1 billion or 1.7 billion?

Because the date at which replacement fertility is experienced can, in part, be influenced by public policy, it is useful to examine the extent to which populations projections are sensitive to assumptions about policy. For example, better-organized and better-funded family planning programs might lead to more rapidly falling fertility, while those that were less well organized or had fewer resources would lead to less rapidly falling, or stalling, fertility. One set of circumstances could bring about replacement level fertility from, say, 1995 onward, while another set might bring it about from 2000 onward, and so on. Each alternative would lead to different population sizes in the future. The sensitivity of population projections to alternative dates of reaching replacement fertility thus permits consideration of the demographic effect of different policy regimes.

The population of the eighteen Asian countries in table 7.4 was 2.7 billion in 1990. World Bank projections—which assume considerable progress in the spread of contraceptive use in the coming decades—show increases in the aggregate total to 4.3 billion in 2030, 4.7 billion in 2050, and 5.1 billion in 2075. If contraceptive prevalence rose less rapidly, resulting in, say, a twenty-year delay in the onset of replacement level fertility, how would the future sizes of Asian populations differ from those projected under the standard World Bank assumptions? The aggregate population of the eighteen countries would be 6 percent larger in 2030, 9 percent larger in 2050, and 12 percent larger in 2075, corresponding to absolute differences of 243 million over forty years, 409 million over sixty years, and 602 million over eighty-five years (table 7.4). The percentage differences are substantially larger in such countries as Nepal, Pakistan, and Papua New Guinea, where the demographic transition is still at an early stage. Initiating and sustaining fertility declines in these countries would have relatively large effects on their long-run population sizes.

If the date of attaining replacement level fertility were delayed by two decades from the date currently used in the World Bank projections, the population of Bangladesh would be about 19 percent higher than it would have been in 2075. In India it would be around 17 percent higher, and around 18 percent higher in Cambodia, Malaysia, the Philippines, and Viet Nam.

The sensitivity of population projections in the shorter run—say, the next forty years—can be illustrated with data for India, showing the effects of a wide range of alternative replacement fertility dates (figure 7.4).[9] The right-hand vertical axis in the figure shows projections of India's population in 2030 assuming that replacement fertility is experienced starting from seven alternative dates, beginning in 1995 and continuing at five-year intervals through 2025. The left-hand vertical axis shows the percentage by which the 2030 population projected under these alternative dates for replacement fertility is larger than the population India would have had if replacement level fertility began in 1995.

Assumptions about the replacement fertility date carry cost and other implications. For example, to achieve replacement level fertility in 1995, India may need to adopt policies and program activities similar to those of China, involving substantial incentives for small families and disincentives for large ones. The degree of coercion necessary would probably be impossible to sustain under India's democratic institutions, as witnessed by the backlash against Mrs. Gandhi's policies of mass sterilization camps during the Emergency Period of the 1970s. On the other hand,

Table 7.4: Comparing Population Sizes under Different Assumptions about Replacement Fertility Date

Country	Projected population under standard World Bank assumptions (millions)			Percentage increase in projected population with 20-year delay in assumed onset of replacement fertility		
	2030	2050	2075	2030	2050	2075
Bangladesh	191	218	236	11	15	19
Bhutan	3	4	5	3	10	16
Cambodia	16	19	21	10	13	18
China	1,501	1,556	1,593	0	0	0
India	1,432	1,623	1,755	9	13	17
Indonesia	275	304	324	5	7	9
Korea, DPR	35	38	39	2	3	4
Korea, Rep. of	54	54	54	0	0	0
Lao PDR	11	14	17	3	12	19
Malaysia	32	36	39	10	14	18
Myanmar	77	89	99	10	15	20
Nepal	41	50	57	9	16	23
Pakistan	259	316	361	14	22	31
Papua New Guinea	8	9	10	10	16	22
Philippines	121	143	160	9	13	18
Sri Lanka	24	27	28	3	5	6
Thailand	83	91	98	0	0	1
Viet Nam	123	142	156	10	14	18
Country average[a]	4,286	4,734	5,052	7(6)	12(9)	16(12)

a. Current fertility is below replacement level in China and the Republic of Korea. Therefore, a 20-year delay in reaching replacement fertility is irrelevant for them. Country average refers to the 16 countries, excluding China and the Republic of Korea. Figures in parentheses refer to percentage increase of the aggregate population of the 18 countries in the sample.

Source: Bos and others 1994, and personal communication from Eduard Bos, September 23, 1994.

replacement level fertility could, possibly, be achieved in 2025 through a set of far less objectionable policies.

What would be the gain, in terms of 2030 population size, of reaching replacement level fertility thirty years earlier? According to figure 7.4, India's population would be about 13 percent larger in 2030 if the onset of replacement level fertility were delayed from 1995 to 2025. Policymakers need to balance the amount of population reduction against the costs of accelerating the decline in fertility. These sorts of computations can give policymakers a feel for the orders of magnitude involved.

The foregoing simulations illustrate two important lessons about future population growth in Asia. First, as indicated earlier, a substantial amount of population growth will occur even with rapid decreases in fertility. Second, relative to the population growth which is preprogrammed because of young age structures, the amount of population reduction associated with advancing the onset of replacement level fertility is small, especially in the short run (say, the next forty years). The differences in projected population size between a faster and slower trajectory to

Figure 7.4: Effect of Alternative Replacement Fertility Dates on the Size of India's Population in 2030

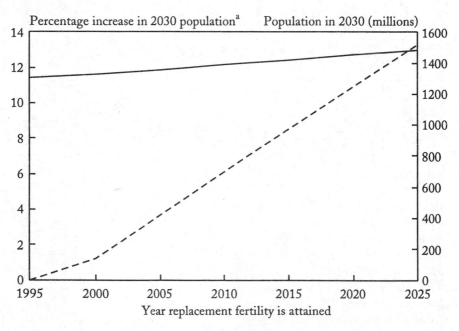

a. Increase over 2030 population with replacement fertility in 1995.
Source: Projections using Hill 1990.

replacement level fertility widen as the time horizon stretches further into the future: with a twenty-year delay in the onset of replacement fertility, the populations of the sixteen Asian countries with above replacement fertility in 1995 would, in aggregate, be 7 percent larger over forty years than projected under standard World Bank assumptions, and 16 percent larger over eighty-five years.

In assessing policies to influence the speed of fertility decline and future population size, there is thus a clear need to weigh the value of the potential reduction in population growth against the cost, pecuniary or otherwise, of those policies. Some may consider the differences presented in the above simulation large because the marginal costs of even small increases on an already large base could be substantial; if so, the marginal benefits of population control would be correspondingly large. On the other hand, accelerating the rate of fertility decline could also entail high marginal costs in that significant additional financial resources, as well as possibly increasingly coercive policies, may be needed.

The balance between costs and benefits is difficult to determine, in part because fertility declines translate into reductions in future population size mainly in the very long run. As a result, judgments about the benefits of accelerating fertility decline necessarily involve conjecture about the implications of alternative population sizes in the distant future. At the same time, the costs of bringing about a faster decline in fertility may entail not only increased financial outlays, but also possibly considerable suppression of personal freedoms and intrusion of the state into individuals' private lives. Value judgments are clearly central to a consideration of these costs. Thus, on both costs and benefits, assessments are fraught with difficulty. The demographic implications of alternative trajectories of fertility decline nonetheless offer a useful, and perhaps even an indispensable, perspective on the choices involved.

Conclusions

In the majority of Asian countries, the World Bank expects the demographic transition to be completed by 2015. Population growth rates are expected to come down quickly, and the percentage increase in population sizes is expected to be only around half as large in the 1990–2030 period as it was in 1950–90. Most of this population growth will come from population momentum. In other words, most of the expected population growth would occur even if fertility fell immediately to replacement level. If countries are on a path that would lead to replacement level fertility sometime before 2025, population sizes in 2030 are not much affected by when replacement level fertility is reached, nor even by whether or not special effort is made in the decade of the 1990s to achieve sharp drops in fertility. What matters most to future population size is having sustainable population policies that would eventually bring the country to replacement level fertility. Population policies have their most significant effects on population sizes in the long run. Therefore, policies that will have a

Notes

1. See Sanderson (1994).

2. These projections are from Bos and others (1994).

3. Replacement level fertility occurs when adults have just the right number of children to replace their generation with a new one of exactly the same size; it corresponds to a total fertility rate of about 2.1 births per woman.

4. The exceptions are Bhutan and Lao People's Democratic Republic. In Bhutan, the population grew by 95 percent during 1950–90 and is projected to grow by 125 percent during 1990–2030. In Lao PDR, the corresponding increases are 136 percent and 164 percent.

5. In this example, population A begins cycling between two sizes (600 and 650) at twenty-year intervals starting in 2050. Similarly, population B also cycles, but between two smaller sizes (480 and 520).

6. For a complete documentation of the World Bank's projection methodology, see Bos and Bulatao (1990), Bulatao and others (1989c), Bulatao and Bos (1992), and Bos and others (1994).

7. Life expectancies by sex are projected forward in time based on logit regressions using the rate of change in life expectancy as the dependent variable and the lagged rate of change and either the percent urban or the female secondary school enrollment rate as independent variables. The results are checked for plausibility, and if they are acceptable they are used for fifteen years. After that time, standard rates of change—based on historical observations—are used. Rates of change in infant mortality rates are projected on the basis of past rates of change in the country and historical observations. After fifteen years, standard rates of decline are used. Various procedures are applied to unify the infant mortality rates and life expectancies into consistent age patterns of mortality. The actual methods used to project mortality are more complex and involve a considerable amount of internal consistency checking. For more details see Bulatao and others (1989c).

8. World Bank population projections assume three phases of fertility change: (a) pretransition, (b) transition, and (c) post-transition. The fertility transition is the period during which fertility shows a sustained decline from a previously high and stable level to a new low and stable level. Combining these phases with data on sterility and life expectancy, nine patterns of fertility change are distinguished. Four concern the movement from phase (a) to phase (b); three concern the movement from phase (b) to phase (c); and two refer to the situation of countries in phase (c) that are at or below replacement level fertility.

The first pattern is pretransition with high sterility (above 6 percent) and low life expectancy (below 50). Here fertility rises as sterility falls. The second pattern is pretransition with low sterility (below 6 percent) and low life expectancy. In this situation, fertility is assumed to remain constant. The fertility transition is assumed to begin when the country's life expectancy reaches 50 years. For a country just beginning its transition, the total fertility rate is assumed to fall by 0.3 births in the first five years of the transition, and by 0.6 births in subsequent five-year periods, until the total fertility rate reaches 3.15. Where the transition begins under circumstances of high sterility, the third pattern, the decline in fertility is adjusted for changes in sterility. Where it begins under circumstances of low sterility, the fourth pattern, no adjustment for sterility change is made.

For countries undergoing the fertility transition but with total fertility rates above 3.15 births per woman, the decline of the total fertility rate in each five-year period is based on the change in the total fertility rate over the previous five-year period. Again, two patterns are differentiated, one with high and one with low sterility. The seventh pattern represents the ending phase of the transition. Roughly speaking, once the total fertility rate falls to 3.15, it begins a fifteen-year period where it follows a geometrically declining path to replacement level. For some countries where the approach to 3.15 level has been slow, a twenty-year period is allowed. After replacement level fertility is achieved—that is, after the country enters its post-transition stage—fertility is assumed to remain at that level.

The last two patterns concern fertility at or below replacement. If a country has below-replacement-level fertility in 1990, it is assumed that fertility will remain constant for fifteen years and then rise gradually until replacement level fertility is achieved in 2030. The only country in the sample which already had below-replacement fertility in 1990 is the Republic of Korea. In the case of a rapid fall in fertility immediately before the projection period, the total fertility rate is allowed to fall below replacement for one five-year period, and then stay constant for another period before gradually returning to replacement level.

To elaborate further on the projection methodology, for a given total fertility rate for a five-year period, age-specific fertility rates are determined using two basic schedules, one defined for total fertility rates of 6 births per woman and above, and the other defined for total fertility rates of 3 births per woman or below. When the total fertility rate is between 3 and 6, an interpolated schedule is used. The schedule for total fertility rates of 6 births per women and above implies a mean age at childbearing of 28.9 years, and the schedule for total fertility rates of 3 and below implies a mean age at childbearing of 28.0. This range is considerably smaller than that documented in chapter 3.

9. While the simulations are performed only on Indian data, the lessons that emerge would be virtually the same for all the other Asian countries in the sample.

8

Coping with Population Growth and Change

OVER THE NEXT FORTY YEARS, the current young age structures of Asian populations imply continued population growth in virtually all countries in the region, including those that have already reached low levels of fertility. In most settings, future increases in population will be smaller than they have been in the past forty years. Nonetheless, they remain large in absolute terms, and will often be accompanied by substantial shifts in age structure as well as geographic distribution. This chapter considers the implications of these changes for the environment, education and health services, employment, and urban development.[1]

Population and the Environment

Like every other part of the world, Asia has environmental problems which deserve serious attention.[2] According to the Asian Development Bank (1991), for example, 15 percent of the land area of Sri Lanka is affected by salinization; in India, that figure is 27 percent, and in Pakistan it is 24 percent. Salinization is produced, in part, by poor irrigation techniques. As the land becomes more saline crop yields decline and eventually, the population can no longer be supported. Desertification produces the same sort of results. Overgrazing and other inappropriate land management practices can cause severe soil erosion which, in time, results in desertification and makes the land unable to support its population. The Asian Development Bank estimates, for example, that 27 percent of Indian land is affected by severe soil erosion. Environmental problems like these can certainly get worse, but with faster population growth, they may get worse more rapidly.

Future income growth is likely to exacerbate the environmental problem. China, for example, had a per capita income of around US$350 in 1989, and its economy was growing very fast. During 1980–89, its per capita income grew by about 8.3 percent a year. Even if the rate of growth slows to, say, 7 percent a year, China's per capita income would increase 15-fold by 2030. At that time its per capita income in 1989 U.S. dollars would be $5,240—higher than the $4,400 per capita income of the Republic of Korea in 1989, and smaller than the $5,350 per capita income of Greece in that year. Currently, China adds 0.35 tons of carbon per capita to the atmosphere per year.[3] A 15-fold increase in per capita income is likely to have a substantial impact on the amount of carbon added to the atmosphere per year, even without any population increase. With population growth, the problem could certainly get worse.

The connection between population growth, development, and the environment is complex, and is treated in detail in the World Bank's *World Development Report 1992.* What we can add here is a highly simplified example that gives a sense of the quantitative importance of changing rates of population growth as a tool for solving certain sorts of environment problems, such as the emissions of greenhouse gases. For many other environmental problems, such as deforestation and the salinization of farmland, the analysis below is not relevant.

Focusing on air quality as the environmental good of interest, consider for a moment an Asian country with a policy of maintaining the emission level of some pollutant at its 1990 level. If the amount of pollutant produced per unit of income remained constant, the rate of growth of emissions would equal the rate of growth of income. In this situation, we can distinguish between two types of policies: (a) policies to reduce the amount of pollution per unit of income, and (b) policies designed to reduce the growth of income. Since few people would advocate reducing the rate of growth of per capita income on environmental grounds, reducing the growth rate of income implies reducing the rate of population growth. In other words, we can think about two different types of policies to maintain a constant level of pollution: a technological policy that reduces the emissions per unit of output, and a population policy that reduces the growth of income (but not per capita income) through reducing the growth of population.[4]

Although this approach is highly simplified, it allows us to take a first step toward disentangling the effects of population growth, income growth, and technical change on pollution. The question we ask is: To what extent can population policy contribute to the goal of stabilizing 2030 emissions levels at their 1990 levels. We first answer this question using data for the Philippines; we then apply the same computational procedure to data for other Asian countries. According to World Bank projections, the Philippine population is expected to grow by 97.5 percent between 1990 and 2030—from 61 million to 121 million—on the assumption that replacement fertility is experienced from 2020 onward. If the average annual rate of growth of per capita income were 5 percent a year, per capita income in 2030 would increase by 604 percent over the period 1990–2030. If pollution per unit of income remains unchanged, the combination of population increase and per capita income growth would produce a level of pollution in 2030 that is 13.9 times the level in 1990—an increase of 1,290 percent over forty years.

If public policy were to maintain the 1990 level of pollution, a 93 percent reduction in the projected pollution in 2030 would be required. This reduction could be achieved by reducing population growth as well as by changing the amount of pollution per unit of income. If fertility fell to replacement level from 1995 onward, the population of the Philippines in 2030 would be 103 million— 68 percent larger than the 61 million in 1990, or 15 percent smaller than the 121 million projected under the assumption that replacement fertility is reached from 2020 onward. With per capita income growth of 5 percent a year, and unchanged pollution per unit of income, the level of pollution in 2030 would be 11.9 times the level in 1990—15 percent less than the level under standard World Bank population projections. Achieving replacement fertility from 1995 onward thus helps to mitigate the increase in pollution, but pollution would still be 1,090 percent greater in 2030 than in 1990. Under the replacement-fertility-in-1995 scenario, pollution in 2030 would need to drop by 92 percent to stay at the 1990 level.

The calculations show that when per capita income is growing at 5 percent a year, population policies and changes in pollution control technology contribute as follows to containing pollution in 2030 at the 1990 level: fertility falls by 15 percent (the replacement fertility effect) and the amount of emissions per unit output is reduced by 90 percent. The contribution of population policies to reducing pollution levels in 2030 would thus be 14 percent, while that of pollution control technology would be 86 percent.[5] Calculations for assumed per capita income growth at 3 percent a year and 7 percent a year were made and the results are comparable in magnitude.

Similar computations were performed for other Asian countries (table 8.1), also assuming a 5 percent a year growth in per capita income. The results show that the Philippine example was fairly typical of Asian countries. In only four out of eighteen countries in the table would immediate replacement level fertility contribute more than 20 percent of the change required to keep pollution in 2030 at the levels in 1990. The highest contribution of immediate replacement level fertility arises in Lao People's Democratic Republic, where it is 29 percent.

The foregoing needs to be qualified in three important ways. First, it assumes that there was no connection between population growth and the rate of per capita income growth. The figures above do not tell us what would actually happen in any particular country. Changes in population policy would affect population size, the rate of per capita income growth, and possibly the path of technological change, as different baskets of goods were produced. The framework allows us to do a simple sort of arithmetic decomposition; it has no predictive power.

Second, the reduction in population growth assumed by maintaining fertility at replacement level from 1995 through 2030 may be more than can be achieved by any change in population policies. The Philippines, for example, did not achieve replacement level fertility in 1995 and it is unlikely to achieve the 68 percent increase by having a period of above-replacement fertility followed by a period of below-replacement fertility. If the best that any population policy could achieve is population growth above 68 percent, then slower population growth could contribute even less than 14 percent to maintaining the 1990 level of pollution. On the other hand, the projected 98 percent increase in the Philippine population assumes a very considerable increase in the use of contraception in the next two decades. If policies were not in place to help service that demand, the increase in population could be considerably larger, perhaps 120 percent, or even more, over forty years. In that case, a strong family planning program could have a larger impact.

Third, many types of environmental degradation clearly do not fit into this framework. This is especially true where the environmental problem is not closely related to increases in income, as is the case, for example, with deforestation in the

Table 8.1: Percentage Contribution of Replacement Level Fertility and Technical Change to the Maintenance of the 1990 Level of Pollution in 2030

Country[a]	Contribution of replacement level fertility	Contribution of changes in emissions levels
Bangladesh	7	93
Bhutan	27	73
Cambodia	13	87
India	8	92
Indonesia	2	98
Lao PDR	29	71
Malaysia	7	93
Myanmar	18	82
Nepal	21	79
Pakistan	21	79
Papua New Guinea	18	82
Philippines	14	86
Sri Lanka	1	99
Viet Nam	9	91

a. Data for China, DPR of Korea, Rep. of Korea and Thailand are not shown in this table because fertility in these countries is currently already at or below replacement level.

Source: Author's computations based on data on populations in 1990 and projected populations in 2030 from Bos and others 1994; and populations assuming replacement level fertility in 1995 from Bos, private communication, 1994.

Himalaya Mountains or erosion due to increased hillside farming in the Philippines.

Asia has significant environmental problems, some caused in part by rapid population growth. Some of those problems would be relieved if population densities were reduced. Because population policies are slow-acting, however, and have their biggest effects on population size in the long run,[6] they do not, in themselves, offer the total, nor indeed the main, answer to environmental problems that require attention in the short or medium term. Such problems require energetic interventions of other sorts.

Education Sector Implications

Asian countries' achievements in education over the last few decades have been impressive. Despite the burden of growing school-age populations, countries have, without exception, raised the proportion enrolled in school and increased the stock, if not the quality, of human capital. In the 1980s, the proportion of literate adults in Asian countries averaged 60 percent, and enrollment ratios averaged 88 percent in primary education, 35 percent in secondary education, and 9 percent in higher education. These aggregate indicators are comparable to the average for developing countries. Asia is unique, however, in achieving these results at relatively modest levels of public spending on education: 3.3 percent of GNP on average (or 12.3 percent of aggregate public spending), compared to an average of 4 percent in developing countries (table 8.2).

Progress in education has nonetheless been uneven across countries in the region. Korea, for example, is at one end of the spectrum, with widespread coverage of the system at all levels, a rational allocation of public spending favoring basic education, and a well-developed and well-diversified system of higher education. At the weaker end of the spectrum are such countries as Bhutan, India, Nepal, Pakistan, and Papua New Guinea, where education development has been, and continues to be, hindered by inadequate resources, poor allocations, unsustainable patterns of student finance, or a combination of those factors. Some of these countries face the added challenge of making progress in the context of relatively grim demographic prospects.

Population pressures on education systems can be appreciated by relating the size of the school-age population (aged 5–14) to that of the population of working adults (aged 15–59), that is, the school dependency ratio (table 8.3). The larger this ratio, the heavier the education sector's fiscal burden on taxpayers and therefore the tighter the constraints on future education development. For example, if Korea had Lao PDR's dependency ratio in 1990, the tax contribution of each Korean adult would need to rise by 85 percent to finance current levels of coverage in Korea's education system, assuming that all else in the system is unchanged. In countries that started the transition to lower fertility early—including China, Republic of Korea, Sri Lanka, and Thailand—dependency ratios were already relatively small by 1990 and are projected to drop still lower. Most other countries in the region had relatively large school dependency ratios in 1990 owing to high and only recently declining fertility. Except for Lao PDR and Cambodia, dependency ratios in these countries are projected to remain stable or to decline, sometimes quite substantially, as in Bangladesh and Indonesia. Where the projected declines materialize, the fiscal constraints on education can be expected to ease.

Demographic trends also affect the size of future school-age populations. At this writing, the World Bank's most recent projections in 1994-95 show changes in this population between 1990 and 2005 ranging from -10 percent (Republic of Korea) to 43 percent (Cambodia). Thus, over the next decade, some countries in the region would experience sizable shrinkage of the school-age population whereas others would have substantially larger school-age populations. These changes reflect the

Table 8.2: Selected Education Indicators in Asian Countries, Mid-1980s

Country	Percentage adults literate	Gross enrollment ratio (percentage)			Public spending on education	
		Primary	Secondary	Higher[a]	Percentage of budget	Percentage of GNP
Bangladesh	33	60	18	5.2	10.3	1.5
Bhutan	15	25	4	0.1	7.3	3.8
China	69	118	39	1.7	7.8	3.3
India	43	92	41	9.0	13.7	3.0
Indonesia	74	118	42	6.5	15.0	3.7
Korea, Rep. of	92	96	75	31.6	16.6	3.4
Lao, PDR	84	94	19	1.5	–	–
Malaysia	74	99	53	6.0 (9.0)	16.0	6.0
Myanmar	–	107	23	5.4	10.9	1.8
Nepal	26	82	25	4.6	9.6	1.8
Pakistan	26	50	15	4.0	7.4	2.2
Papua New Guinea	45	70	13	2.0	17.9	6.9
Philippines	86	106	65	38.0	11.5	1.8
Sri Lanka	87	103	63	4.6 (5.1)	8.1	2.8
Thailand	91	97	30	19.6 (11.9)	19.4	3.6
Country average	60	88	35	9.3	12.3	3.3

a. For Malaysia and Sri Lanka, the data in parentheses refer to the enrollment ratio if nationals studying abroad are included in the numerator; for Thailand, the figure in parentheses refers to the enrollment ratio adjusted for substantial dropout rates and extended duration of study in the open and distance universities.

Source: Tan and Mingat 1992 for all countries except Pakistan; the sources for Pakistan are World Bank, Pakistan–1988, 1989, 1991a, and 1991b. The source for data on Thailand's adjusted higher education enrollment is World Bank (Thailand–1990).

Table 8.3: *School-Age Population and Dependency Ratios in Selected Asian Countries*

Country	Dependency ratio[a]			Population aged 5–14 in 1990 (thousands)	Projected increase 1990–2005 (percentage)	Annual rate of growth 1990–2005 (percentage a year)
	1970	1990	2005			
Bangladesh	56	53	36	30,594	2.9	0.2
Bhutan	45	46	43	356	34.6	2.0
Cambodia	50	44	43	2,073	43.6	2.4
China	45	26	24	187,398	9.4	0.6
India	46	40	35	195,287	17.4	1.1
Indonesia	49	44	30	44,265	-5.4	-0.4
Korea, Rep. of	54	27	20	7,659	-10.1	-0.7
Lao, PDR	48	50	54	1,043	65.7	3.4
Malaysia	57	42	34	4,183	19.9	1.2
Myanmar	48	42	40	9,834	34.9	2.0
Nepal	46	52	48	5,030	42.0	2.3
Pakistan	57	52	46	29,731	43.3	2.4
Papua New Guinea	48	46	44	986	35.7	2.0
Philippines	57	45	39	15,452	28.4	1.7
Sri Lanka	50	37	26	3,705	-8.7	-0.6
Thailand	57	37	20	12,686	-8.8	-0.6
Viet Nam	56	40	37	16,355	21.8	1.3
Country average	51		43	36	-21.6	1.2

a. Defined as size of the population ages 5–14 as a percentage of the size of the population ages 15–59.
Source: Bos and others 1994 for population data for 1990 and 2005; United Nations 1991b for population data for 1970.

effect of the size of the cohort of women in reproductive ages and are sensitive to assumptions in the projections regarding the pace of future fertility and mortality declines. In Bangladesh, for example, the surprisingly small increase in the school-age population—only 3 percent between 1990 and 2005—owes much to the assumption that fertility will fall to replacement level by 2010. In China, the projected increase of 9 percent between 1990 and 2005 contrasts sharply with the projected decrease of 16 percent between 2005 and 2015. The wide shift over relatively short periods reflects the large swings in the cohort sizes of reproductive age women.[7] China's situation is typical of countries (such as Cambodia) with disrupted demographic histories.

Very large shifts in school-age population size over relatively short periods introduce significant difficulties for education planning. Because attrition rates are relatively modest among teachers, these large shifts in the school-age population may cause large shifts in pupil-teacher ratios, and by implication, swings in schooling conditions that affect unit costs, efficiency, and student learning. Finding ways to ameliorate the adverse effects of these swings—including, for example, investments in appropriate in-service training for teachers—thus deserves the serious attention of policymakers. School buildings are another durable school input. Where large swings in the school-age populations are expected, investments in school facilities require especially careful scrutiny to avoid waste while accommodating expanding and then contracting school populations over the usable lifetime—say, twenty years or more—of such investments. Perhaps more so in China and Cambodia than in other countries, agility on the part of policymakers and flexibility in the education system are essential to accommodate the population swings.

In all countries, projections of the future size of school-age populations offer, at best, only a rough guide for planning education services. Uncertainty is greater at the primary than at the secondary level, because the pool of potential entrants to secondary education is limited to those currently in primary education and the size of this population is known; furthermore, coverage in secondary education is, to a large extent, a matter of policy choice. In primary education, most countries view universal coverage as a basic public policy objective, so demographic variables become central in planning investments at this level.

Table 8.4 shows projections of the target population across countries in Asia and some basic education indicators. Two World Bank projections—one done in 1991–92 and the other in 1994–95—illustrate the volatility of the projections, even over relatively short periods. The more recent projection takes into account new information since the previous projection about underlying fertility and mortality trends, including the impact of AIDS. For most countries, the two projections for the primary-school-age population between 1990 and 2000 are comparable. There are exceptions, however. In the Philippines, for example, the earlier projection shows an expected *decrease* of 2.3 percent, compared to a *increase* of 17.4 percent under the more recent one. Large gaps also exist for Cambodia, China, India, Indonesia, Nepal, and Sri Lanka. The volatility of the projections does not necessarily undermine their usefulness for education planning, but it does underscore the need for

Table 8.4: *Primary–School-Age Population (5–9) and Primary Education Indicators in Selected Asian Countries*

Country	Size in 1990 (thousands)	Primary-school-age population Projected increase 1990–2000 (percentage)[a]		Percentage of population entering grade 1, 1980s	Percentage of grade 1 entrants completing cycle, 1980s	Pupils per teacher, 1985
		A	B			
Bangladesh	16,119	-2.6	-2.6	100	24	47
Bhutan	190	35.9	26.8	54	17	39
Cambodia	1,187	12.8	25.4	-	-	-
China	91,619	30.9	15.7	90	68	25
India	103,402	5.8	11.5	83	37	58
Indonesia	22,950	2.0	-8.4	100	60	25
Korea, Rep. of	3,696	-8.1	-7.3	100	97	38
Lao PDR	571	53.4	42.6	100	40	25
Malaysia	2,367	13.9	8.2	100	97	24
Myanmar	5,111	20.1	26.2	-	-	46
Nepal	2,856	22.6	13.7	75	33	36
Pakistan	16,026	28.7	29.5	75	40	-
Papua New Guinea	520	30.4	22.1	75	67	31
Philippines	8,288	-2.3	17.4	100	66	31
Sri Lanka	1,926	-17.5	-9.1	100	85	32
Thailand	6,418	-8.0	-12.0	100	80	19
Viet Nam	8,712	14.3	13.5	-	-	-
Country average	-	13.7	12.5	74	48	28

a. A refers to the increase according to projections made in 1992–93; B refers to projections made in 1994–95.

Source: Data on the size of and projected increase in the population ages 5–9 are from Bulatao and others 1989a, 1989b; Bos, Vu, and Levin 1992 and Bos and others 1994; data on primary education indicators are from Tan and Mingat 1992.

close and continuous monitoring of demographic developments as a check against assumptions in the projections, particularly where underlying conditions are known to be changing rapidly.

Beyond issues of space planning, what do the projections of the primary school-age population imply for education development? In some Asian countries first-grade enrollment is currently still not universal; countries in this group that also expect increases in projected primary-school-age populations—including Bhutan, Cambodia, Lao PDR,[8] Nepal, Pakistan, Papua New Guinea—would face a demanding challenge in reaching universal coverage. In all likelihood, expanded investments in school facilities and teacher training would be needed. In countries where nearly all children enter grade one and where the school-age population is not expected to grow significantly—including, for example, Bangladesh—there is now clearly an opportunity to shift the focus of education planning away from expanding physical facilities toward strengthening schools' ability to retain pupils to the end of the cycle. Such a shift is important because school continuation rates are still poor. More allocations for primary education may be needed—particularly in countries (such as India) where current spending levels are relatively modest—but better allocations among school inputs are important too.

A third group of countries in Asia—notably the Republic of Korea, Sri Lanka, and Thailand—faces the possibly enviable prospect of shrinking primary-school-age populations. The projected decline implies future potential savings in the subsector that could be used to upgrade education quality. Experience nonetheless suggests that these savings do not materialize automatically, but may in fact be lost because of rigidities in the education system. In Thailand, for example, the primary-school-age population has been contracting, but because schools with sharply declining enrollments continue to operate without the benefit of multigrade teaching, and teachers colleges continue to produce new graduates for teaching jobs, the ratio of pupils to teachers has dropped steadily, from 35 in 1970 to only 20 in 1987. This drop has, in effect, absorbed most of the potential savings associated with a shrinking school-age population, leaving little scope for other, possibly more effective arrangements to improve school quality. Because the demographic context has altered so drastically in Thailand, new approaches to primary-school development may need to be considered now, particularly regarding teacher training and teaching methods in schools. Thailand's example illustrates the more general point that in countries facing the prospect of declining school-age populations, the challenge of adjusting education services to the new demographic conditions can also be quite demanding.

To summarize, because demographic trends have important implications for education development but are hard to predict, regular and close tracking of fertility trends—especially where systems of birth registration are weak—is essential for planning investments and services, notably at the lower levels of education. Differences exist across countries in the implications of their demographic prospects for education. In countries with large projected increases in school-age populations and still inadequate coverage, continued focus on mobilizing the resources to expand facilities and teacher training appears, in most instances, to be appropriate. In other countries where population pressure is projected to ease, there remains much scope for improving education outcomes; increased spending may sometimes be needed, but better allocation of existing spending is often just as important. At least two countries—China and Cambodia—face sharp swings in the size of the school-age population owing to disrupted demographic histories. Planning education services becomes even more demanding there, requiring a high degree of flexibility in the use of school resources—particularly physical facilities and teacher inputs.

Health Sector Implications

The age structure of a country's population, coupled with age-specific cause-of-death patterns, is a major determinant of its mortality profile. Overall demographic trends in Asia point to lower crude death rates in the next two decades, as cohort sizes expand rapidly in the lower-mortality age groups (15–64) (table 8.5). Cohorts aged 65 years or more are also expected to expand rapidly, but they start out from tiny bases in 1990. Except in China and the Republic of Korea, which are furthest along in the demographic transition, at least 75 percent of the population in 2010 in most Asian countries will still be under 45 years of age (figure 8.1).

This salutary prospect nonetheless implies changing, rather than lessened, demands on health services. In most Asian countries, scope remains for improvements in life expectancy, smaller incidence of infant and child mortality, and lower fertility (table 8.6). But there is concern that the demographic transition might produce a polarization in health problems, as the incidence of chronic diseases rise as the population at older ages increases, even as large segments of the population, mainly in rural areas, remain exposed to and die from communicable diseases. Health-financing issues, particularly as regards allocation of public resources and private responsibility for health care, are therefore likely to become increasingly prominent as public policy issues.

Fortuitously, the prospect of polarization is, in most Asian countries, on the horizon rather than close at hand because the elderly population is increasing from a tiny base, and will, for at least the next two decades, still comprise a small share of the total population. Sooner or later, however, all countries can expect to face the challenge of developing institutions to ensure that the chronic health needs of the aged are addressed in a cost-effective manner without imposing heavy tradeoffs in public budgets against other basic health services. China and the Republic of Korea (with Sri Lanka and Malaysia not far behind) have already begun to lead the way, choosing to increase health spending while at the same time developing and expanding health insurance mechanisms to spread the risks of costly chronic care services (Griffin 1992). The other Asian countries in the sample still have time to develop and test alternative health-financing mechanisms, but the task of laying the groundwork for such mechanisms to deliver equitable and efficient health services remains inescapable as their demographic transitions proceed.

The more immediate challenges contained in Asia's demographic future concern health services for children and women—groups with clearly identifiable health

Table 8.5: Percentage Change in Size of Each Age Cohort in Selected Asian Countries, 1990–2010

| Country | Age group (years) | | | | All age groups |
	0–14	15–44	45–64	65+	
Bangladesh	0	103	79	65	34
Bhutan	59	56	55	73	59
Cambodia	25	68	110	74	46
China	-6	42	70	58	28
India	11	60	64	77	36
Indonesia	-4	63	68	82	28
Korea, Rep. of	-9	26	79	122	29
Lao PDR	68	63	69	83	68
Malaysia	4	57	112	105	36
Myanmar	25	78	57	67	45
Nepal	39	63	68	92	50
Pakistan	39	94	102	95	60
Papua New Guinea	35	72	61	114	50
Philippines	27	65	117	98	50
Sri Lanka	-8	32	95	69	25
Thailand	-1	62	91	90	35
Viet Nam	17	97	67	44	44
Country average	19	65	80	83	42

Source: Bos and others 1994.

needs. During the decade of the 1980s, the population of children below age five in Asia increased, on average, by about 30 percent, but in the 1990s, the increase is projected at only 8 percent, and in the 2000s, by only 1 percent (table 8.7). In purely quantitative terms, growth in the demand for basic health services for young children, particularly immunizations,[9] can be expected to slow in the next two decades relative to the 1980s. In addition to the prospect of lighter demand, the fact that immunization rates all across Asia rose sharply during the last decade, in the face

Figure 8.1: Age Distribution of Populations in Selected Asian Countries, 1990 and 2010

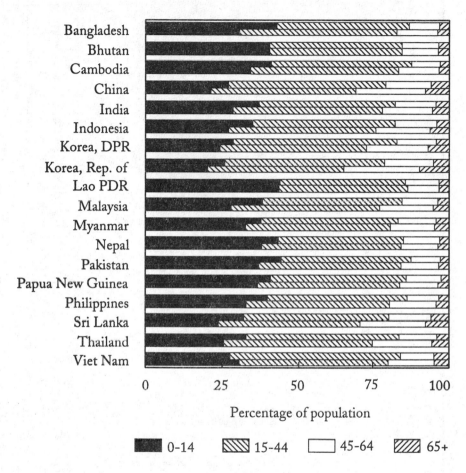

Percentage of population

◼ 0-14   ▧ 15-44   ☐ 45-64   ▨ 65+

For each country, the top bar refers to 1990; the bottom bar, to 2010.
Source: Based on data in Bos and others, 1994.

of very large increases in the target population, suggests that further gains in coverage should be within reach for most countries in the sample.

Demographic change nonetheless suggests shifts in the nature of health services demanded for the young. The typical negative association between infant mortality and total fertility rates—shown using data for Asian countries in figure 8.2—reflects the combined effects of factors relating to the supply of and demand for health care. On the supply side, health interventions, including immunization services, reduce

Table 8.6: *Health and Fertility Indicators in Selected Asian Countries, Selected Years*

Country	Life expectancy at birth, 1989 (years)		Infant mortality rate, 1989 (per 1,000 births)	Child mortality rate, 1990 (per 1,000)	Total fertility rate, 1989[b] (births per woman)	Expenditure on health services, 1986–1987	
	F	M				Total (percentage of GNP)	Public share of total (percentage)
Bangladesh	51	52	106	47	4.2	1.7	41
Bhutan	48	49	125	59	5.5	2.0	60
Cambodia[a]	52	49	119	56	4.7	–	–
China	71	69	30	6	2.0	4.0	20
India	59	58	95	27	3.6	4.3	37
Indonesia	63	60	64	23	3.0	2.4	38
Korea, Rep. of	73	67	23	5	1.5	5.1	12
Lao PDR	51	48	105	67	6.7	–	–
Malaysia	72	68	22	4	3.5	3.5	77
Myanmar	63	59	66	24	3.9	3.2	34
Nepal	51	52	124	58	6.0	1.4	57
Pakistan	55	55	106	32	6.6	2.5	44
Papua New Guinea	55	54	59	20	5.1	3.8	89
Philippines	66	62	42	11	4.1	2.4	25
Sri Lanka	73	69	20	4	2.8	2.3	57
Thailand	68	64	28	6	2.1	3.8	29
Viet Nam	69	64	43	11	4.7	–	–
Country average	61	59	69	27	4.1	2.5	36

a. Data for Cambodia on life expectancy and infant mortality refer to 1990.

b. Data refer to latest available year for the following countries: Bangladesh, 1990; China, 1993; India, 1991; Indonesia, 1988–91; Rep. of Korea, 1985; Malaysia, 1987; Nepal, 1982–86; Philippines, 1990–92; Sri Lanka, 1983–87; Thailand, 1986; and Viet Nam, 1986.

Source: World Bank 1991d for data on life expectancy, infant (ages 0–1) mortality, and total fertility rate for Bhutan, Cambodia, Lao PDR, Myanmar, Pakistan and Papua New Guinea; same source as table 3.2 for total fertility for the remaining countries; World Bank 1991d for data on child (ages 1–4) mortality rate and all data for Cambodia; Griffin 1992 for data on expenditure except Pakistan, for which the source is World Bank, (Pakistan–1992).

mortality among children, thereby reducing the number of births needed to achieve desired numbers of living children. Working on the demand side, parents who choose fewer births are also more likely to invest in better health care for their children, resulting in lower mortality among children that are born. Declining fertility trends in Asia thus imply increasing focus on the sorts of health services for young children for which intermittent delivery modes may be less appropriate or effective. Evolution toward individualized care—including prenatal and postnatal care for mothers as well as services directed specifically toward children—is probably more the pattern of the future.

Women of childbearing age (15–49) are another population group for which the demographic transition holds specific implications. The size of this population is projected to grow slightly more slowly between 2000 and 2010 than in the previous two decades (table 8.8),[10] reflecting the effect of fertility declines associated with increased contraceptive use. In the mid- to late-1980s, contraceptive prevalence averaged 43 percent in Asia. If prevalence rates rose toward the levels characterizing a fully contracepting population (around 70 to 75 percent), substantial increases in the demand for contraceptive services can be expected,[11] raising issues about burden-sharing in the financing of those services, as discussed elsewhere in this study. A benefit of rising contraceptive prevalence and lower fertility is to

Figure 8.2: Relation between Total Fertility Rates and Infant Mortality Rates, Asia, 1989

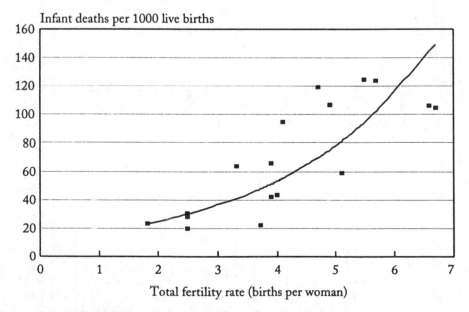

Infant deaths per 1000 live births

Total fertility rate (births per woman)

Source: World Bank 1991c.

Table 8.7: Cobort Size of Population Ages 0–4 and Percentage of One-Year-Olds Immunized, Selected Asian Countries

Country	Population ages 0–4 1980 (thousands)	Percentage increase in population cohort ages 0–4[a]			One-year-olds immunized with full DPT cycle (percentage)	
		1980 –1990	1990 –2000	2000 –2010	1981	1988–89
Bangladesh	16,211	2	-2	-6	1	49
Bhutan	193	17	29	16	13	70
Cambodia	359	299	9	-6	–	22
China	98,468	20	-16	-4	–	95
India	96,705	14	5	-4	31	83
Indonesia	22,374	-7	2	-2	–	75
Korea, Rep. of	6,222	-46	4	-7	61	86
Lao PDR	532	49	22	20	7	21
Malaysia	1,868	39	-5	-9	54	72
Myanmar	4,800	25	16	-6	5	50
Nepal	2,422	32	15	11	16	67
Pakistan	14,476	38	12	8	3	73
Papua New Guinea	484	20	22	1	50	53
Philippines	7,701	16	14	2	51	79
Sri Lanka	1,854	-6	-5	3	45	89
Thailand	6,344	-6	0	5	52	84
Viet Nam	8,394	9	10	-4	–	68
Country average	–	30	8	1	30	67

a. Based on projected population for 1990, 2000, and 2010.
Source: Population data are from Bos and others 1994; immunization data are from United Nations Children's Fund (UNICEF) 1991.

decrease the risks of maternal mortality, as figure 8.3 suggests. Correspondingly, women's health issues can be expected to shift away from problems related to childbearing to those of a more general nature.

Population and Employment

Shifts in the size and age composition of the working-age population affect the pool of potential labor supply, leading to concerns about labor market prospects. In most countries in Asia, past fertility trends imply a slowdown in the growth of that population (table 8.9). Whereas the working-age population increased, on average, by 30 percent between 1970 and 1980, the increase was 27 percent between 1980 and 1990, and is projected at 26 percent between 1990 and 2000, and 24 percent between 2000 and 2010. In purely quantitative terms, these trends suggest a possible modest easing of pressures on employment creation in Asian countries in the coming decades—compared to experiences in the 1970s and 1980s—with a corresponding shift toward concern about potential labor shortages.

Figure 8.3: Relation between Total Fertility Rates and the Ratio of Female to Male Expected Number of Years Lived between Ages 15 and 50

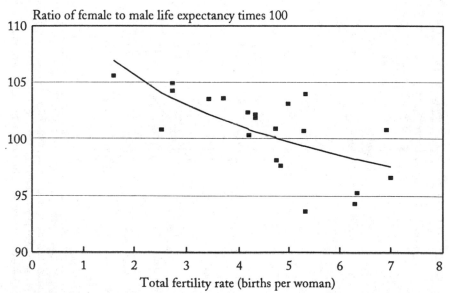

Note: If no deaths occur between ages 15 and 50, males and females would live 35 years in that age interval and the ratio of female to male life expentancy would be 100. Where the ratio exceeds 100, females live more years in that age interval, on average, than males; where it is below 100, males live more years than females.
Source: See table A.8.1 in appendix C.

Table 8.8: *Percentage Increase in Number of Women Ages 15–49 and Contraceptive Prevalence Rates in Selected Asian Countries*

Country	No. of women ages 15–49, 1980 (thousands)	Percentage increase in female cohort ages 15–49[a]			Contraceptive prevalence rate[b] (Percentage)	Year
		1980–1990	1990–2000	2000–2010		
Bangladesh	18,720	35	36	24	30.8	1988
Bhutan	289	15	24	28	–	
Cambodia	1,813	28	21	24	–	
China	236,849	30	10	7	75.0	1988
India	159,835	27	24	21	43.0	1987
Indonesia	36,417	26	26	12	40.0	1983–87
Korea, Rep. of	14,331	–15	9	–3	65.5	1985
Lao PDR	751	24	30	38	–	
Malaysia	3,406	31	27	22	41.5	1987
Myanmar	7,973	30	27	24	–	
Nepal	3,561	20	30	30	11.1	1982–86
Pakistan	18,556	33	38	37	11.9	1990–91
Papua New Guinea	687	32	26	27	–	–
Philippines	11,593	31	29	24	32.1	1984–88
Sri Lanka	3,785	19	17	6	59.8	1983–87
Thailand	11,407	33	22	7	65.5	1986
Viet Nam	12,487	32	32	22	47.0	1983–87
Country average	–	25	25	21	42.6	–

a. Based on projected population for 1990, 2000, and 2010.

b. Refers to contraceptive users among married women ages 15–49.

Source: Bos and others 1994 for population size data for 1990–2010; population data for 1980 are from United Nations 1991; data on contraceptive prevalence rates are from the same sources for table 3.2, except Pakistan, for which the source is National Institute of Population Studies 1991.

Table 8.9: *Growth of the Working-Age Population (15–59) in Selected Asian Countries*

Country	Size of working-age population, 1970 ('000)	Increase in working-age population (percentage)			
		1970–1980	1980–1990	1990–2000	2000–2010
Bangladesh	32,359	33	33	36	25
Bhutan	569	19	14	25	27
Cambodia	3,618	11	18	27	30
China	443,851	28	28	11	12
India	297,326	27	28	24	22
Indonesia	63,217	28	26	27	17
Korea, Rep. of	16,767	36	25	10	5
Lao PDR	1,444	18	23	29	37
Malaysia	5,411	40	32	29	27
Myanmar	14,299	28	28	25	27
Nepal	6,107	31	22	32	31
Pakistan	31,991	36	32	37	38
Papua New Guinea	1,283	28	30	27	26
Philippines	18,862	35	34	30	28
Sri Lanka	6,527	32	17	20	11
Thailand	17,514	46	34	23	12
Viet Nam	21,170	28	33	31	29
Country average		30	27	26	24

Source: United Nations 1991b for 1970 and 1980 data; and Bos and others 1994 for 1990, 2000, and 2010 data.

Among the Asian countries in this study, this shift in concern is clearest in the Republic of Korea, where the working-age population is projected to increase by only 10 percent in 1990–2000 and 5 percent in 2000–2010, compared with the 25 percent increase in 1980–90. Significant slowdown in growth of the working-age population is also projected in China, Thailand, and Sri Lanka. In most other Asian countries, however, the projected increases during the 1990s and 2000s are often only slightly smaller than in the previous decade, suggesting that employment creation and labor absorption will remain significant issues. In a few countries—notably Bhutan, Cambodia, Lao PDR, and Pakistan—increases in the working-age population are in fact projected to accelerate in the 1990s. These countries are therefore likely to face bigger challenges in labor absorption than in the past.

In almost all Asian countries, the potential for labor absorption through agriculture is small, given already heavy rural population densities, high incidence of landlessness, and declining farm size among the landed (Bauer 1991). While investments in land-augmenting infrastructure (such as irrigation and drainage) and technology could help to increase absorption into productive agricultural employment, most of the projected increases in the labor pool would need to shift to employment outside agriculture. Analysis by Bloom and Freeman (1986) using data from 1960–80 shows that "despite . . . unprecedented . . . population growth and imperfections in labor markets, developing countries tended to shift from low-productivity agriculture to the higher-productivity service sector and . . . industrial sector, and to raise incomes per head." The pattern in Asia mirrors this general finding, with the proportion of the labor force in agriculture declining from an average of 69 percent in 1960 to 42 percent in the late 1980s (table 8.10).

Given past trends and cross-country experiences, employment shifts to nonagricultural sectors are likely to continue. But the pattern of absorption will depend importantly on labor market institutions and policies (such as minimum wages, government incentives to join the military or remain in school, etc.) which affect labor costs and the shape of labor demand curves. Experience in industrial economies points to wages and employment/unemployment as the two key dimensions along which adjustment to expanding labor pools takes place. The United States, for example, adjusted to the baby boom after World War II through a lowering of relative wages; in contrast, adjustment in most Western European countries has primarily been through diminished job opportunities for members of the baby boom cohorts (Bloom and Freeman 1986).

In developing countries, the existence of trichotomous labor markets is an added factor, with traditional agricultural and urban informal sectors characterized by self-employment and small-scale enterprise, and a modern sector characterized chiefly by contractual employment. Because minimum wage settings above market rates and government pay policies in the modern sector tend to limit its absorptive capacity, the urban informal sector takes on a particularly critical role as a source of employment. Thus, as labor pools continue to expand at historical rates in the coming decade, the promotion of permissive rather than prohibitive business

Table 8.10: *Percentage of Economically Active Population Engaged in Agriculture, Hunting, and Fishing in Selected Asian Countries*

Country	1950	1960	1970	1980	Latest available data Percentage	Latest available data Year
Bangladesh	–	86	77[b]	59	56	1985–86
Cambodia	–	80	–	–	–	–
China	–	–	–	82	71	1990
India	70	72	72	66	67	1987–8
Indonesia	–	68	64	55	54	1990
Korea, Rep. of	–	61	50	35	19	1989
Malaysia	–	58	47	34	30	1987
Myanmar	–	–	–	–	64	1983
Nepal	–	94	94	91	–	–
Pakistan	65	60	51	51	49	1987–88
Philippines	–	61	52	50[a]	41	1990
Sri Lanka	53[a]	49[b]	41	37	42	1985–86
Thailand	85	82	78	70	66	1988
Viet Nam	–	–	–	–	72	1989
Country average[b]	–	69	63	55	42	

Note: Unless otherwise noted, data for 1950–80 are within one or two years of the specified date.

a. Data for Bangladesh refer to 1974; for Malaysia, to 1957; for Philippines, to 1975; for Sri Lanka, to 1946 and 1963 respectively; and for Thailand, to 1947.

b. Includes only countries with data for 1960, 1970, 1980, and latest available year.

Source: International Labour Office (ILO) 1990 for data for 1950–80; ILO 1991 for latest available data for Bangladesh, Republic of Korea, Malaysia, Myanmar, Pakistan, Philippines, and Sri Lanka; supplemented by Government of China 1991, Government of India 1991, Government of Indonesia 1990, and Government of Viet Nam 1990b.

environments in the informal sector is likely to remain an essential focus of public policy to enhance job creation in that sector (see, for example, de Soto 1989).

Job seekers are likely to include growing numbers of women, as work outside the home becomes increasingly feasible with declining fertility. The ratio of young children (below age 5) to women aged 20–39 has been dropping since 1970 in all Asian countries, and the downward trend is projected to continue (see appendix table A8.1). In most Asian countries, women's increasing availability for outside work adds to the demographically driven pressures on the economy to deliver jobs.

The Republic of Korea's situation—as well as those of demographically advanced Asian countries not shown here, such as Taiwan (China), Singapore, and Hong Kong—is different, however. Given the drastic slowdown of the working-age population, women's increased labor force participation may be part of a possible solution to labor shortage problems which are beginning to surface. But women's labor force participation is already relatively widespread in Korea (figure 8.4), except between ages 20 and 35 when they are most likely to have young children. The U.S. experience suggests there is scope for further increases in Korean women's entry to the labor market, but if culturally similar Japan's experience is a guide, the child-rearing responsibilities of young mothers are likely to remain substantial. As a result, increases in women's labor force participation are likely to occur mainly at younger and older ages.

In contrast to the experience of past decades, the overall prospect in Korea thus remains one of growing labor scarcity, creating real pressures for shifts toward more capital-intensive economic activity accompanied by rising wages. Such a transition calls for changed and enhanced skills in the work force. In growing populations, skill endowments in the labor force improve as young workers enter the labor force with new or upgraded skills. In Korea, however, young cohorts will actually be declining in the coming decades, so this source of change will be limited. A more likely source of new and upgraded skills in the Korean work force is through in-service training for existing workers. Fostering training institutions is therefore likely to become an increasingly relevant focus of public policy in Korea and other demographically advanced countries in Asia.

In contrast to Korea's situation, most of the Asian countries in this study will experience large cohorts of young people (aged 15–19) entering the labor force for the first time, on a scale similar to that in the 1980s, but much smaller than in the 1970s (table 8.11). Job readiness training and school-to-work transition among youth are therefore likely to remain important issues in the 1990s. In a few countries, disrupted demographic histories have created large swings in the cohort size of the youthful population, relaxing the demand for job creation in one decade, but exacerbating it in the next. In China, for example, the coming decade will see a sharp decline in young labor market entrants (owing to past fertility swings), but a large increase is projected in the following decade. Because a sizable proportion of the labor force in China is still in agriculture, the labor shortages evident in Korea are unlikely to surface in China just yet. Large swings in the youthful population are also projected in Cambodia due to the effects of war; in Sri Lanka due to the echo effect of malaria eradication around World War II;[12] and in Myanmar. In all these countries, the swings in labor supply conditions are likely to test the responsiveness of existing labor market institutions, and to increase the political difficulties of addressing unemployment and related problems among youths, particularly during supply upswings.

Among the remaining Asian countries, several features are noteworthy in the projections.[13] In Thailand, the population aged 15–19 is projected to expand much

Figure 8.4: Women's Labor Force Participation Rates in Selected Countries, Late 1980s

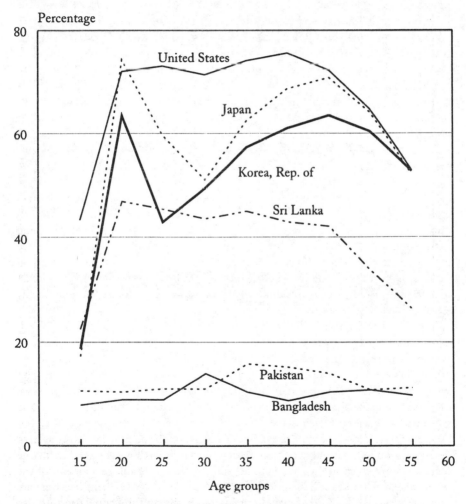

Note: Rates are for five-year age groups starting at ages shown on the x-axis.
Source: Based on data from ILO 1990.

Table 8.11: Growth of the Population Ages 15–19 in Selected Asian Countries, 1970

Country	Size of population ages 15–19, 1970 ('000)	Increase in the population ages 15–19 (percent)			
		1970–80	1980–1990	1990–2000	2000–2020
Bangladesh	6,136	52	34	26	–2
Bhutan	107	18	15	26	27
Cambodia	706	17	5	32	26
China	91,201	19	13	–26	16
India	54,623	30	23	17	12
Indonesia	11,846	33	19	20	–8
Korea, Rep. of	3,129	49	–3	–19	–7
Lao PDR	280	19	22	34	44
Malaysia	1,173	34	15	30	8
Myanmar	2,738	29	30	9	27
Nepal	1,046	39	29	48	14
Pakistan	7,112	34	25	32	30
Papua New Guinea	240	30	39	18	23
Philippines	4,265	24	24	25	18
Sri Lanka	1,211	32	1	17	–9
Thailand	3,793	39	18	3	–12
Viet Nam	4,039	52	16	21	14
Country average	–	32	19	18	13

Source: United Nations 1991b for 1970, 1980 data; and Bos and others 1994 for 1990, 2000, and 2010 data.

more slowly in the 1990s compared to the previous decades, and further slowdown is expected in the 2000s. In countries with intermediate level fertility and reasonable expectations about future declines—including Bangladesh, India, Indonesia, Malaysia, and the Philippines—the same downward trend is expected, but with a delay of a decade or so. Not all countries in Asia share this pattern. Notably in Bhutan, Lao PDR, and Pakistan, the projected increases in the population of youths is expected to accelerate or remain large in the coming two decades. To the extent that large upswings are problematic, these countries face a bigger challenge in addressing the problems of youth than they have had to deal with in the past.

Population and Urbanization

Asian countries are typically less urbanized than those in Latin American and Africa. According to United Nations estimates, 24 percent of Asia's population lived in urban areas in 1970, compared to 60 percent in Latin America and just over 20 percent in Africa (UN 1989).[14] By 1990, Asia's urban population had risen to 30 percent of the total, still modest compared to 72 percent in Latin America and almost 35 percent in Africa. As expected, there is considerable diversity among Asian countries; for example, only one in ten Nepalese are urban residents, whereas more than seven of ten residents of the Republic of Korea are. The Republic of Korea is exceptional, however. In Malaysia and the Philippines, the next most urbanized countries, a little more than 40 percent of the population live in urban areas. In China, India, and Indonesia, between 20 and 30 percent of the population are urban dwellers.

The concentration of people in urban areas is integral to the process of economic development, resulting from both push and pull factors. Rising productivity in agriculture reduces the demand for rural labor, while better job and income prospects in urban areas—which reflect the greater productivity of labor supported by economics of scale and agglomeration—attract migrants. These dynamics underlie the positive correlation observed between the extent of urbanization across countries and per capita incomes. The pattern in Asia is similar to that for countries elsewhere (figure 8.5).

The economic forces of urbanization are powerful, and population growth intensifies them, in large part by expanding the pool of potential migrants. Experience shows that no government—including China's, which adopted explicit policies to restrain the growth of cities—has been effective in checking rural-to-urban migration. As elsewhere in the world, Asian countries can thus expect to continue experiencing rapid urbanization. Accurate projections are elusive at best, and existing estimates offer only a rough indication of the growth to anticipate (table 8.12).[15] For the region as a whole, urban growth between 1990 and 2000 is forecast to average 4.2 percent, marginally slower than the average of 4.5 percent a year during the 1980s.[16] Deviating from the regional trend are such countries as Myanmar, Papua New Guinea, Sri Lanka, and Viet Nam, where urban growth is projected to

Figure 8.5: Correlation between Urbanization and Per Capita GNP in Asia, circa 1990

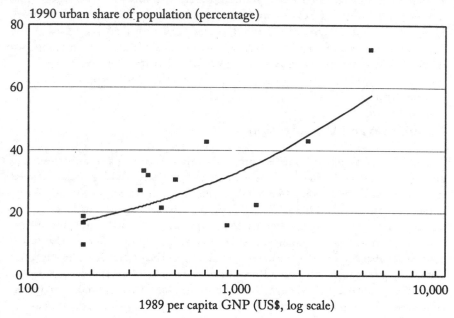

1990 urban share of population (percentage)

Source: UN 1991a, World Bank 1991c.

speed up. Between 1990 and 2000, Asia's urban population is expected to swell by about 450 million people, raising the urban population share from 30 to 40 percent.

Urbanization has been accompanied by the emergence of megacities. In 1950, no Asian city had more than 8 million residents. Shanghai and Beijing reached this size in 1970, while Calcutta, Bombay, Seoul, Tianjin, Jakarta, Delhi, and Manila reached it in 1990. The list is expected to include four more Asian cities by 2000.[17] As elsewhere, Asia's megacities dominate the urban landscape: in 1990 Bangkok had more than half of Thailand's urban population; Seoul, Dhaka, and Manila had, respectively, about one-third of the urban populations of the Republic of Korea, Bangladesh, and the Philippines; and Jakarta, and Karachi accommodated roughly 20 percent of the urban populations of Indonesia and Pakistan, respectively. Many of these cities are generally at least twice the size of the next largest city in the country, and are expected to continue growing (figure 8.6).

Between 1990 and 2000, Asia's main urban centers—with a few exceptions[18]—are projected to expand by an average of 50 percent in population size, adding pressure on what are still inadequate and unreliable basic infrastructure and services (table 8.13). The scale and speed of urbanization are thus likely to present demanding

Table 8.12: Urban Growth in Asia, 1980–2000

| Country | Per capita GNP (1989 US$) | Urban population (thousands) | | Urban population as share of total (percentage) | | Average annual growth rate (percentage a year) | | | |
| | | | | | | Urban population | | Total population | |
		1990	2000	1990	2000	1980–1990	1990–2000	1980–1990	1990–2000
Bangladesh	180	19,005	34,548	16.4	22.9	6.5	6.0	2.7	2.6
China	350	380,803	614,514	33.4	47.3	6.7	4.8	1.3	1.3
India	- 340	230,269	336,542	27.0	32.3	3.7	3.8	2.1	2.0
Indonesia	500	56,293	86,401	30.5	39.5	5.2	4.3	2.0	1.7
Korea, Rep. of	4,400	30,794	37,773	72.0	81.4	3.5	2.0	1.2	0.8
Lao PDR	180	770	1,372	18.6	25.1	5.8	5.8	2.6	2.8
Malaysia	2,160	7,701	11,255	43.0	51.2	4.8	3.8	2.6	2.1
Myanmar	n.a.	10,316	14,523	24.8	28.4	2.4	3.4	2.1	2.0
Nepal	180	1,837	3,446	9.6	14.3	7.0	6.3	2.5	2.3
Pakistan	370	39,250	61,477	32.0	37.9	4.9	4.5	3.6	2.8
Papua New Guinea	890	613	979	15.8	20.2	4.2	4.7	2.3	2.2
Philippines	710	26,602	37,775	42.6	48.8	3.9	3.5	2.6	2.2
Sri Lanka	430	3,679	4,701	21.4	24.2	1.4	2.5	1.5	1.2
Thailand	1,220	12,609	18,738	22.6	29.4	4.4	4.0	1.8	1.3
Viet Nam	n.a.	14,600	22,340	21.9	27.1	3.4	4.3	2.2	2.1
Regional average									
Unweighted	916	835,141[a]	1,286,384[a]	28.8	35.3	4.5	4.2	2.2	2.0
Weighted	–	–	–	30.4	39.3	5.2	4.3	1.9	1.7

a. Total population.
Source: United Nations 1991a; data on 1989 per capita GNP from World Bank 1991c.

challenges for urban management and development. Past models of urban development reserved a leading role for central governments in the financing and provision of services, but experience with such models has been less satisfactory than desired (World Bank 1991b). Notably, policy has tended to focus on public investment, failing to recognize the critical role of local institutions in the operation and maintenance of infrastructure as well as the importance of establishing incentives to maximize the contribution of private sector activity. The public sector's dominance has also constrained and skewed responses to the burgeoning demand for shelter, infrastructure, and services in urban areas. In light of this experience, as well as countries' demographic prospects, it seems clear that sustainable urban development would require substantial reorientation of the government's role in the sector.

A redefined government role would address three emerging priorities in urban development: a) enhancement of the productivity of the urban economy (which typically contributes more than half of the gross domestic product [GDP] in developing countries and is therefore vital to overall economic growth); b) alleviation of increasing urban poverty; and c) protection of the urban environment.[19] Although it is beyond the scope of this paper to elaborate on the precise changes called for, broad directions can be identified. Enhancing urban productivity would require reducing such constraints as infrastructure deficiencies, rigid regulatory frameworks

Figure 8.6: Population Size of Selected Asian Cities, 1970–2000

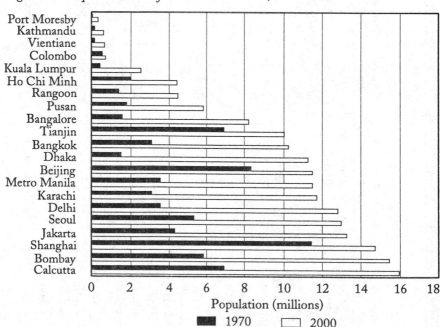

Population (millions)

■ 1970   □ 2000

Source: UN 1991a.

Table 8.13. *Population Size and Measures of Urban Infrastructure and Services in Major Asian Cities*[a,b]

Country	City[a]	Population 1990 (millions)	Projected population increase 1990–2000 (percent)	Percent housing units with		Communications[c]		Rush hour car speed[d] (miles/hour)	Clean air score[e]	Murders per 100,000 population
				Electricity	Running water	Phones per 100 persons	% of calls successful			
Bangladesh	Dhaka	6.4	76	85	–f	1.8	68	21	–	2.4
China	–	6.1	27	74	89	3.7	76	21	3	2.3
India	–	6.0	43	83	64	2.9	68	14	2	2.8
Indonesia	–	4.8	42	78	83	2.0	39	16	1	5.1
Korea, Rep. of	–	8.0	19	85	85	23.2	89	15	5	1.4
Lao PDR	Vientiane	0.4	68	–	–	–	–	–	–	–
Malaysia	Kuala Lumpur	1.7	52	–	–	–	–	–	–	–
Myanmar	Yangon	3.2	40	–	–	–	–	–	–	–
Nepal	Kathmandu	0.4	69	–	–	–	–	–	–	–
PNG	Port Moresby	0.2	65	–	–	–	–	–	–	–
Pakistan	–	5.9	49	84	71	2.8	77	16	9	5.3
Philippines	Manila	8.4	37	93	89	8.8	71	7	6	30.5
Sri Lanka	Colombo	0.6	15	–	–	–	–	–	–	–
Thailand	Bangkok	7.2	43	–	–f	11.9	70	13	3	7.6
Viet Nam	Ho Chi Minh	3.2	39	90	83	0.5	70	20	–	2.1

a. For China, India, Indonesia, Republic of Korea, and Pakistan, data reflect the arithmetic averages of cities that are among the hundred most populous in the world. These are Shanghai, Beijing, Tianjin, Shenyang, Wuhan, Guangzhou, Chonqing, and Nanjing (eight cities) in China; Bombay, Calcutta, Delhi, Madras, Bangalore, Hyderabad, Ahmedabad, Kanpur, and Pune (nine cities) in India; Jakarta, Surabaya, and Bandung in Indonesia; Seoul and Pusan in the Republic of Korea; and Karachi and Lahore in Pakistan.

b. Data on urban infrastructure and services refer to dates in the mid– to late 1980s.

c. Number of phones per 100 people are adjusted for nonworking phones.

d. Estimated by dividing the distance between the nearest airport to the central business district by the time it takes to travel between them during morning rush hour.

e. Scored on a 1 to 10 scale, with scores rising with increasing cleanliness. Based on measures of concentrations of ozone, sulfur dioxide, nitrogen dioxide, and suspended particulate matter.

f. Estimated at 60 percent in 1981 for Dhaka, and at 76 percent in 1980 for Bangkok.

Sources: Camp, Barbers, and Hinds 1990; data on population in columns 3 and 4 are from United Nations 1991a.

that hobble the productive potential of assets, weak municipal institutions, and inadequate financial services for urban development. Developing effective ways to mobilize private sector effort in these areas is an important key to the government's evolving role. On urban poverty, increased urban productivity would help to reduce its incidence, but direct antipoverty efforts and investments in human capital are probably also needed. Designing sustainable programs in these areas is an inescapable challenge in light of the severe demographic pressures facing most municipal governments in Asia. These same pressures can also be expected to exacerbate urban environmental problems—including air and water pollution and degradation of physical surroundings—with serious implications for public health and the urban economy's long-term viability. Establishing incentives to counteract these tendencies, and identifying options for effective and efficient public action, would be needed to protect the urban environment.

Notes

1. The treatment here is by no means exhaustive. Not addressed, for example, are issues related to food production and water resources for Asia's growing populations. The discussion on employment and urbanization draws, in part, on background materials kindly provided by Andrew Mason of the University of Hawaii.

2. These problems occur at every scale from global to local. The list includes global warming, ozone depletion, acid rain, deforestation, desertification, marine resource degradation, erosion and salinization of the soil, depletion of underground water resources, air pollution, water pollution, waste disposal, and loss of biodiversity, among others. In a broad sense, we can think of the planet, each country, and even each community as having a stock of environmental capital. Sustainable development implies that each generation passes on to the next at least as large a stock of environmental capital as it received from its parents. Even today, there may be places in Asia where current population levels and current technological levels cannot be sustained, where people are living off the environmental capital.

3. Asian Development Bank (1991), p. 230.

4. More formally, we specify the framework as $Q = P \cdot I \cdot T$, where Q is the amount of the pollutant, P is the size of the population, I is per capita income, and T is the amount of the pollution produced per unit of income (or output). In the model, the pollutant can be any hypothetical cause of environmental damage. It could easily be carbon dioxide emissions, in which case, the technology variable would be the amount of carbon dioxide emitted per unit of gross domestic product. If the environmental damage is caused by the withdrawal of water from underground aquifers, the technology would then be the amount of water withdrawn per unit of gross domestic product. For simplicity of expression, we call all sources of environmental degradation "pollution."

5. Notice that the sum of 15 percent and 90 percent exceeds the 92 percent reduction indicated under the initial simulation with standard World Bank population projections. The reason is the interaction between population and technology, so that the 15 percent overstates the contribution of population while the 90 percent overstates the contribution of technology. Following convention, we apportion the extra 13 percent according to the relative shares of population and technology in this calculation.

6. As documented in the previous chapter, population growth during the next forty years in Asian countries will be largely due to the effects of population momentum.

7. Mothers of the school-age population in 1990 were born in the 1950s (assuming 30 years to be the average age of mothers); mothers of the school-age population in 2005 were born in the 1960s and 1970s, and mothers of the school-age population in 2015 were born in the 1980s. Because fertility rose sharply in the early 1960s—partly reflecting compensatory childbearing as famine conditions eased following the Great Leap Forward period—the cohort of mothers born during this period is larger than those born in the 1950s. Even though more recent cohorts of mothers were each having fewer children, the cohort size effect results in a larger total number

of school-age population in 2005 than in 1990. During the 1980s the government's one-child policy had been in effect for some time. The smaller cohort size combined with very low fertility to produce smaller school-age populations in 2015 than in 2005.

8. Almost all children in Lao PDR currently appear to enroll in grade one (although this may be overestimated), but because of the very large increase in the primary-school-age population between 1990 and 2000, the country essentially faces similar pressures as others in this group.

9. To economize on space, the data shown in table 8.7 refer only to immunization with the full DPT cycle. Similar trends apply to other child immunization services (see data contained in United Nations Children's Fund [UNICEF] 1991).

10. Only in China and Republic of Korea are the projected changes in this and the next decade relatively small.

11. For example, if the contraceptive prevalence rate in Indonesia rises to 75 percent in the 1990s, the total number of contracepting women would more than double by the end of the decade.

12. Malaria eradication in the 1940s in Sri Lanka reduced mortality in the generation that became parents of youths aged 15–19 in 1990, thus increasing births associated with that generation compared to births in the previous decade.

13. Note that because projections of the population aged 15–19 to 2010 are sensitive to current and projected mortality and fertility trends, they are subject to wider margins of error than projections to 2000 which depend only on mortality assumptions.

14. Urban areas were defined by country-specific criteria which may differ across countries. Although Asia is less urbanized than other world regions, four of the world's ten largest cities are in Asia.

15. A recent study evaluated the application of the UN method for projecting urban populations of five Asian countries from 1960 to 1980 (Cho and Bauer 1987). In three countries, the projected urban population deviated from the actual by over 10 percent. The worst case was the Republic of Korea, where the projected urban population was 24 percent less than the actual 1980 urban population. In retrospect, the difficulty in Korea's case was hardly surprising: who could have anticipated the country's remarkable economic growth over the ensuing two decades?

16. For projections to 2020, see appendix table A8.2.

17. Bangalore, Bangkok, Dhaka, and Karachi.

18. Smaller increases are projected in China's and the Repbulic of Korea's largest cities as well as in Colombo, Sri Lanka.

19. See World Bank 1991b for a fuller treatment.

Appendixes

Appendix A

Parameterization of the Total Fertility Rate

THE TOTAL FERTILITY RATE IS DERIVED by summing age-specific fertility rates across all reproductive ages. These age-specific rates are parameterized in this study into eleven easily understood variables broadly related to marriage, contraceptive practice, abortion, and timing of childbearing:

- Earliest age at which a consequential number of women first marry

- Proportion of women who ever marry

- Mean age at marriage of women

- Mean age at marriage of men

- Proportion currently remarried among 20-year-old ever-widowed women

- Proportion currently remarried among 49-year-old ever-widowed women

- Contraceptive prevalence rate

- Contraceptive effectiveness rate

- Total marital abortion rate

- Length of postpartum nonsusceptibility, or protection against pregnancy following a birth due to breastfeeding and other fertility-influencing behaviors not mentioned above

- Mean age at childbearing.

The approach here permits analysis of a country's demographic development (as in chapter 3), and simulations of scenarios of age-specific fertility rates under alternative assumptions about the behavior of the eleven underlying demographic parameters. The resulting age-specific fertility rates can be used to produce population projections to illustrate the effect of alternative changes in the fertility variables on future population size.

To derive the relevant relationships among the eleven variables, we write age-specific fertility rates as the product of two terms: (a) age-specific proportions currently married; and (b) age-specific marital fertility rates:[1]

$$\phi(a) = \chi(a) \cdot \mu(a) \tag{A.1}$$

where
$\phi(a)$ = the age-specific fertility rate at age a;
$\chi(a)$ = the proportion of women of age a who are currently married; and
$\mu(a)$ = the marital fertility rate at age a.

The age-specific proportions currently married can be expressed in terms of the first six variables in our eleven variables, while age-specific marital fertility rates can be expressed in terms of the remaining five variables, as shown below.

Parameterization of the Age-Specific Proportions Currently Married

We write the proportion of women currently married as follows:

$$\chi(a) = [\gamma(a) - \delta(a)] \cdot [1 - \omega(a)] + [\gamma(a) - \delta(a)] \cdot \omega(a) \cdot \rho(a) \tag{A.2}$$

where
$\chi(a)$ is the proportion of married women[2] at age a in the specified year;
$\gamma(a)$ is the proportion of ever-married women at age a in the specified year;
$\delta(a)$ is the proportion of women at age a who are either divorced or separated[3] in the specified year;
$\omega(a)$ is the proportion of women of age a who were ever-widowed prior to or including the specified year; and
$\rho(a)$ is the proportion of ever-widowed women of age a who are remarried as of the specified year.

Each of the foregoing age-specific schedules can be parameterized. Coale and McNeil (1972) provides a parametric specification of the age-specific proportions of women ever married. This formulation has been thoroughly tested and found to fit the data quite well in a large number of cases. We use this as the basis for parameterizing the proportions ever married. Accordingly, the age-specific proportions ever married are expressed as:

$$\gamma(a) = \frac{0.1946c}{k} \int_0^a \Gamma(a)da \tag{A.3}$$

where

$$\Gamma(a) = e^{\frac{(-0.174)(a - a_0 - 6.06k) - e^{\frac{(-0.288)(a - a_0 - 6.06k)}{k}}}{k}}$$

a_0 is the earliest age at which a consequential number of women first get married;

c is the proportion of women ever married; and

$$k = \frac{smam_f - a_0}{11.37},$$

$smam_f$ is the singulate mean age at marriage for females.[4]

Equation A.3 allows us to express the proportion ever married by age using three parameters, the age at which a consequential number of women first marry, a_0; the mean age at marriage, $smam_f$; and the proportion of women who ever marry, c.

Widowhood is a more complex phenomenon because it depends on the path of past male mortality rates. To our knowledge there are no parametric models of female widowhood as a function of male mortality rates, but there do exist methods for estimating male mortality based on the proportions of women ever widowed. One such method, which appears in United Nations 1983 (pp. 122–26), suggests the use of the following equation for the estimation of male mortality:

$$s_m(a,20) = \alpha_0(a) + \alpha_1(a) \cdot smam_f + \alpha_2(a) \cdot smam_m + \alpha_3(a) \cdot \omega(a-5) \qquad \text{(A.4)}$$

where

$s_m(a,20)$ is the probability of a male's surviving from age 20 to age a[5];

$smam_f$ is the singulate mean age at marriage of females;

$smam_m$ is the singulate mean age at marriage of males;

$\omega(a)$ is the proportion of ever-married women of a who have ever been widowed; and the $\alpha_i(a)$ are sets of age-specific constants.[6]

Since the $\omega(a)$ are exactly what we need for equation (A.2) and the $s_m(a,20)$ can be computed from past male survival rates[7], it is natural simply to rearrange equation (A.4) to obtain:

$$\omega(a-5) = \frac{s_m(a,20) - \alpha_0(a) - \alpha_1(a) \cdot smam_f - \alpha_2(a) \cdot smam_m}{\alpha_3(a)} \qquad \text{(A.5)}$$

Equation (A.5) allows us to express the proportions ever widowed as a function of two parameters, the singulate mean ages at marriage of females and males.

The age-specific proportions of ever-married women who are currently remarried in the period in question, the $\rho(a)$, are bounded between 0 and 1. They are likely to be higher for younger women and lower for older women. We postulate, therefore, that these remarriage rates follow a logistic pattern with respect to age, and so we write:

$$\rho(a) = \frac{e^{\lambda_0 \cdot (a - \lambda_1)}}{1 + e^{\lambda_0 \cdot (a - \lambda_1)}} \tag{A.6}$$

where
$\rho(a)$ is the proportion of ever-widowed women of age a who are currently remarried; and
λ_0 and λ_1 are the logistic parameters.

It would not be appropriate to use the two λ parameters in the model because they have no direct interpretation. So, we take one more step and express the λ's as a function of $\rho(20)$ and $\rho(49)$. A little algebra is all that is necessary to see that:

$$\lambda_0 = \frac{\ln\left[\frac{\rho(49)}{1 - \rho(49)}\right] - \ln\left[\frac{\rho(20)}{1 - \rho(20)}\right]}{29} \tag{A.7}$$

and

$$\lambda_1 = \frac{20 \cdot \ln\left[\frac{\rho(49)}{1 - \rho(49)}\right] - 49 \cdot \ln\left[\frac{\rho(20)}{1 - \rho(20)}\right]}{\ln\left[\frac{\rho(49)}{1 - \rho(49)}\right] - \ln\left[\frac{\rho(20)}{1 - \rho(20)}\right]} \tag{A.8}$$

Equations (A.6), (A.7), and (A.8) allow us to obtain all the necessary age-specific remarriage rates from two parameters, the values of those rates at ages 20 and 49.

In the case of the $\delta(a)$, we deviate from our standard procedure. Instead of formulating a method for parameterizing the $\delta(a)$, we simply use a convenient $\delta(a)$ schedule.[8] As a practical matter, the $\delta(a)$ tend to be small, usually less than 5 percent, and in this range, they have little impact on the projections. It would have been a very simple matter to parameterize the $\delta(a)$, but we did not see the point in it.

In summary, the parameters for the age at which women first start getting married in appreciable numbers, their mean age at marriage, and the proportion of them who ever marry is sufficient to determine all the $\gamma(a)$'s, the age-specific proportions of women ever married. The parameters for the mean ages at marriage for females and males, along with past male mortality rates, is enough to produce the $\omega(a)$'s, the age-specific proportions of women ever widowed. The proportion of ever-widowed women remarried at ages 20 and 49 is what is required to produce all the $\rho(a)$'s, the age-specific remarriage rates. These schedules, along with the $\delta(a)$'s, enter into equation (A.2) to produce our parametric age-specific proportions currently married.

Parameterization of the Age-Specific Marital Fertility Rates

For our purposes, the best analytic representation of age-specific marital fertility rates is due to Coale (1971) and Coale and Trussell (1974). The authors write:

$$\mu(a) = M\eta(a) \cdot e^{m\upsilon(a)} \tag{A.9}$$

where
$\mu(a)$ is the marital fertility rate at age a;
$\eta(a)$ is the "standard" age-specific marital fertility rate at age a in the case of no parity-specific fertility control;
$\upsilon(a)$ is a set of constants reflecting the differential age-specific effects of contraception;[9] and
M and m are the two parameters.

Differences in M values capture variations in age-specific fertility rates which are due to dissimilarities in factors such as the length of breastfeeding, and to the practice of contraception at young ages. Variations in the m's are caused by differences in the extent to which the practice of contraception increases with age. The parameters M and m are not directly useful here because they lack easy interpretation. Our approach, then, is to find a set of easily understood and policy-relevant parameters which can be mapped into M and m.

The Bongaarts proximate determinants approach (see Bongaarts 1978 and Bongaarts and Potter 1983) has been frequently used to decompose changes in the total fertility rate. It is of interest here because it incorporates variables such as the contraceptive prevalence rate and the contraceptive efficiency rate, and so includes factors which may be of concern to decisionmakers.

Bongaarts and Potter (1983) suggests a simple approximation to the total fertility rate (tfr):

$$tfr = C_m \cdot C_i \cdot C_c \cdot C_a \cdot 15.3 \tag{A.10}$$

where

C_m, C_i, C_c, and C_a are a set of indices which range between 0 and 1 and which reflect the proportionate decreases from the maximum possible level of fertility due to marriage, the period of postpartum nonsusceptibility, contraception, and induced abortion respectively; and

15.3 is the maximum possible fertility level.[10]

They also offer the following specifications for the C_m, C_i, C_c, and C_a:

$$C_m = \frac{\sum_{a=15}^{49} \chi(a) \cdot \mu(a)}{\sum_{a=15}^{49} \mu(a)} \qquad (A.11)$$

where

C_m is the proportionate decrease in fertility resulting from marriage rates of less than 100 percent at each age;

$\chi(a)$ are the age-specific proportions of women of age a who are currently married; and

$\mu(a)$ are the age-specific marital fertility rates.

$$C_i = \frac{20}{18.5 + i} \qquad (A.12)$$

where

C_i is the proportionate decrease in fertility resulting from any breastfeeding, postpartum abstinence, or any other factor which lengthens the period of nonsusceptibility between births; and

i is the length of the period of postpartum nonsusceptibility.[11]

$$C_c = 1 - 1.08 \cdot u \cdot e \qquad (A.13)$$

where

C_c is the proportionate decline in the total fertility rate due to the use of contraception;

u is the contraceptive prevalence rate; and

e is the contraceptive effectiveness rate.

$$C_a = \frac{tfr}{tfr + 0.4 \cdot (1 + u) \cdot ta} \qquad (A.14)$$

where

C_a is the proportionate reduction in the total fertility rate due to induced abortions; ta is the total abortion rate;[12]

tfr is the total fertility rate; and
u is the contraceptive prevalence rate.

Now let us return to our task of showing how a set of easily interpretable policy-relevant parameters can be mapped into the two Coale parameters *M* and *m*. Our approach here is determined by what we perceive to be an important policy issue in program design. In some countries, such as India, the family planning program concentrates on providing sterilization. Sterilization programs influence fertility later in the reproductive span and have little direct impact on the fertility of younger women. Other family planning programs offer couples more choice of contraceptive techniques and try to aid younger couples who need a temporary form of contraception in order to space their children. We try to capture this kind of difference in program emphasis by including the mean age at childbearing (MACB) in the analysis.

Before writing the expression of MACB, let us define a set of integers, j = 1, 2 . . . 7, which indexes the age periods 15–19, 20–24, . . . , 45–49. For example, using the notation in equation (A.9), $\eta(2)$ is the baseline marital fertility rate for women aged 20–24. Further, let us define $(AM)_j$ as the age midpoint for the *j*-th group. $(AM)_2$, for example, is equal to 22.5 years.

Now, using equation (A.9), we can write the mean age at childbearing as:

$$MACB = \frac{\sum_{j=1}^{7} (AM)_j \cdot \eta(j) \cdot e^{m\,v(j)}}{\sum_{j=1}^{7} \eta(j) \cdot e^{m\,v(j)}} \tag{A.15}$$

Equation (A.15) is one equation in one unknown, *m*. Therefore, if the mean age at childbearing is known, it is possible to use equation (A.16) to determine the Coale parameter *m*.

Given the $\chi(a)$ determined in equation (A.2), the total fertility rate determined in equation (A.10), and the *m* parameter determined in equation (A.15), it is possible to compute the value of the second Coale parameter, *M*. For example, if the $\chi(a)$'s are fixed, an increase in the contraceptive prevalence rate would decrease the total fertility rate, through equation (A.10). If the mean age at childbearing is held constant, then the *m* parameter is also constant, and the increase in contraceptive prevalence changes only the *M* parameter. In other words, if the contraceptive prevalence rate increases and the mean age at childbearing does not change, then the levels of the age-specific marital fertility rates shift downward proportionally at all ages. If both the contraceptive prevalence rate and *m* increase, then the increase in contraceptive adoption is more concentrated among women in the later childbearing years. For any given increase in contraceptive prevalence, there is a new value of *m* (and therefore, the mean age at childbearing) such that the *M* parameter does not change.

Notes

1. This formulation implies that nonmarital fertility is small enough to ignore. Where informal marriages are common, we include women in those arrangements as being currently married. Where there is a consequential amount of childbearing outside of both formal and informal marriage, the model should include a parametric representation of nonmarital fertility.

2. It is important to recall that our definition of marriages includes women living in informal as well as formal unions.

3. If appropriate data are not available, it may occasionally be necessary to use the proportions currently divorced as a first approximation.

4. The singulate mean age at marriage is what the mean age at marriage would be, given a fixed set of age-specific marriage rates and a population with the same number of women at each age. The singulate mean age at marriage is used here instead of the mean age at which women marry in a given year because it removes the influence of the age structure of the female population.

5. This survival rate has a different reference date from the three right-hand side variables. As age increases, the reference date for the survival rate recedes further back in time. A full discussion of this appears in United Nations 1983 (pp. 111–14).

6. These age-specific constants appear in United Nations 1983 (table 97, p. 112).

7. These "past" male survival dates are rates which predate the period of interest. Suppose, for example, we were making a projection for 2010–14. The "past" male survival rates would be those experienced before 2010–14. Those rates would still be in the future as of this writing, but they are in the past with respect to the reference year of the projection.

8. In general, we use the latest available data.

9. The values of η (a) and υ (a) can be found in United Nations 1983 (p. 24).

10. In their 1983 publication, Bongaarts and Potter use the 15.3 figure in their empirical work, but stress that this figure, which they call TF, is best considered to have a range between 13 and 17 (see pp. 87–99, for example, and Bongaarts 1978).

11. The standard notation is a trifle confusing here. The subscript i in C_i differentiates it from the other Cs. The value of i in equation (A12) is the length of the period of nonsusceptibility.

12. The total abortion rate is defined analogously to the total fertility rate. It is the number of induced abortions that a woman would have over her lifetime if she experienced a given set of age-specific abortion rates (usually those for a particular year).

Appendix B

Government Policies and Their Effects on the Use of Family Planning Services: An Analytical Framework

THIS STUDY HAS DOCUMENTED Asian governments' widespread use of policies to lower fertility through family planning programs. Given that governments choose to intervene, the problem becomes one of finding ways to provide those services as efficiently as possible. The following discussion offers a simple framework for thinking about alternative options in this regard. Two specific roles of the government are considered, namely, as a direct supplier of family planning services, and as a catalyst for enhancing private participation in service delivery.

The Government as a Direct Supplier of Services

The easiest approach is to set the problem in a simple supply-and-demand framework. The demand for contraceptive services depends on the price of those services, the quality of the services, and the level of government activity to provide information, education, and communication (IEC) about contraception. The quality of contraceptive services is a shorthand expression which combines all the attributes of contraceptive services valued by couples. It depends on the accessibility of the services, whether the services are available at times when it is convenient to obtain them, whether the personnel are courteous, whether personnel of the preferred sex are available, whether the mix of contraceptive methods offered is appropriate, whether appropriate follow-up is available, and so on. Collapsing all these quality dimensions into one variable greatly simplifies the problem here. In reality, governments must worry about how to provide packages of attributes desired by couples at minimum cost.

For the moment, imagine that the government is providing family planning services at some fixed price, perhaps zero. In this case, the demand function depends only on the quality of services and on the level of IEC activity. Figure B.1 shows the demand curve for contraceptive services, holding constant the level of IEC activity. The unusual thing about this demand curve is that it is upward sloping. It slopes upward because the relationship between quality and demand is positive, while the relationship between price and demand is negative. The upward-sloping demand curve indicates that holding price and IEC constant, the higher the quality of contraceptive services offered by the government, the greater will be the demand for contraception.

Figure B.1: Excess Capacity of Public Facilities to Supply Contraceptive Supplies

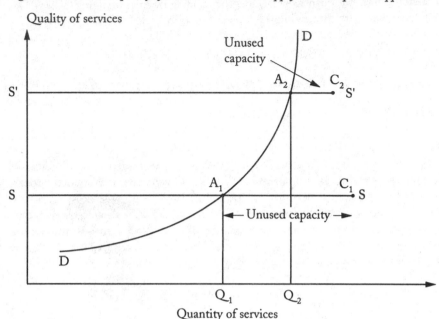

Quantity of services

On the supply side, the government fixes two variables: the level of quality it supplies to the population, and the capacity for providing these services. The capacity for providing the services is simply the number of people who can give contraceptive services in government facilities. Quality and capacity are related. Suppose the government of India decided that all family planning services would be offered in one gigantic complex in New Delhi. The capacity of this complex might be large, but the quality of service would be low because obtaining contraceptive services would be terribly inconvenient for most Indians. Another strategy would be to take the same capacity and spread it out closer to the users. In this case, capacity would remain constant, but quality would increase. It would be possible also to decrease capacity and spend the money saved on increasing quality.

In the figure, the initial supply curve, SS, is horizontal at the government-provided quality level. The SS curve intersects the demand curve at point A_1 and, therefore, the quantity of contraceptive services used by the public will be Q_1. The capacity to produce services, though, is point C_1. Hence, the distance C_1–A_1 measures the extent of unused capacity. In this case, the government has built in too much capacity at too low a quality level. The telltale sign of this condition is the large amount of unused capacity. If, for example, government facilities stock condoms, but these are rarely requested, it is a sign that the government has built too much low-quality capacity.

The government has two alternatives to diminish its wasted capacity. First, it can shift some funds from the quantity of facilities to providing facilities of higher quality. This shift is represented by the new higher supply curve S'S' in figure B.1. Not only is this curve higher than SS, indicating a higher level of quality, but C_2 lies to the left of C_1, indicating that capacity has been reduced. The higher-quality contraceptive service strategy has increased the use of contraception from Q_1 to Q_2. The amount by which contraceptive use would increase depends on the size of the upward shift from SS to S'S' and the quality-elasticity of demand for contraceptive services. The second option to reduce wasted capacity, not shown in the figure, is to increase spending on IEC, using the money saved from reducing the quantity of facilities, thus shifting the demand curve to the right and reducing the extent of unused capacity. For governments to make appropriate tradeoffs between these options, they need to know the responsiveness of their customers to changes in quality and IEC interventions. Studies of this sort are virtually nonexistent, but without them, policymakers are just shooting in the dark.

Instead of excess capacity, there could well be a situation of shortage, as depicted in figure B.2. Here the government's initial supply curve, SS, is one in which it has produced too little high-quality capacity, C_1. The distance between A_1 and C_1 is the extent of the shortage. In this case, the quantity of contraceptive provided by the government is its full capacity Q_1 (= C_1). The government can reduce the shortage

Figure B.2: Shortage of Public Facilities to Supply Contraceptive Services

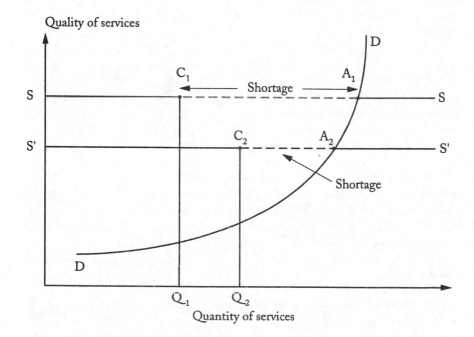

of facilities by producing more and lower-quality capacity. This is shown by the lower and longer supply curve S'S'. In this case, there still is too little capacity, but contraceptive use has risen from Q_1 to Q_2. Since there are shortages in both instances, the increase in contraceptive use, in this example, is simply the increase in capacity. In this case, the government could have saved money by reducing its expenditures on IEC, which were inefficiently large given its capacity constraint. Lower levels of IEC spending would cause the demand curve to shift to the left, but until capacity was reached there would be no change in the use of contraception.

Mobilizing and Influencing Private Participation in Service Delivery

Suppose the government wants to ensure that people receive family planning services but does not want to provide these services itself. How would it try to affect the use of contraceptive services in such situations? Figures B.3 and B.4 provide a framework for answering this question. The government can influence private firms to provide these services by regulating quality and giving the firms a subsidy. The quality level could be be a licensing stipulation requiring every firm receiving the subsidy to meet certain minimum quality standards. For example, it might have to provide at least a specified list of services and have a doctor available for patients for a certain number of hours per week, among other things. For each patient seen, the government would give the firm a certain subsidy. (This subsidy could vary with the type of service given, but this is a complication which can be ignored here.) Given the subsidy level, the supply curve of services will be downward sloping, because the higher the quality standard, given the subsidy, the fewer firms will find it profitable to enter the market.

Given an initial subsidy level, the supply curve is depicted as S_1S_1 in figure B.3. Suppose now that the government stipulated a quality level of q_1; then the quantity of contraceptive use would be Q_1 and there would be a shortage because, at the quality level q_1, couples want a quantity of contraceptive services of Q_2. The government, in this case, can easily erase the shortage by increasing the subsidy and thus shifting the supply curve from S_1S_1 to S_2S_2. At the intersection of the new, higher supply curve and the demand curve, there would be neither an excess nor a deficit of contraceptive services.

A different situation is shown in figure B.4, in which excess capacity is caused by a combination of a subsidy which is too high and a quality level which is too low. To reduce the wasted capacity, the government has two choices: lower the subsidy and shift the supply curve to the left, or raise IEC expenditures and shift the demand curve to the right. The latter option is depicted in the figure.

Summary

The government can affect people's use of family planning services through its policies on the supply of public services and by attracting the participation of private

Figure B.3: Subsidizing Private Suppliers of Contraceptive Services

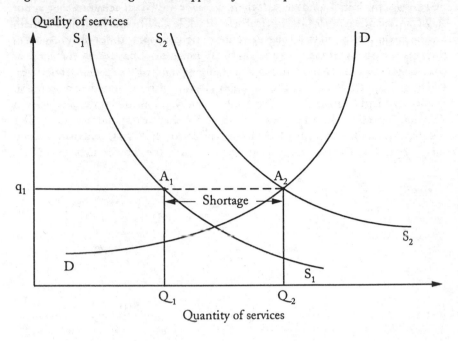

Figure B.4: Shifting the Demand for Contraceptive Services

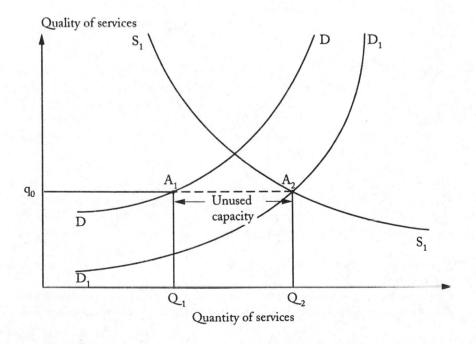

providers. As a first step, the formulation of appropriate policies requires a clear diagnosis of the initial conditions. Is there excess or wasted capacity or a shortage of services? Are private providers oversubsidized while quality standards set for them are too modest? Beyond these questions, the design of appropriate policy responses involves a clear assessment of the tradeoffs involved. Changes in the level of contraceptive use can be brought about by changing the quality of public services, the extent of IEC activities, and the subsidies given to private providers along with quality standards set for them. The optimal intervention to choose in any given situation depends on how people's contraceptive behavior responds to these policy options. Although only empirical evidence can provide the basis for choosing among them, the framework presented above helps to clarify the choices involved.

Appendix C

Supplementary Data

The following tables provide additional information on family planning services in Asian countries. The reference to each table begins with the letter "A," to indicate that it is an appendix rather than text table, followed by two numbers separated by a period. The first number refers to the chapter to which it most closely relates, while the second simply indicates the sequence in which it is cited in the chapter.

Table A4.1: Gross National Product (GNP), Selected Asian Countries, 1985 and 1989 (millions of local currency)

Country	1985	1989
Bangladesh	414,642	646,138
China	854,890	1,383,171[a]
India	2,607,040	4,339,100
Indonesia	93,063,031	158,196,047
Korea, Rep. of	78,088,421	141,066,051
Lao PDR	92,162	358,099
Malaysia	72,039	97,447
Myanmar	55,408	109,495
Nepal	45,078	79,128
Papua New Guinea	2,335	2,898
Philippines	597,743	822,725[a]
Sri Lanka	161,694	250,128
Thailand	996,800	1,767,408
Viet Nam	783,950[b]	27,603,512

a. Refers to 1988.
b. Refers to 1986.
Source: World Bank Economic and Social Indicators (BESD) database.

Table A4.2: Public Expenditure on Health and Family Planning, Selected Asian Countries, 1985 and 1989 (units of local currency)

Country	Units	Overall health expenditure[a] 1985	1989	Expenditure on family planning programs 1985	1989
Bangladesh	million	3,547	6,304	1,271	2,399
China[b]	million	9,437	12,540	754	1,004
India[c]	million	34,565	55,882	4,289	7,356
Indonesia	billion	685[d]	1,014[d]	110	199
Korea, Rep. of	million	419,800	985,100	30,237	22,028
Malaysia	million	1,256	1,450	23	22
Nepal (i)[e]	million	394	867	55[f]	93[f]
(ii)[g]				70	127
Philippines	million	2,466[h]	5,197[h]	294[i]	232
Sri Lanka	million	1,955	15		
Thailand	million	9,044	11,733	373	480
Viet Nam	million	4,760[j]	239,561	489[j]	13,001

a. Data include expenditures on health and family planning. In some countries budget documents provide separate records for these items, in which case the total would be their sum; in other countries, family planning expenditures are already included in the line for health, in which case summation would lead to double counting.

b. Public expenditure includes spending by central, provincial, and local governments. Data for fourth and sixth columns refer to 1988.

c. Data reflect consolidated central and state expenditures. Aggregate reflects expenditure on "medical, public health, sanitation, and water supply," as well as family welfare.

d. Includes BKKBN expenditures.

e. Data reflect actual recurrent and development expenditures. These are often substantially different from allocation and released budgets. They also do not include donors' in-kind contribution and other direct payments to projects.

f. Reflects actual expenditure (which differs significantly from allocated and released budgets).

g. Data include estimated value of in-kind contribution and direct payments of the two principal donors in the sector, United States Agency for International Development (USAID) and UNFPA. Data are based on information provided by FP/MCH Division of the Ministry of Health.

h. Reflect the sum of DOH and POPCOM expenditures.

i. Reflect POPCOM expenditure and that part of DOH expenditure on family planning. Data for last column is for 1988, as the reporting of accounts has yet to be adjusted to the major administrative changes involving POPCOM and DOH that took place after 1986.

j. Data refer to 1986, the same year for which GNP data are available.

Source: India 1989; World Bank (Indonesia–1989), and World Bank (Indonesia–1990); World Bank (China–1990), and Banister and Harbaugh 1991 for China; Nepal 1990 and personal communication from Nepal Ministry of Health, Family Planning/Maternal Child Health Division, for data on expenditure on family planning; World Bank (Philippines–1990); Gertler, Molyneaux and Tanok 1991 for Thailand; World Bank (Viet Nam–1991); Institute of Business Administration (IBA) 1988 for Bangladesh; Bank of Korea 1991 and personal communication from Korea Ministry of Health, Family Health Division; and Malaysia 1989 and personal communication from Malaysia Ministry of Health as well as Malaysia National Population and Family Development Board.

Table A4.3: Public Expenditure on Selected Components of Family Planning Programs, Selected Asian Countries, Most Recent Year (millions of local currency)

	Contraceptive supplies	Staff training	Demand generation IEC[a]	Demand generation Compensation[b]	Demand generation Total	Married women of reproductive age[c] ('000)	Year
Bangladesh	399.4	46.8	20.2[d]	77.0	97.2	20,253	1990
China	98.5	na	na	na	na	193,743	1990
India	480.5	91.5	118.5	1,030.0	1,148.5	153,457	1990
Indonesia	27,402.0	7,703.0	8,621.0	0.0	8,621.0	30,843	1989
Korea, Rep. of	789.0[e]	273.6[f]	2,747.5	2,303.8	5,051.3	6,671	1989
Malaysia	3.4[g]	0.1[h]	0.3	0.0	0.3	2,766	1990
Nepal	12.6[i]	3.3	5.8	13.1	18.9	3,271	1990
Philippines[j]	14.8	2.9	4.7	0.2	4.9	8,108	1986
Sri Lanka	24.8	2.8	0.9	1.8	2.7	2,469	1990
Thailand	332.0	29.4	55.7	0.0	55.7	8,956	1990
Viet Nam	1,000.0	850.0	1,080.0	0.0	1,080.0	8,910	1990

a. Information-education-communication (or sometimes motivation) activities.
b. Includes payment (cash and in-kind) to acceptors of contraception and payment (usually cash) to eligible providers of service (usually for sterilization and IUD insertion).
c. That is, ages 15-44.
d. Includes development activities in family planning programs intended to stimulate demand for family planning services.
e. In 1989, W 13,461 million was spent by the government to reimburse private providers of sterilization services.
f. Amount equals the total number trained multiplied by the average cost of their training.
g. Estimated from trends in contraceptive expenditures between 1985 and 1987.
h. Includes the training expenditure of MOH and the National Population and Family Development Board (NFDB).
i. Reflects average for 1989-91 to smooth out the volatility of figures over the period.
j. Data refer to average for 1984-88 to smooth out extreme year-to-year fluctuation during this period.

Source: Banister and Harbaugh 1991 for China; Bangladesh (various years) and World Bank Loan Disbursement database for Bangladesh; India n.d. World Bank (Indonesia-1990); Gertler, Molyneaux and Tanok 1991 for Thailand, based on data supplied by Ministry of Health, Family Health Division. Personal communications from Nepal Ministry of Health, FP/MCH Division; Sri Lanka Ministry of Health and Women's Affairs, Population Division; Philippines Commission on Population (POPCOM); Korea Institute of Health and Social Affairs; Malaysia National Population and Family Development Board. Data on the number of women of reproductive age (15-44) are from Ross and others 1988, except for Viet Nam, the source of which is Viet Nam 1990b.

Table A4.4: External Financing of Family Planning Programs in Asian Countries, 1985 and 1989 (millions of local currency)

Country	1985	1989
Bangladesh	807	1,441
China[a]	37	58
India[b]	911	973
Indonesia	40,680	90,945
Korea, Rep. of	1,502	899
Malaysia	1	1
Nepal[c]	49	45
Philippines	142	102[d]
Thailand	124[e]	83[e]

a. Data do not include foreign aid channeled through NGOs.

b. The time profile of foreign aid expenditures shows an unusually large increase for 1989–90, due mainly to a large increase disbursed under a project financed by the World Bank, by far the largest external donor. Since retroactive expenses were financed, a more representative profile of foreign financing would require smoothing the World Bank data. The data here reflect average World Bank financing during 1985–90 (coinciding with the seventh five-year plan period) and reported disbursements of other donors.

c. Data include value of donors' in-kind contribution and direct payments.

d. Data refer to 1988.

e. Data refer to annual average between 1982 and 1986; foreign funding was down to 82.8 million baht in 1990, a large drop from 1989. The foreign share in 1990 was 2%.

Source: IBA 1988 and Bangladesh (various years); UNFPA 1989 and personal communication from Ministry of Health, FP/MCH Division; World Bank (Philippines–1991); Gertler, Molyneaux and Tanok 1991; World Bank (Indonesia–1990); India n.d.; UNFPA 1991 for China, with conversion of U.S. dollars into yuan using exchanges rates in the World Bank BESD database; personal communication from Korea Institute of Health and Social Affairs; and Malaysia National Population and Family Development Board.

Table A4.5: Payment to Acceptors of Sterilization and IUD in Bangladesh, India, Korea, Nepal, and Sri Lanka

| Country | Year | Target population | Payment per client in local currency | | | Per capita GNP (local currency) | |
| | | | Sterilization[a] | | IUD | | |
			Cash	In kind			
Bangladesh	1991	None	175	125[b]	15[c]	5,790	takas
India	1989	None	100	45[c]	9	5,212	rupees
Korea, Rep. of	1989	Low-income: 1 Child	300,000	66,000[d]	0	3,328,598	won
		2 Children	100,000	132,000[d]	0		
Nepal	1991	60 of country's 75 districts	100	10	5	4,293	rupees
Sri Lanka	1991	None	500	0	0	12,907	rupees

a. Rates for tubectomies; vasectomy clients get slightly different rates.

b. Value of sari given to clients.

c. Allowance for food and transportation.

d. Annual value of free delivery services and free medical services for children up to age 6. Estimates based on average annual medical expenses per child ages 0–6 years reported in KNFMI 1988.

Source: India 1990a; Korea National Federation of Medical Insurance (KNFMI) 198; personal communication from Bangladesh Ministry of Health, Directorate of Family Planning; Nepal Ministry of Health, FP/MCH Division; Korea Institute of Health and Social Affairs; and Sri Lanka Ministry of Health and Women's Affairs, Population Division.

Table A4.6: Own Price Elasticities of Contraceptive Demand in Thailand, 1984

	Price elasticity		Average price per year's contraceptive protection (as percentage of per capita GNP[a])		
	Nonmunicipal areas	Municipal areas	Nonmunicipal areas	Municipal areas	Mean
Public source					
Pill	−0.04	−0.09	0.19	0.36	0.28
Injection	−0.25	−0.12	1.04	0.52	0.78
IUD[b]	−0.02	−0.04	0.08	0.16	0.12
Sterilization[b]	−0.02	−0.04	0.10	0.18	0.14
Private source					
Pill	−0.26	−0.19	n.a.	n.a.	1.11
Injection	−0.31	−0.26	n.a.	n.a.	1.26
Condom[b]	−0.24	−0.26	n.a.	n.a.	n.a.
IUD	n.a.	n.a.	n.a.	n.a.	0.35
Sterilization	n.a.	n.a.	n.a.	n.a.	0.58

a. Thailand's per capita GNP in 1984 was 18,967 bahts or US$860.
b. Ashakul 1989 does not differentiate between public and private sources of service because most IUD insertions and sterilizations are performed in the public sector while condoms are supplied predominantly by the private sector.
Source: Adapted from Ashakul 1989, tables 1–3. The analysis was based on data from the 1984 Thailand Contraceptive Prevalence Survey of 7,574 currently married women ages 15–49.

A5.1: Number of Public Sector Outlets by Type of Contraceptive Services Offered, Selected Asian Countries, Most Recent Year

	Number of facility-based outlets offering			Persons acting as resupply points for pills/condoms[c]	Year
	Sterilization & other methods[a]	Commodity-based methods only[b]	All Methods		
Bangladesh	504[d]	3,404[d]	3,908	23,500	1990
China	-	-	-	-	
India (upper-bound)[e]	24,968	120,767	145,735	239,104[f]	1989
(adj. estimate)[e]	23,649	116,919	140,568	239,104	
Indonesia	1,886	17,518	19,404	-	1987
Korea, Rep. of	10,012	5,634	15,646	-	1989
Lao PDR	-	-	-	-	
Malaysia	31	1,117	1,148[g]	-	1990
Myanmar	-	-	-	-	
Nepal	36[h]	834	870	17,217	1989
Papua New Guinea	-	-	-	-	
Philippines	331	5,049[i]	5,380	-	1989
Sri Lanka	119	796	915	-	1990
Thailand	642	8,402	9,044	35,968	1990
Viet Nam	900	1,000	1,900	1,000	1990

a. Sterilizations are usually performed in hospitals, and sometimes also in lower-level facilities. Other methods of contraception may also be offered, most notably in systems that do not rely heavily on referral arrangements, as in Bangladesh.

b. Includes IUD, injectables, implants, and oral pills.

c. In most cases, these would be community-based workers or volunteers authorized to resupply oral pills and distribute condoms.

d. Reflects number of facilities that perform female sterilizations. For male sterilizations, services are offered at slightly fewer facilities (415); for commodity-based methods, the number shown excludes mobile "satellite" clinics, of which there are currently 13,500.

e. Upper-bound estimates for sterilization outlets include all hospitals, Community Health Centres, and Primary Health Centers; for commodity-based outlets, they reflect all subcenters. The adjusted figures include only Urban Family Welfare Centers, including those attached to Post Partum Centers (of which there are 554), subdistrict hospitals sanctioned for extension of Post Partum Programmes, all Community Health Centres (CHCs), and all Primary Health Centres (PHCs) with at least one doctor. The number of commodity-based outlets is the number of subcenters staffed with an auxiliary nurse midwife. Dispensaries which generally serve urban and semiurban areas have an unclear status with respect to the delivery of family planning services and are not included in the numbers shown here. In 1989, there were 12,639 public dispensaries, including those belonging to local bodies. According to the Concurrent Survey, however, the availability of contraceptives is not assured in all subcenters throughout the year. For example, in a sample of 179 facilities in 15 states, the proportion reporting year-round availability for condoms was 68%, for pills 61%, and for IUD 50%.

f. A total of 410,204 Village Health Guides were trained as of 1990, but only the number shown here were reported to be actually working.

g. Includes outlets in West Malaysia under the National Population and Family Development Board and the Ministry of Health. In addition to the static facilities, a substantial number of mobile units are also in operation. In a small number of these facilities, sterilization is available. The number of facilities differs from that reported in the Ministry of Health's Annual Report 1988 (1,999 for 1988). Data are from Tey Nai Peng, head of the National Population and Family Development Board.

h. Reflects the number of facilities that perform vasectomy; the number of facilities equipped to perform mini-laparotomy and laparoscopy is respectively 20 and 17. In many districts sterilization is available only during "camps."

i. Includes rural health centers without lying-in facilities and the estimated one-third of barangay health stations currently staffed to provide family planning services.

Source: Personal communications from Directorate of Family Planning, Ministry of Health, Bangladesh; Korea Institute of Health and Social Affairs; Family Planning Service, Department of Health, Philippines; and Population Division, Ministry of Health, Sri Lanka. Document sources are India 1990a and 1991; World Bank (Indonesia–1990); Malaysia n.d.; Vaidya, Tuladhar, and Dhungana 1990 for Nepal; Gertler, Molyneaux, and Tanok 1991 for Thailand; and Ross and others 1988 for number of women of reproductive age.

Table A6.1: Total Fertility Rates, China, 1950–1993

Year	National	Urban	Rural
1950	5.81	5.00	5.96
1951	5.70	4.72	5.90
1952	6.47	5.52	6.67
1953	6.05	5.40	6.18
1954	6.28	5.72	6.39
1955	6.26	5.67	6.39
1956	5.85	5.33	5.97
1957	6.41	5.94	6.50
1958	5.68	5.25	5.78
1959	4.30	4.17	4.32
1960	4.02	4.06	4.00
1961	3.29	2.98	3.35
1962	6.02	4.79	6.30
1963	7.50	6.21	7.78
1964	6.18	4.40	6.57
1965	6.08	3.75	6.60
1966	6.26	3.10	6.96
1967	5.31	2.91	5.85
1968	6.45	3.87	7.03
1969	5.72	3.30	6.26
1970	5.81	3.27	6.38
1971	5.44	2.88	6.01
1972	4.98	2.64	5.50
1973	4.54	2.39	5.01
1974	4.17	1.98	4.64
1975	3.57	1.78	3.95
1976	3.24	1.61	3.58
1977	2.84	1.57	3.12
1978	2.72	1.55	2.97
1979	2.75	1.37	3.05
1980	2.24	1.15	2.48
1981	2.63	1.39	2.91
1982	2.86	1.58	3.32
1983	2.42	1.34	2.78
1984	2.35	1.22	2.70
1985	2.20	1.21	2.48
1986	2.42	1.24	2.77
1987	2.58	1.36	2.94
1988	2.52	–	–
1989	2.35	–	–
1990	2.31	–	–
1991	2.17	–	–
1992	2.01	–	–
1993	2.00	–	–

Note: "–" means not available. Data for 1950–81 are from China's 1982 one-per-thousand-population fertility survey. Data for 1982–87 are from China's 1988 two-per-thousand-population fertility survey. Data for 1988–90 were estimated from China's 1990 census and 1990 annual survey of population change.

Source: Data for 1950–90 are from Banister and Harbaugh 1991, table 1; data for 1991–92 are calculated from the crude birth rates in China Population Information and Research Centre (CPIRC) 1993c; data for 1993 are calculated from the crude birth rate in CPIRC 1994.

Table A8.1: Life Expectancy of Males and Females at Ages 15 and 50, Selected Asian Countries in Selected Years

| | Year of data | Life expectancy at (years) | | | | Gap in life expectancy between ages 15 and 50[a] | | |
| | | Age 15 | | Age 50 | | | | |
		Male	Female	Male	Female	Male (years)	Female (years)	Female-to-male ratio
Bangladesh	1974	46.3	46.1	20.9	20.5	25.4	25.6	101
	1981	52.9	52.2	21.5	22.6	31.4	29.6	94
	1988	54.1	52.6	23.1	23.6	31.0	29.0	94
China[b]	1981	55.6	58.6	24.0	26.7	31.6	31.9	101
	1973–75	55.2	57.7	24.0	26.4	31.2	31.3	100
India	1976–80	50.3	52.1	20.5	23.0	29.8	29.1	98
	1981–85	53.8	55.7	23.3	25.8	30.5	29.9	98
Korea, Rep. of	1970	50.0	56.3	19.5	25.2	30.5	31.1	102
	1978–79	50.9	58.6	19.9	26.2	30.9	32.4	105
	1989	53.3	61.4	22.1	28.4	31.2	33.0	106
Malaysia[c]	1978	55.4	60.5	23.9	28.3	31.5	32.2	102
	1988	55.4	59.5	23.4	26.3	32.0	33.1	104
Myanmar	1974	49.0	53.2	21.0	24.1	28.0	29.1	104
	1978	50.3	54.8	21.3	24.9	29.0	29.9	103
Nepal	1981	47.3	46.9	20.3	21.2	27.0	25.7	95
Pakistan	1976–78	56.8	56.3	26.6	27.0	30.3	29.2	97
Philippines	1988	53.0	55.9	22.7	25.0	30.3	30.9	102
Sri Lanka	1981	56.2	59.9	25.4	28.0	30.8	31.9	104
Thailand	1974–75	51.6	56.2	22.4	26.7	29.2	29.4	101
	1985–86	53.5	58.0	23.0	26.2	30.5	31.8	104
Viet Nam	1979	55.0	59.2	23.6	27.6	31.4	31.6	101

a. The gap in life expectancy between ages 15 and 50 may be interpreted as the average years of life a person expects to live between those ages.
b. The source data for China refer to life expectancies at ages 10, 20, 40, and 60. They were interpolated to obtain the expectancies at ages 15 and 50.
c. Data refer to peninsular Malaysia.
Source: United Nations 1991c; supplemented by United Nations 1987 for Bangladesh 1974 and 1981, Myanmar 1974, Republic of Korea 1970 and 1978–79, Malaysia 1978, and Thailand 1974/5; Ruzicka and Kane 1987 for China; India 1989 for India 1981–85.

Table A8.2: Urban and Total Population Size, Asian Countries, Selected Years 1970–2020

Country	Urban population						Total population					
	1970	*1980*	*1990*	*2000*	*2010*	*2020*	*1970*	*1980*	*1990*	*2000*	*2010*	*2020*
Bangladesh	5074	9968	19005	34548	56999	83984	66671	88219	115593	150589	188196	220119
China	144537	195370	380803	614514	782538	927185	830675	996134	1139060	1229180	1395328	1476852
India	109616	158851	230269	336542	480806	648265	554911	688856	853094	1041543	1223483	1371767
Indonesia	20534	33514	56293	86401	117767	151036	120280	150958	184283	218661	246680	273349
Korea, Rep. of	12995	21678	30794	37773	42568	45172	31923	38124	42793	46403	49459	51178
Lao PDR	261	431	770	1372	2229	3263	2713	3205	4139	5463	6838	8046
Malaysia	2929	4769	7701	11255	14702	18479	10852	13763	17891	21983	25169	28503
Myanmar	6190	8108	10316	14523	21422	29814	27102	33821	41675	51129	60567	68743
Nepal	450	909	1837	3446	5794	8878	11488	14857	19143	24084	28900	3308
Pakistan	16354	23946	39250	61477	93385	131802	65706	85299	122626	162409	205496	248116
Papua New Guinea	237	403	613	979	1560	2342	2422	3086	3874	4845	5846	6828
Philippines	12380	18064	26602	37775	51201	65707	37540	48317	62413	77473	92095	105384
Sri Lanka	2736	3196	3679	4701	6605	9126	12514	14819	17217	19416	21520	23656
Thailand	4750	8088	12609	18738	26669	35346	35745	46718	55702	63670	71594	78118
Viet Nam	7820	10350	14600	22340	33855	47306	42729	53700	66693	82427	97396	110638
Total	346863	497645	835141	1286384	1738100	2207705	1853271	2279876	2746196	3269275	3718567	4104377

Source: United Nations 1991a, tables A.2 and A.4.

References

(a) General

Abramovitz, Moses. 1962. "Economic Growth in the United States." *American Economic Review* LII(4): 762–82.

Adioetomo, Sri Moertiningsih, Ayke S. Kitting, and Alman Taufik. 1990. "Fertility Transition in Indonesia: Trends in Proximate Determinants of Fertility." In *Population Studies in Sri Lanka and Indonesia Based on the 1987 Sri Lanka Demographic and Health Survey*, Demographic and Health Survey Further Analysis Series, No. 2, The Population Council, New York; and Demographic and Health Surveys, IRD/Macro, Columbia, Maryland.

Ahn, Namkee. 1990. "An Economic Analysis of Fertility Choice: Measuring the Value of Children." Ph.D. dissertation, State University of New York, Department of Economics, Stony Brook, New York.

Ashakul, Teera. 1989. "Analysis of Contraceptive Method Choice and Optimum Contraceptive Pricing Structures." *Thailand Development Research Institute Newsletter* 4(3): 10–13.

Asian Development Bank (ADB). 1991. *Asian Development Outlook 1991*. Asian Development Bank, Manila.

Bangladesh, Government of. 1989. *Bangladesh Contraceptive Prevalence Survey–1989*. Mitra and Associates, Dhaka.

Bangladesh, Government of. Various years. *Annual Development Programme*. Planning Commission, Dhaka.

Bangladesh, Government of. Various years. *Demand for Grants and Appropriations (Non-Development)*. Ministry of Finance, Dhaka.

Banister, Judith, and Christina Wu Harbaugh. 1991. "China's Family Planning Program: Inputs and Outcomes." Mimeo, United States Bureau of the Census, International Research Center, Washington, D.C.

Bank of Korea (BOK). 1991. *Economic Statistics Yearbook*. BOK, Seoul.

Bauer, John. 1991. "Demographic Change and Asian Labor Markets." *Population and Development Review* 16(4): 615–46.

Birdsall, Nancy. 1988. "Economic Approaches to Population Growth and Development." In Hollis B. Chenery and T. N. Srinivasan, eds., *Handbook of Development Economics*. Amsterdam: Elsevier Science Publisher.

Bloom, David E., and Richard Freeman. 1986. "The Effects of Rapid Population Growth on Labor and Employment." *Population and Development Review* 12(3): 381–414.

Bongaarts, John. 1978. "A Framework for Analyzing the Proximate Determinants of Fertility." *Population and Development Review* 4(1): 105–29.

Bongaarts, John, and R. G. Potter. 1983. *Fertility, Biology and Behaviour*. New York: Academic Press.

Bongaarts, John, and Susan Greenhalgh. 1985. "An Alternative to the One-Child Policy in China." *Population and Development Review* 11(4): 585–617.

Bos, Eduard, and Rodolfo A. Bulatao. 1990. *Projecting Fertility for All Countries*. Working Paper Series 500, World Bank, Policy, Research, and External Affairs, Washington, D.C.

Bos, Eduard, and Rodolfo A. Bulatao. 1992. "The Demographic Impact of AIDS in Sub-Saharan Africa: Short and Long-Term Projections." *International Journal of Forecasting* 8(1992): 367–84.

Bos, Eduard, My T. Vu, and A. Levin. 1992. *World Population Prospects 1992–93 Edition*. Baltimore: Johns Hopkins University Press for the World Bank.

Bos, Eduard, My T. Vu, Ernest Massiah, and Rodolfo A. Bulatao. 1994. *World Population Projections, Estimates, and Projections with Related Demographic Statistics 1994–95*. World Bank, Washington, D.C.

Boskin, Michael J., and Lawrence J. Lau. 1992. "Postwar Economic Growth in the Group-of-Five Countries: A New Analysis." Mimeo, Stanford University, Department of Economics, Stanford, California.

Bruce, Judith. 1990. "Fundamental Elements of the Quality of Care: A Simple Framework." *Studies in Family Planning* 21(2): 61–91.

Bulatao, Rodolfo A., Eduard Bos, Patience W. Stephens, and My T. Vu. 1989a. *Europe, Middle East, and Africa (EMN) Region Population Projections, 1989–90 Edition.* Working Paper Series 328, World Bank, Population and Human Resources Department, Washington, D.C.

Bulatao, Rodolfo A., Eduard Bos, Patience W. Stephens, and My T. Vu. 1989b. *Asia Region Population Projections. 1989–90 Edition.* Working Paper Series 331, World Bank, Population and Human Resources Department, Washington, D.C.

Bulatao, Rodolfo A., Eduard Bos, Patience W. Stephens, and My T. Vu. 1989c. *Projecting Mortality for All Countries.* Working Paper Series 337, World Bank, Population and Human Resources Department, Washington, D.C.

Bulatao, Rodolfo A., and Eduard Bos. 1992. *Projecting the Demographic Impact of AIDS.* Working Paper Series 941, World Bank, Population and Human Resources Department, Washington, D.C.

Bulatao, Rodolfo A., and Ronald D. Lee, eds. 1983. *The Determinants of Fertility in Developing Countries*, 2 vols. New York: Academy Press.

Camp, Sharon L., Mary Barbers, and Judith Hinds. 1990. *Cities: Life in the World's 100 Largest Metropolitan Areas. Statistical Appendix.* Population Crisis Committee, Washington, D.C.

Casterline, John B., Susheela Singh, John Cleland, and Hazel Ashurst. 1984. "The Proximate Determinants of Fertility." *Comparative Studies: Cross National Summaries.* Report No. 39, International Statistical Institute, Voorburg, Netherlands.

Chernichovsky, Dov, Henry Pardoko, David De Leeuw, Pudjo Rahardjo, and Charles Lerman. 1991. *The Indonesian Family Planning Program: An Economic Perspective.* Working Paper Series 628, World Bank, Population, Health and Nutrition Department, Washington, D.C.

China, Government of. 1991. *China Statistical Yearbook 1991.* State Statistical Bureau, Beijing.

China Population Information and Research Centre (CPIRC). 1993a. "Policy and Perspectives." *China Population Today* 10(2): 3.

China Population Information and Research Centre (CPIRC). 1993b. "Chinese Government Prohibits Gender Identification of Foetus." *China Population Today* 10(4): 3.

Cho, Lee Jay, and John G. Bauer. 1987. "Population Growth and Urbanization: What Does the Future Hold." In Ronald J. Fuchs and others, eds., *Urbanization and Urban Policies in Pacific Asia*. Boulder: Westview Press, pp. 169–82.

Chomitz, Kenneth M., and Nancy Birdsall. 1991. "Incentives for Small Families: Concepts and Issues." *Proceedings of the World Bank Annual Conference on Development Economics 1990*, pp. 309–40.

Ciszewski, R. L., and P. D. Harvey. 1991. "The Effect of Price Increases on Contraceptive Sales in Bangladesh." Mimeo (April), Population Services International, Washington, D.C.

Coale, Ansley J. 1971. "Age Patterns of Marriage." *Population Studies* 25(2) (July) : 193–214.

Coale, Ansley J., and Donald R. McNeil. 1972. "The Distribution by Age of the Frequency of First Marriage in a Female Cohort." *Journal of the American Statistical Association* 67(340)(December) : 743–49.

Coale, Ansley J., and T. James Trussell 1974. "Model Fertility Schedules: Variation in the Age Structure of Childbearing in Human Populations." *Population Index* 40(2)(April) : 185–258.

Coale, Ansley J., F. Wang, N. E. Riley, and F. D. Lin. 1991. "Recent Trends in Fertility and Nuptiality in China," *Science* 251 (4992) : 389–93.

Cochrane, Susan H. 1979. *Fertility and Education: What Do We Really Know?* World Bank Staff Paper No. 26. Baltimore: Johns Hopkins Press.

Cochrane, Susan H., and David K. Guilkey. 1991. "Fertility Intentions and Access to Services as Constraints on Contraceptive Use in Colombia." *Demographic and Health Surveys World Conference Proceedings*, Vol. 2. World Bank, Washington, D.C.

Cochrane, Susan H., and David K. Guilkey. 1992. "How Access to Contraception Affects Fertility and Contraceptive Use in Tunisia." Working Paper 841, World Bank, Population and Human Resources Department, Washington, D.C.

Cross, Harry E., Virginia Poole, Ruth Levine, and Richard M. Cornelius. 1991. "Contraceptive Source and the For-Profit Private Sector in Third-World Family Planning: Evidence and Implications from Trends in Private Sector Use in the 1980s." Paper presented at the Annual Meeting of the Population Association of America, Washington, D.C., March 21–23, 1991.

David, Paul A., and Warren C. Sanderson. 1986. "Rudimentary Contraceptive Methods and the American Transition to Marital Fertility Control, 1855–1915." In S. L. Engerman and R. E. Gallman, eds., *Long-Term Factors in American Economic Growth*. Chicago: University of Chicago Press.

Denison, Edward. 1967. *Why Growth Rates Differ: Postwar Experience in Nine Western Countries*. The Brookings Institution, Washington, D.C.

Denison, Edward. 1976. *How Japan's Economy Grew So Fast: The Sources of Postwar Expansion*. The Brookings Institution, Washington, D.C.

Denison, Edward. 1985. *Trends in American Economic Growth, 1929–1982*. The Brookings Institution, Washington, D.C.

de Soto, Hernando. 1989. *The Other Path: The Invisible Revolution in the Third World*. New York: Harper and Row.

Donaldson, Peter, and Amy O. Tsui. 1990. "The International Family Planning Movement." *Population Bulletin* 45(3).

Ehrlich, Paul R. 1968. *The Population Bomb*. New York: Ballantine Books.

Ehrlich, Paul R., and Anne H. Ehrlich. 1991. *The Population Explosion*. New York: Simon and Schuster.

Easterley, William, Robert King, Ross Levine, and Sergio Rebelo. 1992. *How Do National Policies Affect Long-run Growth? A Research Agenda*. World Bank Discussion Paper #164, World Bank, Washington, D.C.

Easterlin, Richard A., and Eileen M. Crimmins. 1985. *The Fertility Revolution: A Supply-Demand Analysis*. Chicago: University of Chicago Press.

Gertler, Paul, L. Locay, and W. Sanderson. 1987. "Are User Fees Regressive? The Welfare Implications of Health Care Financing Proposals in Peru." *Journal of Econometrics* 36 : 67–88.

Gertler, Paul, John W. Molyneaux, and S. Yosephine Tanok. 1991. "Thailand National Family Planning Program: Overview, Organization and Management." Draft mimeo, based on data supplied by Family Health Division, Ministry of Health, Government of Thailand.

Gertler, Paul, and John W. Molyneaux. 1994. "How Economic Development and Family Planning Programs Combined to Reduce Indonesian Fertility." *Demography* 31(1): 33-63.

Gillespie, Duff G., Harry E. Cross, John G. Crowley, and Scott R. Radloff. 1989. "Financing the Delivery of Contraceptives: The Challenge of the Next Twenty Years." In Sheldon Segal, Amy O. Tsui, and Susan Rogers, eds., *The Demographic and Programmatic Consequences of Contraceptive Innovation*. New York: Plenum Publishing.

Greenhalgh, Susan. 1990. "State-Society Links: Political Dimensions of Population Policies and Programs, with Special Reference to China." Research Division Working Papers No. 18, The Population Council, New York.

Griffin, Charles C. 1992. *Health Care in Asia*. World Bank, Washington, D.C.

Guilkey, David K., and Susan H. Cochrane. 1992. "Zimbabwe: Determinants of Contraceptive Use at the Leading Edge of Fertility Transition in Sub-Saharan Africa," Mimeo, World Bank, Population, Health and Nutrition Department, Washington, D.C.

Havonon N., John Knodel, and W. Sittitrai. 1989. "Family Size and Family Well-Being in Thailand," Briefing Paper, Family Health International, Research Triangle Park, North Carolina.

Hill, Kenneth. 1990. "PROJ3S – A Computer Program for Population Projections." Prepared for the World Bank, Population and Human Resources Department, Washington, D.C.

Hull, Terrance H., and Sri Harijati Hatmadji. 1990. "Regional Fertility Differentials in Indonesia: Causes and Trends." Working Papers in Demography, No.22, The Australian National University, Canberra.

Huq, Md. Najmul, and John Cleland. 1990. *Bangladesh Fertility Survey–1989*. National Institute of Population Research and Training, Dhaka.

India, Government of. Various years. *Sample Registration System Annual Report*. Ministry of Home Affairs, Office of the Registrar General, New Delhi.

India, Government of. 1988. *Family Welfare Programme in India. Yearbook 1986–87*. Ministry of Health and Family Welfare, Department of Family Welfare, New Delhi.

India, Government of. n.d. *National Family Welfare Programme–Proposal for Eighth Five Year Plan and Annual Plan 1991–92*. Ministry of Health and Family Welfare, Department of Family Welfare, New Delhi.

India, Government of. 1989a. "SRS-Based Abridged Life Tables 1981–85." Occasional Paper #1. Ministry of Home Affairs, Office of Registrar General, New Delhi.

India, Government of. 1989b. *Utilization of Family Planning Services*, National Sample Survey Organization, Forty-Second Round, #369. Department of Statistics, New Delhi.

India, Government of. 1990a. *Family Welfare Programme in India: Year Book 1988–89*. Ministry of Health and Family Welfare, Department of Family Welfare, New Delhi.

India, Government of. 1991. *Health Information India 1990*. Ministry of Health and Family Welfare, New Delhi.

Indonesia. 1989. *National Indonesia Contraceptive Prevalence Survey 1987*. Central Bureau of Statistics and National Family Coordinating Board, Jakarta; and Institute for Resources Development/ Westinghouse, Columbia, Maryland.

Indonesia, Government of. 1990. *Statistical Yearbook of Indonesia 1990*. Central Bureau of Statistics, Jakarta.

Institute of Business Administration (IBA). 1988. *Bangladesh Health Finance and Expenditure Study*. University of Dhaka, Dhaka.

International Labour Office (ILO). 1986. *Economically Active Population. Estimates and Projections 1950–2025*. Volume 1, *Asia*. ILO, Geneva.

International Labour Office (ILO). 1990. *Yearbook of Labour Statistics 1989-90*. ILO, Geneva.

International Labour Office (ILO). 1991. *Yearbook of Labour Statistics 1991*. ILO, Geneva.

International Planned Parenthood Federation (IPPF). 1989. *Family Planning in Five Continents*. IPPF, London.

Jain, Andrudh. 1989. "Fertility Reduction and the Quality of Family Planning Services." *Studies in Family Planning* 20(1): 1–16.

Janowitz, Barbara, John H. Bratt, and Daniel B. Fried. 1990. *Investing in the Future: A Report on the Cost of Family Planning in the Year 2000*. Family Health International (FHI), Research Triangle Park, North Carolina.

Johnson, D. Gale, and Ronald D. Lee, eds. 1987. *Population Growth and Economic Development: Issues and Evidence*. Madison, Wisc.: University of Wisconsin Press.

Kanagaratnam, Kandiah. 1980. "Population and Family Planning Programs: Trends in Policy and Administration." World Bank Staff Working Paper No. 411, World Bank, Washington, D.C..

Kelley, Allen C. 1988. "Economic Consequences of Population Change in the Third World." *Journal of Economic Literature* 26(Dec): 1685–1728.

Knodel, John, and M. Wongsith. 1991. "Family Size and Children's Education in Thailand: Evidence from a National Sample." *Demography* 28(1): 119–31.

Korea National Federation of Medical Insurance (KNFMI). 1988. *1987 Medical Insurance Statistical Yearbook*. KNFMI, Seoul.

Lapham, Robert J., and George B. Simmons, eds. 1987. *Organizing for Effective Family Planning Programs*. Washington, D.C.: National Academy Press (for National Research Council [US], Working Group on Family Planning Effectiveness).

Lau, Lawrence, Dean T. Jamison, and Frederic Louat. 1991. *Education and Productivity in Developing Countries: An Aggregate Production Function Approach*. Working Paper Series 612, World Bank, Policy, Research, and External Affairs, Washington, D.C.

Lau, Lawrence, and Jong-Il Kim. 1992. "The Sources of Economic Growth of the Newly Industrialized Countries on the Pacific Rim." Paper presented at the Conference on the Economic Development of the Republic of China, and the Pacific Rim in the 1990s and Beyond, Taipei, Taiwan (China), May 25–28, 1992.

Lee, Ronald D., and Timothy Miller. 1991. "Population Growth, Externalities to Childbearing, and Fertility Policy in Developing Countries." In *Proceedings of the World Bank: Annual Conference of Development Economics 1990*, World Bank, Washington, D.C.

Lewis, Maureen. 1986. "Do Contraceptive Prices Affect Demand?" *Studies in Family Planning*. 17(3): 126–35.

Lewis, Maureen. 1987. "Cost Recovery in Family Planning." *Economic Development and Cultural Change* 36(1): 161–82.

Lewis, Maureen, and Genevieve Kenny. 1988. *The Private Sector and Family Planning in Developing Countries.* Working Paper No. 96, World Bank, Population and Human Resources Department, Washington, D.C.

Malaysia, Government of. 1988. *Ministry of Health Annual Report.* Ministry of Health, Kuala Lumpur.

Malaysia, Government of. 1989. *Belanjawan Persukutuan 1989* (Annual Budget, in Bahasa). Ministry of Finance, Kuala Lumpur.

Malaysia, Government of. n.d. *Laporan Penerima Tahunan Malaysia 1989* (Annual Acceptor Report). National Population and Family Development Board, Kuala Lumpur.

Malaysia, Government of, and Rand Corporation. 1988–89. *Second Malaysian Family Life Survey.* Rand Corporation, Santa Monica.

Mauldin, Parker, and John A. Ross. 1989. "Historical Perspectives on the Introduction of Contraceptive Technology." In Sheldon Segal, Amy O. Tsui, and Susan Rogers, eds., *Demographic and Programmatic Consequences of Contraceptive Innovation.* New York: Plenum Press.

Mauldin, Parker, and John A. Ross. 1991. "Family Planning Programs: Efforts and Results, 1982–1989." Paper presented at the Annual Meeting of the Population Association of America, Washington, D.C., March 21–23, 1991.

Molyneaux, Jack, and Tohir Diman. 1991. "Impacts of Contraceptive Prices on Indonesia Contraceptive Choices." Forthcoming in Kanter and Palmer, eds., *Further Analysis of the 1987 Indonesia Demographic and Health Survey.* East-West Center, Honolulu.

Montgomery, Mark. 1987. "A New Look at the Easterlin 'Synthesis' Framework." *Demography* 24(4): 481–96.

Moreno, Lorenzo, and Noreen Goldman. 1991. "Contraceptive Failure Rates in Developing Countries: Evidence from the Demographic and Health Surveys." *International Family Planning Perspectives* 17(2)(June): 44–49.

Mun, Hyon-Sang, I. C. Yi, Y. H. Oh, and S. Y. Yi. 1989. *1988 National Fertility and Family Health Survey* (in Korean). Korean Institute for Population and Health, Seoul.

National Institute of Population Studies (NIPS) and Demographic Health Surveys (DHS). 1991. *Pakistan Demographic and Health Survey 1990/91*, Institute for Resource Development (IRD)/Macro International, Columbia, Maryland.

National Research Council (U.S. Working Group on Population Growth and Economic Development). 1986. *Population Growth and Economic Development.* Washington, D.C.: National Academy Press.

Nepal, Government of. 1990. *Economic Survey.* Ministry of Finance, Kathmandu.

Newman, Alfred, and Wen-Pin Chang. 1988. "Paying for Family Planning in China." *Health Policy and Planning* 3(2): 119–30.

Operations Research Group (ORG). 1983. *Family Planning Practices in India: Second All India Survey.* Ministry of Health and Family Welfare, New Delhi.

Operations Research Group (ORG). 1990. *Family Planning Practices in India: Third All India Survey.* Ministry of Health and Family Welfare, New Delhi.

Pakistan, Government of. 1986. *Pakistan Contraceptive Prevalence Survey.* Population Welfare Division (Monitoring and Statistics Wing), Islamabad.

Philippines, Government of. 1988. *1988 National Demographic Survey.* National Statistical Office, Manila.

Phillips, James F., John Cleland, Sajeda Amin, and G. M. Kamal. 1994. *The Determinants of Reproductive Change in Bangladesh: Success in a Challenging Environment.* World Bank, Regional and Sectoral Studies, Washington, D.C..

Population Information Program (PIP). 1991. "Paying for Family Planning." Mimeo, Johns Hopkins University, Center for Communication Programs, Baltimore.

Romer, Paul. 1990. "Capital, Labor and Productivity." *Brookings Papers on Economic Activity: Microeconomics*, Special Issue: 337–67.

Rosenzweig, Mark R., and Kenneth I. Wolpin. 1986. "Evaluating the Effects of Optimally Distributed Public Programs: Child Health and Family Planning Interventions," *American Economic Review* 76(3): 470–82

Ross, John A., and Stephen L. Isaacs. 1988. "Costs, Payments, and Incentives in Family Planning Programs: A Review for Developing Countries." *Studies in Family Planning* 19(5): 270–83.

Ross, John A., Marjorie Rich, Janet Molzanl, and Michael Pensk. 1988. *Family Planning and Child Survival: 100 Developing Countries.* Columbia University, Center for Population and Family Health, New York.

Ruzicka, Lado, and Penny Kane. 1987. "Trends and Patterns of Mortality in the ESCAP Region: Comparative Analysis." In *Mortality and Health Issues in Asia and the Pacific.* Asian Population Studies Series No.78, Economic and Social Commission for Asia and the Pacific (ESCAP), Bangkok.

Ryder, Norman B. 1979. "Consistency of Reporting Fertility Planning Status." *Studies in Family Planning* 10(4): 115–28.

Sanderson, Warren C. 1991. *Parametric Population Projection and Its Usefulness for Policy Analysis.* Asia Regional Series No. IDP93, World Bank, Washington, D.C.

Sanderson, Warren C. 1994. "Predictability, Complexity, and Catastrophe in a Collapsible Model of Population, Development, and Environmental Interactions." Working Paper WP-94-75, August. International Institute for Applied Systems Analysis, Laxenburg, Austria.

Schultz, T. Paul. 1986. Review of *The Fertility Revolutions: A Supply-Demand Analysis,* by Richard A. Easterlin and Eileen M. Crimmins, *Population and Development Review* 12(1): 127–40.

Schultz, T. Paul. 1989. "The Relationship between Local Family Planning Expenditures and Fertility in Thailand, 1976–81." Mimeo (April 10), Yale University Economic Growth Center, New Haven.

Schwartz, J. B., J. S. Akin, David K. Guilkey, and V. Paqueo. 1989. "The Effect of Contraceptive Prices on Method Choice in the Philippines, Jamaica, and Thailand." In Rodolfo A. Bulatao, J. A. Palmore, and S. E. Ward, eds., *Choosing a Contraceptive: Method Choice in Asia and the United States.* Boulder: Westview Press.

Simmons, George, and James F. Philips. 1987. "The Integration of Family Planning with Health and Development." In Robert J. Lapham and George B. Simmons, eds., *Organizing for Effective Family Planning Programs.* National Academy of Sciences, Washington, D.C.

Simon, Julian L. 1981. *The Ultimate Resource.* Princeton: Princeton University Press.

Sinding, S. W. 1991. "Strengthening the Bank's Population Work in the 90s." Working Paper No. 802, World Bank, Population, Health and Nutrition Department, Washington, D.C.

Srikantan, K. S. 1982. "Quality and Comparability of Family Planning Data from Surveys and Service Statistics." In A. I. Hermalin and B. Entwistle, eds., *The Role of Surveys in the Analysis of Family Planning Programs*. Liege, Belgium: Ordina Press.

Tan, Jee-Peng, and Alain Mingat. 1992. *Education in Asia: A Comparative Study of Cost and Finance*. World Bank, Washington, D.C.

Thailand, Government of. 1990a. *Fiscal Year Budget 1989–90*. Ministry of Public Health, Bangkok.

Thailand, Government of. 1990b. *Statistical Yearbook 1990*. Office of the Prime Minister, National Statistical Office, Bangkok.

Thapa, Shyam, S. S. Kumar, J. Cushing, and K. Kennedy. 1991. "Contraceptive Use and Needs among Postpartum Women in 25 Developing Countries: Recent Patterns and Implications." In *Demography and Health Surveys World Conference Proceedings*. Vol. II. IRD/Macro International Inc., Columbia, Maryland.

Tsui, Amy O., and Peter J. Donaldson. 1987. "The Role of Private Physicians and Clinics in Third World Family Planning." In R. J. Lapham and G. B. Simmons, eds., *Organizing for Effective Family Planning*. Washington, D.C.: National Academy Press.

Tsui, Amy O., and Luis Hernando Ochoa. 1989. "Service Proximity as a Determinant of Contraceptive Behavior: Evidence from Cross-National Studies of Survey Data." Paper presented at the IUSSP Seminar on the Role of Family Planning Programs as a Fertility Determinant, Tunis, June 26–30, 1989.

Tuladhar, J. M. 1989. "Supply Aspects of Meeting the Demand for Family Planning." In *South Asia Study on Population Policies and Programmes. Nepal*. United Nations Fund for Population Activities, New York.

United Nations. 1983. *Manual X: Indirect Techniques for Demographic Estimation*. Population Studies No. 81 ST/ESA/SER.A/81. United Nations, Department of International Economics and Social Affairs, New York.

United Nations. 1987. *1985 Demographic Yearbook*. No. ST/ESA/STAT/SER.R/ 15. United Nations, Department of International and Economic and Social Affairs, Statistical Office, New York.

United Nations. 1989a. *Prospects on World Urbanization*. United Nations, New York.

United Nations. 1990. *World Population Prospects 1988.* Report No. ST/ESA/ SER.A/106. United Nations, Department of International Economic and Social Affairs, New York.

United Nations. 1991a. *World Urbanization Prospects 1990.* Report No. ST/ESA/ SER.A/121. United Nations, Department of International Economic and Social Affairs, New York.

United Nations. 1991b. *The Age and Sex Distribution of Population. The 1990 Revision of the United Nations Global Population Estimates and Projections.* No. ST/ESA/STAT/SER.A/122. United Nations, Department of International and Economic and Social Affairs, Statistical Office, New York.

United Nations. 1991c. *1989 Demographic Yearbook.* No. ST/ESA/STAT/SER.R/ 79. United Nations, Department of International and Economic and Social Affairs, Statistical Office, New York,

United Nations Children's Fund (UNICEF). 1991. *The State of the World's Children.* UNICEF, New York.

United Nations Fund for Population Activities (UNFPA). 1989. *South Asia Study on Population Policies and Programmes. Nepal.* UNFPA, New York.

United Nations Fund for Population Activities (UNFPA). 1990a. *South Asia Study of Population Policy and Programmes. Bangladesh*, UNFPA, Dhaka.

United Nations Fund for Population Activities (UNFPA). 1990b. *South Asia Study of Population Policy and Programmes. India*, UNFPA, New Delhi.

United Nations Fund for Population Activities (UNFPA). 1991. *Global Population Assistance Report, 1982–89.* UNFPA, New York.

United Nations Population Fund (UNPF), and The Population Council (PC). 1990. *International Family Planning Programme Study. Questionnaire.* UNPF and PC, New York.

University Research Corporation (URC). 1991. *Family Planning Operations Research/Asia: Lessons from the Field, Final Report.* URC, under USAID Sponsorship, Washington, D.C.

Vaidya, T. M, J. M. Tuladhar, and S. P. Dhungana. 1990. *Nepal: Population and Health Project FP/MCH Service Delivery System.* Paper submitted to the World Bank, Kathmandu.

Viet Nam, Government of. 1990a. *Viet Nam Demographic and Health Survey 1988.* National Committee for Population and Family Planning, Hanoi.

Viet Nam, Government of. 1990b. *Viet Nam Population Census–1989. Sample Results.* Central Census Steering Committee, Hanoi.

World Bank. 1984. *World Development Report 1984.* Washington, D.C.: Oxford University Press for the World Bank.

World Bank. 1990a. *World Development Report 1990.* Washington, D.C.: Oxford University Press for the World Bank.

World Bank. 1990b. *The World Bank Atlas 1990.* Washington, D.C.

World Bank. 1991a. *Population and the World Bank: A Review of Activities and Impacts from Eight Case Studies.* Operations Evaluation Department, Report No. 10021, Washington, D.C.

World Bank. 1991b. *Urban Policy and Economic Development. An Agenda for the 1990s.* Washington, D.C.

World Bank. 1991c. *World Development Report 1991.* Washington, D.C.: Oxford University Press for the World Bank.

World Bank. 1991d. *Global Health Statistics. Database Prepared for World Development Report 1993 (preliminary version).* Population, Health and Nutrition Division, Population and Human Resources Department, Washington, D.C.

World Bank. 1992. *Effective Family Planning Programs.* Population, Health and Nutrition Division, Population and Human Resources Department, Washington, D.C.

World Bank. 1993. *World Development Report 1993. Investing in Health.* Washington, D.C.: Oxford University Press for the World Bank.

World Bank, China–1990. *China Long-Term Issues and Options in the Health Transition.* Asia Region Country Department III, Report No. 7965-CHA, Washington, D.C.

World Bank, India–1989. *Family Planning Strategy in India: Changing the Signals.* Asia Region Country Department IV, Report No. 7900-IN, Washington, D.C.

World Bank, Indonesia–1989. *Indonesia Issues in Health Planning and Budgeting.* Asia Region Country Department V, Report No. 7291-IND, Washington, D.C.

World Bank, Indonesia–1990. *Indonesia Family Planning Perspectives in the 1990s.* World Bank Country Study, Washington, D.C.

World Bank, Indonesia–1991. *The World Bank and Indonesia's Population Program.* Operations Evaluation Department, Report #9370, Washington, D.C.

World Bank, Pakistan–1988. *Pakistan Education Sector Strategy Review.* Europe, Middle East, and North Africa Region Country Department I, Report No. 710-PAK, Washington, D.C.

World Bank, Pakistan–1989. *Higher Education and Scientific Research for Development in Pakistan.* Europe, Middle East, and North Africa Region Country Department I, Report No. 8231-PAK, Volumes I and II, Washington, D.C.

World Bank, Pakistan–1991a. *Pakistan Review of Secondary and Intermediate Education.* Europe, Middle East, and North Africa Region Country Department I, Report No. 9887-PAK, Washington, D.C.

World Bank, Pakistan–1991b. *Pakistan Current Economic Situation and Prospects.* Europe, Middle East, and North Africa Region Country Department I, Report No. 9283-PAK, Washington, D.C.

World Bank, Pakistan–1992. *Pakistan Health Sector Study. Key Concerns and Solutions.* South Asia Region Country Department III, Report No. 10391-PAK, Washington, D.C.

World Bank, Philippines–1991. *New Directions in the Philippines Family Planning Program.* Asia Region Country Department II, Report No. 9579-PH, Washington, D.C.

World Bank, Thailand–1990. *Thailand's Education Sector at a Cross-Roads: Selected Issues.* Asia Region Country Department II, Report No. 9011-TH, Washington, D.C.

World Bank, Viet Nam–1991. *Viet Nam Restructuring Public Finance and Public Enterprises: An Economic Report.* East Asia Region Country Department II, Report No. 10134-VN, Washington, D.C.

World Bank, Viet Nam–1992. *Viet Nam Population, Health and Nutrition Sector Review.* East Asia Region, Country Department II, Report No. 10289-VN, Washington, D.C.

Zeng, Yi, and J. W. Vaupel. 1989. "The Impact of Urbanization and Delayed Childbearing on Population Growth and Aging in China." *Population and Development Review* 15(3): 425–45.

(b) Sources for Table 3.2

Agyei, W. K. A. 1988. *Fertility and Family Planning in the Third World: A Case Study of Papua New Guinea.* New York: Croom Helm in association with Methuen, Inc.

Arshat, H., Tan Boon Ann, Tey Nai Peng, and N. Subbiah. 1988. *Marriage and Family Formation in Peninsular Malaysia.* Analytic report on the 1984/85 Malaysian Population and Family Survey. National Population and Family Development Board, Kuala Lumpur.

Bangladesh, Government of. 1985. *Bangladesh Contraceptive Prevalence Survey– 1983.* Mitra and Associates, Dhaka.

Burma, Socialist Republic of the Union of (now called Myanmar). 1986. *Burma, 1983 Population Census.* Ministry of Home and Religious Affairs, Immigration and Manpower Department, Rangoon.

China, Government of. 1985. *Population Census of China–1982 (result of computer tabulations).* Beijing: Statistical Publishing House.

China, Government of. 1990. *Quanguo Shengyu Jieyu Chougang Diaocha Guanguo Shuju Juan Heiji* [National Sample Survey on Fertility and Family Planning, Summary Volume]. State Family Planning Commission, Beijing.

China Population Information and Research Center (CPIRC). 1993c. "Surveys and Data." *China Population Today* 10(4): 4.

China Population Information and Research Center (CPIRC). 1994. "Populations and Economic Development." *China Population Today* 11(3): 5.

Huq, Md. Najmul, and John Cleland. 1990. *Bangladesh Fertility Survey–1989.* National Institute of Population Research and Training, Dhaka.

India, Government of. 1983. *Sample Registration System–1980/81*, Ministry of Home Affairs, Office of the Registrar General, New Delhi.

India, Government of. 1989. *Family Welfare Programme in India, Year Book 1987–88.* Ministry of Health and Family Welfare, Department of Family Welfare, New Delhi.

India, Government of. 1990a. *Family Welfare Programme in India. Yearbook 1988–89.* Ministry of Health and Family Welfare, Department of Family Welfare, New Delhi.

India, Government of. 1990b. *Sample Registration System 1988.* Ministry of Home Affairs, Office of the Registrar General, New Delhi.

Indonesia, Government of. 1987. *National Indonesia Contraceptive Prevalence Survey–1987.* Central Bureau of Statistics, Jakarta.

Indonesia, Government of. 1992. *Indonesia Demographic and Health Survey 1991.* Central Bureau of Statistics, Jakarta.

International Insttute for Population Sciences. 1994. *National Family Health Survey, India 1992–93. Introductory Report.* Bombay.

Koh, Kap Suk, Hee Soon Hahm, and Jong Hwa Byun. 1980. *1979 Korea Contraceptive Prevalence Survey Report.* Korean Institute of Family Planning and Westinghouse Health Systems, Seoul.

Korea, Government of. 1985. *1985 Census of Population and Housing.* National Bureau of Statistics, Economic Planning Board, Seoul.

Korea Institute for Population and Health (KIPH). 1985. *Fertility and Family Health Survey, 1985.* KIPH, Seoul.

Malaysia, Government of. Various years. *Quarterly Review of Malaysian Population Statistics.* Department of Statistics, Kuala Lumpur.

Malaysia, Government of. 1987. *Social Statistics Bulletin.* Department of Statistics, Kuala Lumpur.

Malaysia, Government of. 1989. *Vital Statistics of Peninsular Malaysia–1986.* Department of Statistics, Kuala Lumpur.

Malaysia, Government of, and Rand Corporation. 1989. *Malaysian Family Life Survey II.* National Population and Family Development Board and Rand, Kuala Lumpur.

Maung, M. I. K. 1986. *The Population of Burma: An Analysis of the 1973 Census*. Papers of the East-West Population Institute, #97, East-West Center, Honolulu.

Nepal, Government of. 1983. *Nepal Contraceptive Prevalence Survey Report–1981*. Ministry of Health, Kathmandu; and Westinghouse Health Systems, Columbia, Maryland.

Nepal, Government of. 1984. *Population Census 1981 Social Characteristics*. Central Bureau of Statistics, National Planning Commission Secretariat, Kathmandu.

Nepal, Government of. 1986. *Nepal Fertility and Family Planning Survey*. Ministry of Health, Kathmandu.

Operations Research Group (ORG). 1983. *Family Planning Practices in India: Second All India Survey*. Ministry of Health and Family Welfare, New Delhi.

Operations Research Group (ORG). 1990. *Family Planning Practices in India: Third All India Survey*. Ministry of Health and Family Welfare, New Delhi.

Philippines, Government of. 1978. *1978 Philippines Fertility Survey*. National Statistical Office, Manila.

Philippines, Government of. 1990. *1988 National Demographic Survey Preliminary Results*. Special Release of the Office of the Administrator, National Statistics Office, Manila.

Philippines, Government of. 1994. *National Demographic Survey 1993*. National Statistics Office, Manila.

Plampiti, S., and J. Knodel. 1978. *Revised Estimates of Age-Specific Fertility Rates from the Survey of Fertility in Thailand*. Chulalongkorn University, Institute of Population Studies, Bangkok.

Population Research Centre (PRC). 1986. *Almanac of China's Population*. PRC, Beijing.

Sri Lanka, Government of. 1978. *World Fertility Survey–1975, Sri Lanka, First Report*. Ministry of Plan Implementation, Department of Census and Statistics, Colombo.

Sri Lanka, Government of. 1983. *Sri Lanka 1982 Contraceptive Prevalence Survey Report*. Ministry of Plan Implementation, Department of Census and Statistics, Colombo; and Westinghouse Health Systems, Columbia, Maryland.

Sri Lanka, Government of. 1984. *Sri Lanka Census of the Population and Housing–1981*. Ministry of Plan Implementation, Department of Census and Statistics, Colombo.

Sri Lanka, Government of. 1987. *Sri Lanka Demographic and Health Survey–1987*. Ministry of Plan Implementation, Department of Census and Statistics, Colombo.

Sri Lanka, Government of. 1988. *Sri Lanka Demographic and Health Survey 1987*. Ministry of Plan Implementation, Department of Census and Statistics, Colombo; and Institute for Resource Management/Westinghouse, Columbia, Maryland.

Supraptilah, B. 1982. *Evaluation of the Indonesia Fertility Survey*. Scientific Reports No. 38, International Statistical Institute, Voorburg, Netherlands.

Tey, Nai Peng, Tan Boon Ann, Tan Poo Chang, and Kwok Kwan Kit. 1988. *Direct and Indirect Determinants of Fertility in Peninsular Malaysia*. A report submitted to the National Population and Family Development Board, and the United Nations Fund for Population Activities, Kuala Lumpur.

Thailand, Government of. 1981. *Report of the Survey of Population Change, 1974–76*. National Statistical Office, Bangkok.

Thailand, Government of. 1982. *A New Decade of Fertility and Family Planning in Thailand: 1981 Contraceptive Prevalence Survey*. Westinghouse Health Systems, Bangkok.

Thailand, Government of. 1985. *1980 Population and Housing Census*. Office of the Prime Minister, Bangkok.

Thailand, Government of. 1988. *Thailand Demographic and Health Survey–1987*. Chulalongkorn University, Institute of Population Studies, Bangkok; and Institute for Resource Development/Westinghouse, Columbia, Maryland.

United Nations. Various years. *Demographic Yearbook*. United Nations, New York.

United Nations. 1982. *Model Life Tables for Developing Countries, Far Eastern Pattern*. United Nations, New York.

United Nations. 1986. *Population of Malaysia*. Country Monograph Series #13. ST/ESCAP/389. United Nations, Economic and Social Commission for Asia and the Pacific, New York.

United Nations. 1989b. *Compendium of Social Development Indicators in the ESCAP Region*. United Nations, Economic and Social Commission for Asia and the Pacific, Bangkok.

United Nations. 1989c. *Global Estimates and Projections of Population by Age and Sex–1988*. United Nations, New York.

United Nations. 1989d. *Levels and Trends of Contraceptive Use as Assessed in 1988*. Population Studies 110. ST/ESA/SER.A/110. United Nations, Population Division, New York.

United Nations. 1991b. *The Sex and Age Distributions of Population. The 1990 Revision of the United Nation's Global Population Estimates and Projections*. Population Studies No. 122. ST/ESA/SER.A/122. United Nations, Department of International Economic and Social Affairs, New York.

United Nations. 1991d. *World Population Prospects 1990*. Population Studies 120, ST/ESA/SER.A/120. United Nations, Department of International Economic and Social Affairs, New York.

United Nations Fund for Population Activities (UNFPA). 1989. *South Asia Study on Population Policies and Programmes, Nepal*. UNFPA, New York.

Viet Nam. 1990a. *Viet Nam Demographic and Health Survey 1988*. National Committee for Population and Family Planning, Hanoi.

Viet Nam. 1990b. *Viet Nam Population Census: 1989 Sample Results*. Central Census Steering Committee, Hanoi.

World Fertility Survey (WFS). 1976. *Indonesia Fertility Survey–1976*. Principal Report, Vols I and II. Central Bureau of Statistics, Jakarta.

World Fertility Survey (WFS). 1976. *Nepal Fertility Survey–1976 First Report*. International Statistical Institute, Voorburg, Netherlands.

World Fertility Survey (WFS). 1977. *The Survey of Fertility in Thailand*. Country Report, Vol 1. Chulalongkorn University, Institute of Population Studies and National Statistical Office, Population Survey Division, Bangkok.

World Fertility Survey (WFS). 1978. *Bangladesh Fertility Survey–1975*. Ministry of Health and Population Control, Population Control and Family Planning Division, Dhaka.

World Fertility Survey (WFS). 1979. *Malaysia Fertility and Family Survey, First Country Report.* International Statistical Institute, Voorburg, Netherlands.

World Fertility Survey (WFS). 1979. *The Korean National Fertility Survey–1974, First Country Report.* Economic Planning Board, National Bureau of Statistics; and Korean Institute for Family Planning, Seoul.

Yatim, M. H. 1982. *Evaluation of the Malaysian Fertility and Family Survey–1974.* Scientific Reports No. 27, World Fertility Survey. International Statistical Institute, Voorburg, Netherlands.